Developing Masterful Management Skills for International Business

THE GLOBAL WARRIOR SERIES
Series Editor: Thomas A. Cook

Developing Masterful Management Skills for International Business
Thomas A. Cook (2018)

Enterprise Risk Management in the Global Supply Chain
Thomas A. Cook (2017)

Excellence in Managing Worldwide Customer Relationships
Thomas A. Cook (2016)

Growing and Managing Foreign Purchasing
Thomas A. Cook (2016)

Managing Growth and Expansion into Global Markets:
Logistics, Transportation, and Distribution
Thomas A. Cook (2016)

Driving Risk and Spend Out of the Global Supply Chain
Thomas A. Cook (2015)

Mastering the Business of Global Trade: Negotiating Competitive
Advantage Contractual Best Practices, Incoterms®,
and Leveraging Supply Chain Options
Thomas A. Cook (2014)

Developing Masterful Management Skills for International Business

Thomas A. Cook

CRC Press
Taylor & Francis Group
Boca Raton London New York

CRC Press is an imprint of the
Taylor & Francis Group, an **informa** business

CRC Press
Taylor & Francis Group
6000 Broken Sound Parkway NW, Suite 300
Boca Raton, FL 33487-2742

© 2019 by Taylor & Francis Group, LLC
CRC Press is an imprint of Taylor & Francis Group, an Informa business

No claim to original U.S. Government works

Printed on acid-free paper

International Standard Book Number-13: 978-1-4822-2610-2 (Hardback)

Library of Congress Cataloging-in-Publication Data

Names: Cook, Thomas A., 1953- author.
Title: Developing masterful management skills for international business / by
Thomas A. Cook.
Description: 1 Edition. | Boca Raton : CRC Press, [2018] | Series: The global
warrior series | Includes bibliographical references and index.
Identifiers: LCCN 2018004043 | ISBN 9781482226102 (hardback : alk. paper) |
ISBN 9781315118154 (e-book)
Subjects: LCSH: International business enterprises--Management.
Classification: LCC HD62.4 .C656 2018 | DDC 658/.049--dc23
LC record available at https://lccn.loc.gov/2018004043

Visit the Taylor & Francis Web site at
http://www.taylorandfrancis.com

and the CRC Press Web site at
http://www.crcpress.com

Taylor and Francis
Global Warrior Book Series
Book #3
Mastering Management Skill Sets for Business and International Commerce
Thomas A. Cook

*To our combat soldiers and veterans who serve and served to protect our way of life and as protectors of democracy and freedom worldwide. "**May peace always be with you**".*

Contents

Foreword xvii
Preface xix
Acknowledgments xxi
Author xxiii

Chapter 1 Understanding and Executing Successful
Leadership and Management 1

Defining Leadership and Management......................................2
Innate or Learned?..5
Quality Leadership Skills 7
These Traits Can Be Both Represented or Argued as
Positives and Negatives...10
They Are All Positive and Negative to an Extent...................10
Where Do We Stand as Individuals in All These Traits?......11
And How Do We Know Where We Really Stand? 11

Chapter 2 Business Management Skill Sets 13

Business Management 101..13
Finance 14
Communication..14
Be a Student Always..15
Be Articulate..16
Be Interesting...16
Be Direct, No Nonsense..17
Utilize Storytelling 18
Create Feedback 19
Be Timely 19
Make Sure Your Points Are Understood by Keeping
It as Simple as Possible...19
Do Not Waste People's Time 20
Learn to Speak to Groups, Publicly, and to Utilize
PowerPoint.. 20
Create a "Communication Style"..21

Project Management 21
Problem Resolution 24
   Stop the Bleeding 25
   Assessment...25
   Strategy...26
   Action 26
   Reassessment 27
   Revision..27
   Outreach... 28
   Mitigation 28
   Closure..29
Negotiation 30
Time Management 31
   Delegating... 34
Time Management and Communicating...............................35
People Skills...36
Business Development 37
Growth Strategies 38
   Raising the Bar of Sales Management..............................38
      In Organic Sales 38
   Creating a Viable Sales Strategy 39
   Hiring Quality Business Development and Sales
   Personnel..41
   Building a Sales Pipeline of Opportunity........................ 43
   Creating an Inventory of Prospects................................. 44
   Closing More Deals 46
   Price 46
   Customer Service 47
   Specific Sales Strategy 48
   Concluding Remarks.. 48
Operations 49
Strategic Planning as an Operational Responsibility............52
   Strategic Planning Considerations 52
      Mantra 52
      Goals and Deliverables..53
   Specific...53
   Measurable...53
   Attainable...53

Relevant 54
Time Frame 54
Collaboration 54

Chapter 3   Financial Considerations 57

Financial Controls 57
Controlling Spend through Procurement Management 61
Senior Management's Role in Procurement 61
Overview 61
Sourcing 63
Purchasing 63
Vendor Management 66
The RFP Tool in Managing the Purchasing Function 67
Risk Management in Procurement 68
Summary 70

Chapter 4   Going Global—The Business Case to Go Global:
Foreign Purchasing and Export Sales 71

The "Case" to Go Global 72
Export Sales 73
Choice of INCO Terms 75
Utilization of Freight Forwarders 76
Landed Costs 77
Competitive Pressures 77
Trade Compliance Issues 77
Use of Distributors and Agents 78
Global Expansion 78
Global Sourcing 79
Foreign Asset Expansion 79
Developing the Skill Sets of Global Business 79
Understanding Foreign Cultures 80
Understanding Import and Export Operations,
Regulations, and Procedures 80
Global Supply Chain 81
International Legal, Accounting, and Finance Issues 82
International Marketing, Sales, and Customer Service 82
Technology on a Global Scale 85

International Purchasing 86
Benefits to Americans and the World 88
Foreign Purchasing 88
Sourcing Globally: Senior Managements Guide to
"Twelve Key Best Practices" 88
Trade Compliance and Regulatory Responsibilities 92
Buying Internationally: Import Supply Chain 93
Duties and Fees 94
Harmonized Tariff Classification 94
Country of Origin Marking 95
Trade Compliance with Customs 96
Reasonable Care Standard 96
Customhouse Brokers 100
Internal Supervision and Control 103
Supply Chain Security 104
Invoice Requirements 106
Bonds 107
Record Retention 108
Selling Internationally: The Export Supply Chain 109
Government Agencies Responsible for Exports 109
International Traffic in Arms Regulations 110
Export Administration Regulations 110
Commerce Control List 111
Electronic Export Information 112
U.S. Principal Party in Interest 112
Schedule B Number/Harmonized Tariff Number 113
Valuation 113
Recordkeeping Requirements 114
Denied Party Screening 114
Embargoed Country Screening 114
Consularization and Legalization 115
Solid Wood Packing Material Certificates 115
Preshipment Inspections 116
Free Trade Affirmations 116
Getting Paid 116
Customs-Trade Partnership against Terrorism Benefits 117
Background 118

Customs-Trade Partnership against Terrorism
Approach and Guiding Principles.......................... 120
External Factors... 122
Customs-Trade Partnership against Terrorism for
Exporters.. 122
Additional Consideration: Drawback, Free Trade
Agreements, Foreign Trade Zones, and Bonded
Warehouses... 123

Chapter 5   Mastering Business Development 125

Developing an International Business Strategy 125
Understanding the Cultures of the World 126
  Business Culture 127
  Considering Cultural Factors.................................127
  Twelve Steps to Building a Successful International
  Business Model...132
E-Commerce in Global Trade.................................... 134
Creating an E-Commerce Website Globally.......................148
  Step 1—Select a Domain Name 148
    Using Country-Level Domain Codes......................148
    Internationalizing Your Domain Name 148
  Step 2—Register with Search Engines 149
  Step 3—Choose a Web Host............................149
  Step 4—Website Content: Localize and
  Internationalize..150
  Step 5—Execute Orders 151
    Policy-Advice 152

Chapter 6   Decision Management 155

Better Decision Making: Qualitative versus
Quantitative.. 155
  Understand the Decision 161
  Mine..161
  Build a Team..163
  Establish Preliminary Findings 163
  Build a Metrics and Quantitative Model....................164

Evaluate Qualitative Criteria...164
Complete the Analysis 164
Make the Decision and Implement 165
Follow-Up and Tweak 165
Emotional Intelligence 165

Chapter 7   Delivering Successful Negotiations 171

Defining What We Want to Accomplish in Negotiation
and Developing a Strategic Plan..172
Goal Setting..172
Assessment...173
Mining..173
Planning 173
Action 174
Tweaking...174
Closure..174
Negotiating Globally 174
The Essence of Compromise 175
Trust Is the Critical Asset..176

Chapter 8   Building the Sustainable Business Model...................... 189

Overview of the Sustainable Business Model........................189
The Ten Steps of Sustainable Business.................................. 190
Integrative Management...191
Developing and Managing Team Initiatives..........................194
Team Building...194
Collaboration..194
Camaraderie 194
Effective Delegation 195
Mentoring Effectiveness...195
Crossing Company Silos 196
Better Results 196
Choosing Team Members...196
Managing the Team..197
Commercial Example...197
Cyber Security Issues in Global Trade 199
Avoiding Costly Mistakes..199

Overview of Cyber Security 200
Cyber Security Impacts... 200
    Application Security... 200
    Information Security... 200
    Network Security 201
    Disaster Recovery and Continuity Planning 202
    Operational Security.. 202
    Technology Bullying.. 202
    End-User Education and Training 202
Cyber Security Cases.. 203
Best Practices in "Mitigating" Potential Security
Issues 203
    Assessment... 204
    Professional Support.. 204
    Mindset ... Cyber Security Is a Very Real Threat!....... 204
    Establish Cyber Security Initiative 204
    Train and Educate Staff... 205
Personnel Issues in Cyber Security 205
Additional International Cyber Concerns 205

Appendix 207
Index.. 323

Foreword

I have read all of Tom's books and am continually impressed by the depth and intensity of his experience, along with his ability to articulate an array of subject matter on global trade and business.

This book is an important asset to the Global Warrior Series and runs deep from general management and leadership skill sets to negotiating effectiveness in international commerce.

This book complements the other seven books of the series and is an important read for executives, students, and business entities to learn the expansive subject matter involved in general and global business, as well as managing your expansion and development into the international arena.

I was taken back in the first chapter to some very deep discussion Tom created on management and leadership styles that brought me back to my over 60 years of experience in running companies and operating in numerous countries around the world.

I found the book easy to read, though comprehensive and interesting material on every page. It is a must read for all business executives looking to expand their horizons and do the very best they are capable of.

Spencer Ross
National Institute for World Trade

Preface

Business is now a global phenomenon, moving at the speed of light. And every day international onset is growing, becoming deeper, more comprehensive, and a necessary strategy, not only for survival, but for prosperity. For business models to compete, for managers to develop, and real-time sustainability realized, the corporate executive in the second and third decade(s) of the new millennium must master a whole set of skill sets, led by leadership, communication style, technology, management prowess, and product and service differentiation.

This book lays the critical foundation and blueprint for students, executives, and corporations to utilize as a strategy and tactical approach to business model success.

Each chapter of the book, not only offers comprehensive information flow on each central topic, but prepares the reader to understand the significance of the topic in making the company a competitive force to be reckoned with.

Some of the key topics: leadership, management, communicating, negotiating, problem resolution, time management, financial considerations, decision making, and business development ... are all covered in detail, simply put forth, but with striking definition.

The author with over 35 years of international trade experience and 19 business books to his credit has reached another level of prowess in the design and execution of this books' content, making it one of the most all-inclusive texts on the skill sets of what it takes to effectively compete in the global economy.

All the subject matter contained in this book will have benefit to both domestic and international business models.

> Information technology and business are becoming inextricably interwoven. I don't think anybody can talk meaningfully about one without the talking about the other.

Bill Gates

Acknowledgments

This book acknowledges Kelly Raia, VP of Blue Tiger International, and also acknowledges the Department of Commerce in Washington, DC.

Author

Thomas A. Cook is a managing director of Blue Tiger International (bluetigerintl.com), a premier international business and management consulting/training company on leadership, general management, supply chain, freight operations, port and terminal services, risk management, trade compliance, purchasing/sourcing, global trade, e-commerce, logistics, and business development/sales. Blue Tiger International owns the National Institute of World Trade (niwt.org), a nonprofit 30+ year corporate training school on global trade and supply chain management.

Tom was former CEO of American River International in NY and Apex Global Logistics Supply Chain Operation in LA.

He has over 30 years' experience in assisting companies all over the world manage their business models, supply chain risk and spend, sales and business development, purchasing, business decision making, vendor/contract management, and import/export operations.

Tom's practice includes business mentoring in sales, leadership, project, presentation skills, risk management, supply chain, purchasing/sourcing management, and international and management capabilities enhancement.

He is a member of the NY District Export Council, sits on the board of numerous corporations, and is considered a leader in the business verticals he works in ... Institute for Supply Management (ISM), Council of Suppl Chain Management Professionals (CSCMP), District Export Council (DEC) ... to name a few of the organizations he works with.

He has now authored over 19 books on business management, global trade, and business development ... in 2016 was in the middle of an 8 book series, titled ... *The Global Warrior* ... Advancing on the Necessary Skill Sets to Compete Effectively in Global Trade. Tom is also a veteran advisor, developer, and instructor of the AMA ... American Management Association in NYC, the largest corporate training association in the world. His latest book … Enterprise Risk Management in the Global Supply Chain is receiving great praise and accolades from the professional community.

Tom is also the director of the National Institute of World Trade (niwt. org), a 30-year-old educational and training organization, based here on Long Island.

Tom is a frequent lecturer and keynote speaker several times a year at various management, leadership, transportation, supply chain, insurance, and business development venues here and abroad.

Tom also is a lecturer/teacher and course developer at Stony Brook University in Long Island, Baruch College, and the Fashion Institute of Technology in NYC.

He graduated from Maritime College where he holds both a BS and MS/MBA in international transportation management. He additionally received his commission in the U.S. Navy where he served from 1971–1984, honorably discharged.

Tom also founded and chairs … *Soldier On* … soldieronathome.org …, a nonprofit organization engaged in helping wounded combat veterans, wounded combat dogs, and supporting specially trained dogs to assist soldiers with Post Trauma Stress Syndrome (PTSD). Tom can be reached at tomcook@bluetigerintl.com or 516-359-623.

1

Understanding and Executing Successful Leadership and Management

This chapter explores the differences and similarities along with the connective tissue of quality leadership and effective business management.

This chapter also outlines the difference in developing comprehensive business strategies and in executing tactics, actions, and plans.

It sets a solid platform for understanding the role of leaders and managers in global business models looking for the best opportunities in sustainability and long-term growth.

And in managing a team of personnel, keeping them headed in one direction and all on the same page.

The other seven chapters delve into the following areas:

- Defining leadership and management
- Quality leadership skills
- Business management skill sets
- Emotional intelligence
- *Better decision making*: Qualitative versus quantitative
- Strategic planning
- Negotiating
- Going global
- Global regulatory and trade compliance
- Action plans and accountability systems
- Financial prowess
- Risk and cyber security
- Training and education
- Creating sustainability

Great things in business are never done by one person. They're done by a team of people.

Steve Jobs

DEFINING LEADERSHIP AND MANAGEMENT

There has been an ongoing debate among philosophers, academics, entre-preneurs, and business professionals for over 10,000 years on just:

- What is leadership?
- What is management?
- Are they the same or different?
- What makes good leaders and good managers?

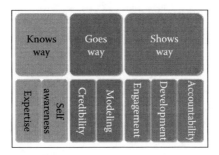

Defining leadership: There are many definitions outlined by various sources ... one I prefer is ... that leadership is the art of motivating a group of people to act toward achieving a common goal. Or in other words ... creating a distinct group of followers for a common cause.

Defining management: The best definition I have found is: The process of dealing with or controlling things or people.

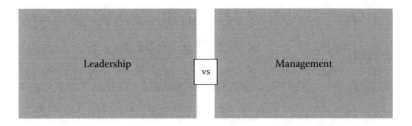

Leadership and management, though closely aligned, are two separate things. Individuals that have both characteristics and skill sets are in the best position to be effective powers of change in any organization, which will always allow the best opportunity for growth, profits, and sustainability.

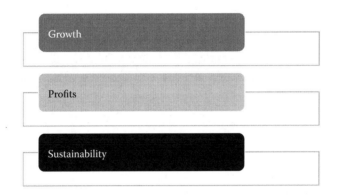

Growth

Profits

Sustainability

The three key components of business management and driving success!!!

In much of the consulting work I do, I have noticed that everyday people assume that being a good leader means that you are also a good manager and the two are interchangeable.

The two concepts are both theoretically and functionally quite different and comprehending that distinction is relevant to how one navigates their executive path.

Management overview: Tactical execution is a critical aspect of the manager's path in any organization, and management is smaller scale and more focused on details than leadership. The leader creates a strategic plan, then sets the vision. Management then executes what is needed to achieve the desired results of the strategic plan.

Management traits are:

- Ability to follow the direction provided by the strategic plan and guidance of leadership
- A practical and tactical focus on executing strategy
- Executing on defined areas within their responsibilities
- Formulating and enforcing the policies of a business to achieve its goals
- Directing and monitoring their team to achieve their specific goals

- Reducing risk and spending in the organization
- Communication intermediary between personnel and corporate leadership

Effective skill sets in:

- Organization
- Communication
- Finance and Accounting
- Human Resources
- Project Management
- Risk Management
- People Handling
- Accountability and Responsibility Systems
- Problem Resolution
- Decision-Making Prowess

Leadership is not necessarily getting caught up in all the details, but rather setting the plan and inspiring people to follow them.

Leadership traits are:

- Ability to determine, visualize, structure, and communicate a vision
- Ability to earn a *following, loyalty, and support* from a following group of people
- Strategic focus on the organization's needs
- Establishing company values, missions, goals, and direction
- Creating a corporate culture that allows success of the mission
- Empowering and mentoring the team to lead them to meeting corporate objectives and deliverables
- Risk taker
- Long-term, high-level focus
- Be the *face* of the company

Management versus leadership
  "Tactical versus Strategic"

In other words ... leadership is setting the culture or nature of an organization, the broad objectives, strategies, and long-term goals.

Managers become the instruments within a company structure that execute the plan to attain corporate goals.

Any organization or business needs people who are good at both leadership and management if they are going to succeed.

The quandary that can exist is that ... with good management and poor leadership, they will be able to execute tactics successfully, but will be doing so without a clear direction and overall strategy. With good leadership and bad management, a company will have the goals and inspiration to succeed, but no one with an ability to achieve the desired results, deliverables, and company goals.

A quality balance of leadership and management creates the best opportunity for a company to succeed.

INNATE OR LEARNED?

A question often raised ... is good leadership innate or is it learned? Most academics and professionals would agree that there is a certain *DNA* factor in both successful and quality management and leadership.

Meaning that there are certain people who are born with leadership and management traits.

As youngsters, we see certain individuals as children take the *lead*, solve problems, and create a following of the peers.

We also know that leadership is not always utilized for positive or to the benefit of society. Genghis Khan, Adolf Hitler, Fidel Castro, and Sadam Hussein would be four examples of individuals who would be clearly defined as *leaders* ..., but their legacies and history paints these leaders with clearly clandestine and unscrupulous strategies and tactics to achieve their desired goals.

Our sensibilities may not want to define these individuals as *leaders*, but by most accounts and definitions ... they certainly had established goals, strategies, and a huge following, with an ability to move people in a specific direction.

In retrospect, as leaders, they convinced hundreds of thousands of people to commit horrific atrocities and unforgivable acts on humankind.

Having said all of that … our focus in this book is on leadership that generally works within the realms of society, business, and the world and certainly not in a clandestine or negative way.

Most professionals have determined that there are those who are born leaders and managers and those that are not so lucky.

I believe there are three categories:

- Those that have it, clearly defined … 20% of the population
- Those that do not have it at all … 40% of the population
- And those that have a little, but it can be potentially enhanced … 40% of the population

Therefore, those that have it a lot or a little … the skill sets … they can be furthered, enhanced, and taught.

Those that do not have it at all … probably are somewhat at a disadvantage. This does not mean that these people cannot contribute or be of great value … just the opposite … this group is the necessary, critical, and important *worker bees* that every business needs.

Good followers are a necessary component of all business models and society in general.

The other 60% made up of those that have it and have it a little ... these two groups must take steps to enhance their leadership and management skill sets, keep them contemporary, and continually grow and develop.

I discuss this further at the end of this chapter, where we discuss training and education.

The bottom line in this discussion on leadership and management in regard to its innateness and learnability ... we should agree that leadership and management are certainly *built-in* qualities that can be further developed and learned through specialized training and continued exposure to experience and education.

Some individuals will *have it*, some will not, and most can develop it, to some extent.

We all observe Olympic athletes every four years whose spectacular feats and accomplishments bedazzle us. And they make it look easy.

It is clear these Olympic athletes *have it*. Can it be further developed and enhanced ... absolutely yes ... their continued training and learning curve occurs every day.

We know some athletes have to work harder than others. And we all know people who have no or very little athletic ability, no matter what they do.

Athleticism can easily be compared to leadership. There are born great athletes. There are born people who have some athleticism, and there are those that have none. All very similar to leadership.

I think the most important factor coming out of this discussion is that leadership is a skill set that requires continued education, development, and training. Those individuals with innate leadership traits have advantages, but to achieve the greatest results and capabilities ... a continuous process of development must be part of any executive's equation.

QUALITY LEADERSHIP SKILLS

In my management classes that I teach, I go through an exercise and ask the students to think about a person in their past life or current situation that they would consider a great leader.

Once identified ... what were their traits ... make up a list. Over 30 years of this banter ... here are some of the common traits that the students put forth:

Persistent	Talented	Mentor/coach
Articulate	Goal oriented	Great advocate
Organized	Open minded	Client focused
Good communicator	Self-motivated	Resilient
Fair	Optimistic	Mentally strong
Visionary	Thick-skinned	Health conscious
Motivational	Charismatic	Generous
Inspirational	Money hungry	Fun
Responsible	Successful	Dependable
Diligent	Caring	Determined
Risk taker	Honest	Challenges
Responsive	Persuasive	Good negotiator
Follow through	Respectful	Champion
Collaborative	Admits mistakes	Closer
Detailed	Hard working	Adaptable
Tenacious	Accessible	Ambitious
Hustler	Emphatic	Credible
Unafraid	Sympathetic	Compassionate
Knowledgeable	Takes advice	Effective delegator
Competitive	Sense of humor	Professional
Team player	Complimentary	appearance
Flexible	Decisive	Manages time well
Personable	Calm in crisis	Technically savvy
Punctual	Trustworthy	Resourceful
Innovative	Show by example	Relationship builder
Creative	Transparent	

So we need to ask a few questions about this list to place in perspective its relevance to becoming a better leader?

1. These traits can be both represented or argued as positives and negatives
2. They are all positive and negative to an extent
3. Where do we stand as individuals in all these traits?
4. And how do we know where we really stand?

THESE TRAITS CAN BE BOTH REPRESENTED OR ARGUED AS POSITIVES AND NEGATIVES

What we mean here is that while most of these character traits for leadership would be considered clear and outright virtues ... that one could argue that some might be viewed as disabilities.

As an example, someone compassionate may lack the *killer* instinct to do what is necessary to get the job done.

As another example, someone so hardworking, *without a life* lacks any empathy for those who have families and external commitments to work obligations, that they take seriously.

THEY ARE ALL POSITIVE AND NEGATIVE TO AN EXTENT

What we mean here is that all these character traits are valued greatly, but only to an *extent* ..., meaning that anything in minutia or in excess can bring more harm than good.

An example may be in the area of *being tenacious* ... where, in excess, it can be called aggressive and that may place a person's action *over the line* as a manager.

Another example ... someone is so *accessible* all the time that they get very little accomplished in their daily responsibilities.

Open door policies have great value, but *accessibility* must be managed and handled within an executive's total scope of responsibilities and in consideration of responsible time management.

A *too little* example might be in the area of being *detailed*. Some managers do not pay attention to *detail* sufficiently and as a result get into compromising scenarios. A good manager or leader knows when to delegate detail and when to assume detail. They recognize that certain tasks require focus, stone-turning, mining, and just simple painstaking detail initiative.

Great executives can discern these differences and know when and to what extent to make all these positive character traits and attributes come alive and work for them, their companies, and for their employees.

WHERE DO WE STAND AS INDIVIDUALS IN ALL THESE TRAITS?

These traits must be self-evaluated by any caring executive wanting to be a better leader or manager.

A suggestion is to mull over this list and create a smaller version with areas requiring your priority attention. Then rate yourself as to where you think you stand in those areas on a 1–10 basis … with 1 being the least and 10 being the best.

One would assume that quality leadership would place you minimally at a "7" in all those areas with a hope of being closer to an 8–9. Being a "10" would be superb!

In most analysis that I have seen with the executives I have worked with, exceeding well over 1000 … would place the majority of having a greater placement of where they stand, then reality would tell them in a core comprehensive review.

Which brings us to the next question …

AND HOW DO WE KNOW WHERE WE REALLY STAND?

The gap between perception and reality must be closed for an executive to develop truly amazing management and leadership skill sets.

They must be able to "see the forest through the trees." Knowing your strengths and weaknesses correctly is the only path for self-improvement. This is where certain aspects of leadership and management can be learned and more importantly … developed.

The critical step is evaluating intelligently and comprehensively. This requires outreach to your peers, colleagues, and subordinates where open dialogue can take place, and you can ask how you are doing in all these areas and get defined feedback.

This can be accomplished through:

- Quality open and honest relationships
- Continual outreach through surveys ... and in sending in *salvos of questions* that ask the hard questions
- The important aspect of obtaining real quality feedback in creating a working environment that allows straight forward dialogue without fear of retribution, embarrassment, one getting upset, and an allowance for criticism
- One must not fear the truth, when they know the truth can be utilized as leverage for advancement, growth, and moving forward to betterment

Good feedback allows one to seek trends and consensus. This then can create the necessary actions to modify or change behavior.

This then creates a culture where others see your willingness to accept criticism and feedback to make yourself a better leader, manager, and person. This then demonstrates your leadership by example.

Keep in mind ... that leadership gets others to follow those that lead by example.

A lot of good will is established when you can:

- Accept criticism and behavior commentary
- Make necessary behavior and style changes
- Show leadership by example

The benefits keep rolling in, with little downside, when managed in balance with all other responsibilities and taken into portion of its relevance in running the business.

2

Business Management Skill Sets

One of the most significant determining factors of business success is organizations that have a *boat load* of executives with skill sets that allow them to be competitive, run well, and develop aggressively.

This chapter reviews those key skill sets.

BUSINESS MANAGEMENT 101

There are a number of key business skill sets that all executives must have, develop, and lead on:

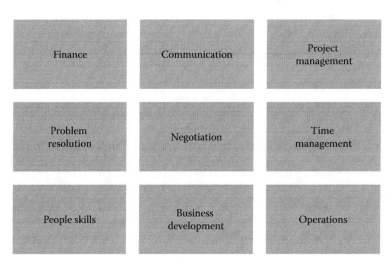

Finance	Communication	Project management
Problem resolution	Negotiation	Time management
People skills	Business development	Operations

FINANCE

Chapter 2 provides an excellent overview of all the financial considerations for executives to follow in the overall management responsibilities.

It has been my experience that managers involved in primary business development, purchasing, sales, customer service, manufacturing, and distribution, to name a few areas are just not as engaged as they need to be when it comes to:

- Understanding basic financial terms, practices, and modus operandi
- Relating to the financial impact of operating decisions
- Studying *landed cost* modeling for working areas of cost of goods sold or cost of goods purchased as well as they should
- Comprehending tax implications
- Working the financial technology well enough
- Leveraging financial options in operational decision making

All these areas are reviewed in Chapter 2.

COMMUNICATION

Our ability to communicate is possibly the most important skill set of successful managers. It allows us to manage, lead, instruct, supervise, and make things happen!

Quality communication capabilities help define who we are and how effective we can be in our responsibilities.

Many possess great ideas, but it is our ability to impart these ideas to others that can lead to successful strategies followed by favorable results.

Communication skill sets are both innate and learnable. We must always be studying and practicing our ability to communicate well.

All great leaders are well-defined communicators. Quality communication skill sets can vary greatly from one person to another and often allow *personality* to be an influential factor.

In 2018, as we enter the second year of President Trump …, we certainly notice a very different style of communicating … direct, brash, and opinionated with *tweets* as the sounding mechanism. But to an extent … it works for him!

We all know executives of every culture, age, and demographic who are successful and communicate very differently from one another.

Some recommendations for being a quality communicator are:

- Be a student always.
- Be articulate.
- Be interesting.
- Be direct, no nonsense.
- Use storytelling.
- Create feedback.
- Be timely.
- Make sure your points are understood by keeping it as simple as possible.
- Do not waste people's time.
- Learn to speak to groups, publicly, and to utilize PowerPoint.
- Create a *communication style*.

Quality Communication Skill Sets … they allow us to manage, lead, instruct, supervise, and make things happen!

Thomas Cook

Be a Student Always

Communication capability is best defined as a *learning process* that continues as an executive moves forward and up in their business growth.

A good communicator is always learning and adapting to contemporary times for how best to get their message across to others.

Keep in mind, as we outlined in Chapter 1, that leadership gets others to follow. Communication is the sounding piece that others listen to before they follow. Quality communications are clearly a leadership trait that continually gets developed by formal, informal, and conductive training.

Communication methods, styles, and outreach channels are always developing and changing in which you must be closely aligned with.

Technology also has impacted communication options. Facebook, LinkedIn, Twitter, Instagram, YouTube, and social media outlets all present various options that we must understand, work, and master to become a good communicator ... leading us to achieve our desired goals.

Always considering yourself a student of communication will assure the best opportunity to succeed in your business goals both on a personal and business level.

As communication options, channels, and technology develop, we must keep learning and developing our communication skill sets to reach across the ages, demographics, and the new challenges we will face as we grow our business models.

Be Articulate

Executives who can articulate well ... communicate well. It allows consistent, pronunciation, annunciations, and generally speaking smoothly.

> In phonetics and phonology, articulation is the movement of the tongue, lips, jaw, and other speech organs (the articulators) in ways that make speech sounds.

It allows the executive to come across well, with confidence, and a sensibility of being knowledgeable.

In comparison, those that articulate poorly ... come across poorly.

Be Interesting

If you come across as a "bore ..." few will listen, irrespective of the importance of the message.

You need to be an *interesting* speaker to increase your effectiveness. You must develop a *style* and project in a manner that keeps people focused on what you are saying and what your message is.

The audience must understand and more importantly *feel* the relevance of your message, and the more you can gain their interest, the more likely you will be able to get your message across.

Being interesting means being relevant, contemporary, timely, and credible.

Being an interesting communicator will exponentially increase your odds of having an audience listen and then respond in a direction you were hoping for.

Be Direct, No Nonsense

Learn to be more direct, not abrasive, but direct. Learn to be no nonsense. This will lead to people willing to listen more intently and your case will come across more believable.

People want you to be upfront, transparent, and straight forward in your communication style. They will listen better and perform better when you communicate with a style that is more plausible and tenable.

A direct communication model also fosters trust. Trust is one of the most important character traits in good leadership and management.

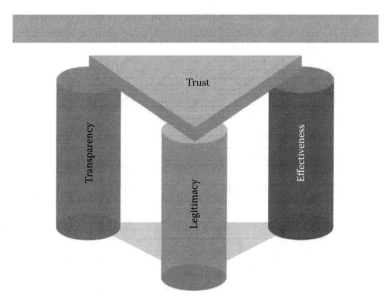

Communicating when trust is established creates a state of comfort between the communicator and their audience, which affords listening, interaction, and better results.

Utilize Storytelling

People love stories, and particularly those stories that personify what you are talking about. I almost always try and come up with a brief story that will relate to what I am trying to accomplish.

An example ... I told the story ... Back in 1987, when my business was only six years old, the economy took a turn for the worse; I had to temporarily reduce the staff's compensation to keep the company financially stable. At that time, I promised to everyone that the reductions were temporary and when circumstances changed for the better ... I would quickly reverse the reductions and add back what was lost.

A year later, the economy improved, and we made good on our promises. Here it was in 2010, and the economy tanked again, and I had to advise the staff of the same senior management steps.

The story created a truth, credibility, and instilled hope. It made it much easier to deliver bad news, but at the same time ... created camaraderie, team initiative, and a future with hope.

This communication style created a calm in turbulent waters and allowed the staff, "though not very happy," to be proactive and willing participants in a direction, I needed them to go and participate in.

Storytelling settles people down, engages, and connects the audience and validates and resonates on the eventual message you are sending, increasing the odds of achieving your desired goals.

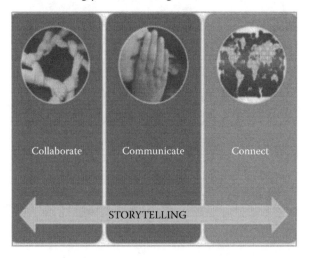

Collaborate   Communicate   Connect

STORYTELLING

Create Feedback

You need to develop methods to obtain feedback on your communication style. This allows you to measure the effectiveness of how you approach communicating and ultimately establishing *your communication style.*

Good and experienced communicators and presenters are usually anxious to obtain an immediate feedback from their audience in order to gauge how they are doing at that moment.

It is a very sensitive and emotionally intelligent person who can pick-up from the audience at the time of delivery how their message is being received.

Eye contact, their demeanor, their sounds, and their body language will all tell a lot.

Be Timely

Communication needs to be timely …, meaning we need to have a strong sense when to project, advise, and inform.

Timing can be as important as the message itself. Too often we are late in communicating, particularly *bad news*, which should always be communicated quickly.

We have to deliver our messages when they will have the most impact balanced off when the message requires delivering based upon the nature of the message.

Taking the *high road*, when we are unsure is usually a good option in the decision-making process.

MAKE SURE YOUR POINTS ARE UNDERSTOOD BY KEEPING IT AS SIMPLE AS POSSIBLE

We too often become too complex and complicated in how we deliver our communication, making the message recipients unsure of what we were trying to say.

We have it in *our mind* organized, but the message comes out unclear. We always have to keep in mind the people we are talking to and how they receive information.

Keeping it simple, well organized, and in synch are important in thinking out how we send out the message.

Do Not Waste People's Time

Make sure the message is important and relevant. You do not want to waste people's time, sending out trivial, meaningless communications just to irritate your audience. Make sure your messages have something to say that is of value.

Learn to Speak to Groups, Publicly, and to Utilize PowerPoint

Most leaders and executives will have to speak to audiences made up of several people to even large audiences.

Becoming comfortable and confident in being able to speak to larger groups is a necessary aspect of overall quality management and is important in successful communications.

Many executives have found the utilization of PowerPoint a powerful tool in communicating visually to a larger group and creating an effective method for making a point, sending a specific message, or informing in a large scale.

Mastering these basic skills will make you a much more effective communicator in delivering your message across to your audience.

Create a "Communication Style"

The most successful communicators over time create a *unique style* that people acknowledge, identify with, and usually find distinct.

If this style is interesting, articulate, and received well ..., then the style is identified with the speaker and the message, as well.

This allows the communicator to develop consistency in presentation, format, and messaging which becomes their *persona* which can be a leadership skill.

Creating a communication style allows for *originality*, which again can be construed as a leadership skill set.

PROJECT MANAGEMENT

The tasks we take on in business can often be described as projects, particularly those that will take considerable time, initiative, and resources.

Mastering project management will make you a much more successful manager.

Project management

The skill sets of good project managers are diverse, as outlined in this pictorial.

Many skill sets are required:

- Conflict and crisis management
- Flexibility and creativity
- Leadership and communication

- Learning and development
- Negotiation and compromise
- Organizational effectiveness
- Problem solving and decision making
- Professionalism, morals, and ethics
- Trustworthiness
- Self-discipline
- Teamwork
- Managing up, down, in, and out within an organization

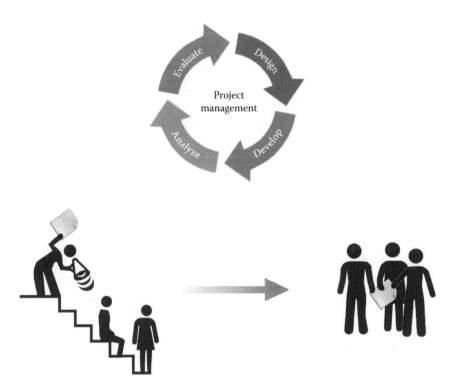

Projects allow:

- A show of your capabilities
- Leading a team
- Bringing matters to a favorable closure

Project management as defined by Wikipedia:

Project management is the discipline of initiating, planning, executing, controlling, and closing the work of a team to achieve specific goals and meet specific success criteria at the specified time. A project is a temporary endeavor designed to produce a unique product, service or result with a defined beginning and end (usually time-constrained, and often constrained by funding or staffing) undertaken to meet unique goals and objectives, typically to bring about beneficial change or added value. The temporary nature of projects stands in contrast with business as usual (or operations), which are repetitive, permanent, or semi-permanent functional activities to produce products or services. In practice, the management of such distinct production approaches requires the development of distinct technical skills and management strategies.

The primary challenge of project management is to achieve all of the project goals within the given constraints. This information is usually described in project documentation, created at the beginning of the development process. The primary constraints are scope, time, quality, and budget. The secondary—and more ambitious—challenge is to optimize the allocation of necessary inputs and apply them to meet predefined objectives. The object of project management is to produce a complete project, which complies with the client's objectives. In many cases the object of project management is also to shape or reform the client's brief in order to feasibly be able to address the client's objectives. Once the client's objectives are clearly established, they should impact on all decisions made by other people involved in the project-project managers, designers, contractors, sub-contractors, and so on. If the project management objectives are ill defined or too tightly prescribed, it will have a detrimental effect on decision making.

Managing projects and the teams that participate in the work is an effective tool of managers and one that will make you be overall a competent leader and business manager.

PROBLEM RESOLUTION

Problems and difficulties will arise every day in every business. It becomes a daily activity for those engaged in growing and developing companies.

Your success in navigating these problems and moving toward a favorable resolution will be an important element of how you are defined by your colleagues, peers, subordinates, clients, vendors, and business associates.

The ability to resolve problems and disputes is an important behavior, skill set, and capability and can prove invaluable to running and managing people and organizations.

The following nine steps are involved in dispute resolution:

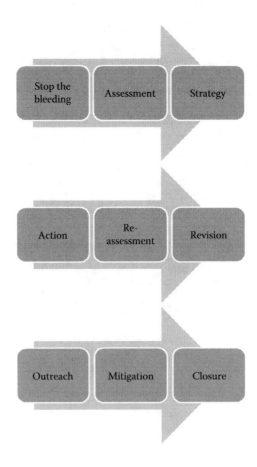

Stop the Bleeding

Often when a problem occurs, there is a panic that sets in requiring immediate action. In the military ... *triage* and *field corpsman* are there to serve this purpose for wounded combat soldiers.

In business, we must very quickly assess the situation and apply tourniquets or Band-Aids to prevent further damage from occurring.

Our ability to quickly assess and apply immediate mitigation and action, typically without the proper allotment of neither time nor resource, is a leadership/management trait that is often required and needed to be applied.

When no immediate action is taken, too often the consequential damages can be costly and devastating. Additionally, when the incorrect action is applied that can often be harmful, as well.

Many times, the initial action is just that ... *initial* and further action and steps will be necessary to bring closure to the issues at hand.

Assessment

A review and study will need to be accomplished to see what went wrong. This is not necessarily a time to place blame ... that can be done later ... now you are working to resolve a problem. Time is of the essence.

The assessment process includes interviews, conference calls, meetings, scrutiny, and so on. The process will drive you to preliminary conclusions, so you know what best actions to undertake.

Strategy

Developing a concept of how you plan to resolve the problem is by default creating a *strategy* for resolution.

The strategy will often contain:

- Defining the problem
- Identifying stakeholders and impacted parties
- Setting the goals of resolution
- Evaluating consequences on inaction and action
- Evaluating impact of potential action steps
- Creating an action plan

Keep in mind that strategies are developed to be amended and modified as time progresses and circumstances and events change and dictate.

Strategies are designed to be a work-in-progress, that get tweaked as actions cause same.

Action

The action becomes the *tactical* side of executing the strategy and becomes the actual steps and activity that will be introduced and followed by your team.

Actions will be successful, unsuccessful, or somewhere in between. It is your job as the problem resolution leader to assess how the actions are doing and then recreate a new or revised strategy.

Sample Action Plan

Action	Point Person	Expectation	Status	Follow-Up
Call all impacted clients	John S.	Done by Oct 1st	9/28 ... 60% complete	Next update by 10/1
Evaluate consequential damages	Sally B. & Bob W.	Need initial response tomorrow 9/29	Waiting update	Will depend upon update tomorrow

All action plans need to identify the action, which is responsible, expectations, status updates, and next steps for follow-up. This sets up clear and concise lines of accountability and responsibility between management and staff.

It clearly becomes a centralized communication document of who is doing what by when and how. This action plan document becomes an important management tool to show how risk is managed and mitigated that face the organization.

Reassessment

All strategies and actions will need to be tweaked, modified, and even changed as much as 180 degrees.

When we first create a strategy and action steps ... we may be guessing on what we need to do. As the situation matures as more information and insight are gained ... and we know how effective our initial steps are working ... we will most likely now take action to tweak what we have done.

This refinement is designed to bring about more favorable results quicker and robustly.

Reassessment can be made directly to the action plan as line item changes or modifications. You can even explain the redirection within the expectation column, as an option, if you think necessary and relevant.

Revision

Revision becomes the following step after the reassessment, which will impact the action plan and to who is doing what, by when, and how.

Outreach

Outreach is a communication strategy that reaches out to all parties impacted, stakeholders, senior executives, and staff to advise of the status of the problem resolution and any changes that have made to the original plan.

Outreach needs to be accomplished as follows:

Following the three guidelines will assure all those impacted and engaged of feeling included, important, and fully informed
That belief will typically mean stratified parties to the issue at hand

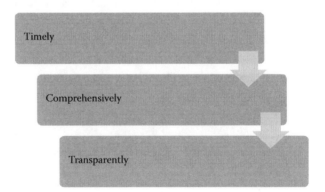

Timely

Comprehensively

Transparently

Mitigation

Mitigation is part of the resolution strategy.
It primarily offers and accomplishes two benefits:

1. Resolution completed
2. Resolution relief

This means that whatever was accomplished worked 100%, everyone is happy, and business has moved forward again as planned. This is a perfect scenario, and while it happens … it happens infrequently.

Option 2 is the more likely scenario. Meaning the steps you took were favorably received by all, but moving forward may be done more cautiously and with certain controls in place to prevent future disruptions.

Mitigation also means that some compromise was offered … with a client, it might be lowering the price, shipping more quantity, or sacrificing margin on future sales.

Mitigation does not necessarily eliminate the problem, but it offers some solace that helps the relationship move forward despite the dispute or problem.

Closure

The problem or dispute will become a *thing of the past* once closure is initiated. Closure becomes a very open and transparent communication between all stakeholders and those impacted by the event that the situation has been finalized and all parties have agreed to move on.

It might outline mitigation steps, future preventative measures, and a general understanding that the situation is over, been resolved, and all parties have agreed to move forward.

It is better accomplished as a *declaratory acknowledgement* so there is no misunderstanding of where the resolution initiative has and is going.

Closure may also identify cause and outline what will happen to make sure that the event does not happen again. And if it does … what preparatory measures have been drawn up from a preventive perspective.

If there are *heroes* in the mix, closure might also identify them and their actions …, which typically is always well received by the impacted and interested parties.

NEGOTIATION

Developing and growing executives as they navigate through their daily responsibilities will be *negotiating* every day.

There will be purchases made, new staff hired, problems resolved, contracts completed, and bosses and subordinates dealt with ... to name a few of the daily challenges every executive will need to make.

Each challenge becomes a negotiation. Negotiation is covered in great detail in Chapter 7.

We must be able to negotiate well for a number of reasons:

- We expect our staff to negotiate well, so we must be in a position to mentor them in this area. The more we understand and can accomplish with negotiation skill sets, the better off we will be in leading our coaching and mentoring efforts
- We will have more success in obtaining the successes we need to move the company forward
- Successful negotiations have a direct line of achievement in reducing risk and spending in any organization ... two principal responsibilities of all senior management

Negotiation is both an art and science. Some of us will have greater innate abilities to negotiate and there are numerous skill sets that we can be trained in.

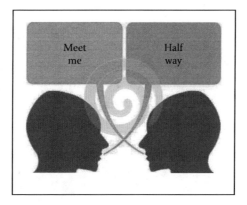

One of the key elements in negotiation management is the ability to obtain a compromise.

The typical negotiation is between two or possibly multiple parties.

Each side has the desired results that each is seeking to obtain. Most successful negotiations are a result of all sides compromising to some extent and obtaining their goals to some extent.

Each party walks away somewhat satisfied. A *win–win* gets created.

TIME MANAGEMENT

If we do not manage our time well, we will not be effective leaders and managers. Executives who are expanding, growing, and accepting new responsibilities will always be busy.

They will always have more to accomplish then they have time to handle. A *quandary* is created that must be managed. Because if the *quandary* is not managed, you will be faced with numerous disappointed colleagues and partners and a consistent flow of problems that will be absorbing all your time.

The *quandary* simply stated:

A state of perplexity or uncertainty, especially as to what to do; dilemma.

We do not want to have quandaries. They take up time, cause anxiety, and have severe consequences to our business model, career, and in being successful.

The better option is to manage our time and avoid quandaries altogether.

We manage our time by believing in the following:

As human beings, our brains have an unlimited capacity to perform. It is our ability to harness these performance capabilities … that is the challenge

We can take on more then we think, and we can handle or manage more then we believe we can

The key is to organize and prioritize properly. If we do those two, then managing our time becomes easier, and we become proficient at managing time better.

Managing time better equates to succeeding in our tasks, responsibilities, and the goals we have as individuals and in our business mantra.

How to organize better:

1. Do not depend on your memory It fails often.
2. Utilize lists. The lists can be written on paper or maintained in your electronics.
3. The list needs to be viewed first thing in the morning, several times throughout the day, and at the end of the work day.
4. The list needs to be updated and maintained throughout the day.
5. It is okay to combine both personal *to do's* and business activity.
6. The list needs to be concise and simple.
7. Get into the habit of writing everything down that will need to be responded to, cause an action, or has to be accomplished.

How to prioritize better:

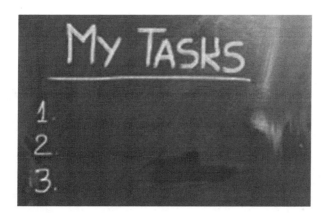

1. Understand what your goals are and what you are trying to accomplish. This will help you determine your priorities.
2. On a personal basis, your priorities are only a few items: living, health, family, religion, career, etc.

3. On a business basis, the list will be much longer and can be organized into funnels of specific concerns: that is ... finance, personnel, sales, customer service, etc.
4. Prioritizing must be coordinated with all the stakeholders, those impacted, bosses, subordinates, colleagues, vendors, and clients and if combined with personal ... then with family and friend members.
5. When you keep a list as outlined earlier ... then the list gets prioritized by the most important first, followed by a declining checklist of importance.
6. Keep in mind that priorities will change as time moves forward ... on a micro scale ... daily. On a macro scale ... yearly.
7. Keep your lists *transparent* to all parties interested, engaged, and impacted. This is a form of higher communication, which keeps everyone on the same page.

Delegating

Delegating is a *tool* executives can utilize to help them manage time better. It accomplishes a number of benefits:

- Delegating can be a form of showing confidence in subordinates.
- It can be a training, coaching, and mentoring tool.
- It allows you to move some responsibility to others, so you can better focus on other maybe more important priorities.
- Delegating some of your weaker areas can strengthen your overall teams' performance.

In delegating, you must also create a set of guidelines:

- Learn the discretion of what to delegate and what to keep to yourself.
- Learn who and when to delegate to.
- Learn to develop reasonable expectations when you do delegate.
- Set responsible deadlines.
- Create systems for follow-up and accountability.
- Keep in mind that as stated previously, that delegating is a form of mentoring and coaching so patience and training are inclusive elements of what you need to contribute during the process.
- Delegation review should be set up to provide immediate feedback. Delays in communicating will lose some of their zeal and effectiveness.

TIME MANAGEMENT AND COMMUNICATING

Those who have mastered time management will still not get everything done they desired to do. This is also reviewed in Chapter _____.

There will always be some things, tasks, responsibilities left over.

This makes communicating these *leftovers* as a next step in responsible time management ..., which is to communicate to all impacted parties the status of where you are at. Do you need more time? Do you want to alter to a new delivery date?

No one typically will have a problem in moving a date out ... as long as they have been proactively communicated to.

Mastering time management can become one of the most important skill sets of managing and leading a business successfully.

PEOPLE SKILLS

Handling and managing people are a daily part of every executive's overall responsibilities.

Leading and managing, which are interchangeable, is a job skill set that all effective business models require of its senior management staff.

Organizations thrive on managers being able to lead people in a positive, mutually beneficial direction that serves the interest of the organization and the individual and their family, as well.

Attributes of an executive with quality people skills are:

- They are active and good listeners
- Create mutually beneficial goals
- Can be driving hard on performance, but not be brash
- Cognizant of how others feel
- Build team initiatives
- Problem solving
- Shows discretion when necessary
- Lead by positive example
- East to work with and for ..., but not be a pushover and firm when needed
- Goal oriented
- Makes good decisions
- Highly responsible
- Good communicator
- Disciplined

Executives with good people skills tend to move along faster and with greater ease. They know how to get along, get things done, and create an atmosphere for most employees to perform well in.

Business owners and senior management are always looking for executives who have good people skills. It makes their jobs easier and creates the best opportunity for the company to prosper and grow.

BUSINESS DEVELOPMENT

Growing businesses always will have new business as a goal as they expand and become more diversified in numerous ways.

While many firms have specific personnel dedicated to sales and business development, it is often a fact that it becomes all managers' responsibilities to take on activities and some functionality to grow their businesses.

Business development can be broken into three major components:

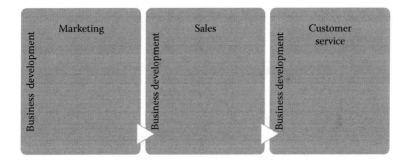

In larger corporations these responsibilities in business development may be very distinct silos of operation. In medium and smaller organizations, these responsibilities often are mutually shared and managed under a singular entity.

Business development includes in the area of marketing: branding, outreach, identifying marketplace, and initial prospect contact.

Sales includes moving prospects from an opportunity to a client … closing deals.

Customer service includes maintaining and renewing existing client relationships.

All three disciplines are important to any growing organization. And are connected to one another's success.

GROWTH STRATEGIES

Raising the Bar of Sales Management

In Organic Sales

In 2018, companies looking to expand and grow have two primary options. One is to become involved with merger and acquisition (M&A) activity where opportunities are purchased.

The other option and central to this article is the expansion by building your company and developing your growth *organically*.

Most companies that are successful in their business models that are aggressively looking to expand and grow their business will work both options simultaneously with a focus on one or the other.

This part of the book will focus on growth organically.

The challenges in organic sales management are numerous, such as, but not limited to:

- This author boldly states that in almost any industry sector … quality sales personnel are one of the hardest hires to make??
- To discern who really is the prospect and/or a serious opportunity??
- Price is a very significant factor in the decision-making process of many purchasing executives??
- No one likes to spend their dollars on various expenditures when other less expensive options may exist??

- Many sales personnel are great at selling against cost only. What really makes one a *great* sales person is one that protects the necessary margins to make decent profits for their organizations and tries to eliminate cost as a driving factor??
- Organic growth, and particularly when compared to M&A growth strategies, is a slower process to mature and the return on investment (ROI) may take longer to make senior management happy??

All these challenges can be managed successfully through the proper management of sales, business development, and opportunity leveraging.

The author has been involved in sales management for over 35 years. He has tried a number of ways, methods, and sales processes to grow the businesses he has been involved with. Some initiatives have worked, some have failed, and both to certain degrees.

But in the past 15 years he has been very successful at helping companies grow their business models organically, being guided by following this outlined formula.

The formula has five primary areas of engagement. These areas of engagement are the focus and platform for a successful organic growth model to be utilized by and sector of the freight, logistics, or supply chain business.

The five cornerstones are:

- Creating a viable sales strategy
- Hiring quality personnel
- Building a sales pipeline of opportunity
- Creating an inventory of prospects
- Closing more deals

The author says ... learn these cornerstones, master them, and organic sales can be very successful!

Creating a Viable Sales Strategy

The sales strategy becomes the blueprint for a plan of attack. The quality and realistic approach of that plan will determine the success of the organic sales initiative.

The steps in the planning process are:

- Where do we want to be? How big do we want to grow? How realistic are these goals?

  Do these goals pass the SMART test? Are the goals specific, measurable, attainable, realistic, and trackable?
- Do a SWOT analysis ... strengths, weaknesses, opportunities, and threats

  What you are doing here is an assessment of your current operations. You are asking questions like ...
- What types and size clients are in our portfolio ... is there a *trend* or reason we have these clients?
- What verticals are we in and why? What verticals should we be in?
- What are the strengths and weaknesses of our existing sales staff? Do they need to be trained further ... in what skill sets? Will they ever be successful sales personnel?

The sales strategy once ready to establish will include:

- Growth goals
- Specific action plan to achieve the goals
- Accountability structure from stakeholders to senior management
- Timing and milestones
- Contingency plans

Once the strategy is in place, we move to the personnel who will make it happen.

Hiring Quality Business Development and Sales Personnel

The first hire, promotion, or internal designation to be made is who is in charge of sales.

A major mistake many companies make is to take their top sales person and make him or her the sales manager.

Believing that the skill sets to sell well ... equate to managing well? This is very often a big misnomer.

THOUGHTS TO SELL BY ...

Gratitude unlocks the fullness of life. It turns what we have into enough, and more. It turns denial into acceptance, chaos to order, confusion to clarity. It can turn a meal into a feast, a house into a home, a stranger into a friend.

Melody Beattie

The head of the sales snake ... has to both sell and manage and more importantly have the capacity to make the new sales strategy in organic growth ... be successful!

Some companies look internally to operations personnel. Another potential mistake. You need a person who can sell. I would agree that an operations person, with all that experience, if they also have sales skills, could be a great option ..., but finding that combination is extremely rare.

When we look outside our company we are met with primarily two choices ... the seasoned candidate or the newbie.

The seasoned candidate may bring some baggage and will more likely cost more. But they often can bring books of business, so their ROI is more immediate.

The newbie has the advantage of no baggage or preconceived notions. But they may require more attention, training, and time for that ROI.

In either case, your choice needs to mirror what your strategy requires.

Attributes of quality sales personnel include some of the following traits:

- High energy
- Persistent
- Flexible
- Good negotiator
- Excepts rejection well
- Likes socialization and people in general
- Creates a high level of trust with others
- Understands the importance of compromise
- Will not allow objections, challenges, and walls to interfere with finding a way to move forward
- Is likeable
- Is able to motivate others
- Learns the technical side of what they are selling
- Knows how to create opportunity
- Deliver compelling arguments
- Close deals
- Protects company margin requirements
- Continually learns
- Has a boatload of emotional intelligence and street smarts

Additionally:

- Making sure you have a robust sales compensation strategy that is not only contemporary, but offers value add to the sales team, which attracts more and better sales talent.

- Spend money to create the initial pipeline of opportunities. Invest in information, marketing, branding, memberships, and travel & entertainment (T&E) … to allow the interface to start the building of prospects and relationships.
- Go after low hanging fruit. Assess where you can obtain easier and quicker results.
- You can never replace experience … seasoned sales talent are always a great option and typically provide faster and better results.
- Moving your company and your sales initiatives into global and international business opportunities will enhance your business profile and increase the number of serious prospects and a door to differentiation.
- The utilization of CRM Systems and technology should be a serious consideration where and when sales become robust and too cumbersome to manage manually.

Building a Sales Pipeline of Opportunity

The sales pipeline begins with establishing a flow of opportunities of companies to engage in a dialog with you.

Sales at the end of the day … is sometimes considered a *numbers* game. Meaning that there has to be a certain number of opportunities that will lead into sales.

In my sales management strategy … I believe there are three stages of the sales process as outlined in the pictorial.

The *first stage* is … opportunities.
The *second stage* is … prospects.
The *third stage* is … closing deals.

Stages 2 and 3 are covered in the following in more detail.

The first stage of creating opportunities can be an infinitum number of companies. You can never have too many opportunities.

But an opportunity may not also be a *prospect*. Because *opportunities* need to go through a vetting process to determine whether or not:

- You have something to specifically sell them
- Is the effort going to pay off?
- Is what they need and what you can deliver … compatible?
- Are there values aligned with yours?
- How do they pay?
- Can you make your margin?
- Do you have the internal expertise necessary to handle the account well? (Side note … you do not want a new client to come in that you cannot service well. You will lose it horribly and the opportunity will be lost forever)

The vetting process of opportunities will pay back in spades and in a quality sales management structure will prove to be a very valuable business process.

Creating a robust supply of opportunities can come in many forms. Cold calling is a common method, but a lot of time is wasted here.

Telemarketing, networking, attendance at industry events, buying vetted lists, and with certain verticals, and their associations are better methods.

Creating an Inventory of Prospects

Here is where the real numbers game starts. Here is where you most likely need a certain number of prospects.

A prospect that has been vetted has the trademarks of an opportunity moved down the pipeline … closer to a deal that can be won!

A vetted opportunity which has turned into a *prospect* might look like this:

- You know who the *real* decision makers are in the company you are soliciting.
- You have established a working relationship with the necessary personnel at the prospects business (The higher up you can go will increase the likelihood of a favorable close).
- Your company has the right tools, services, and expertise to handle the client's needs.
- You are receiving all the necessary information to provide a responsible proposal.
- You can offer competitive pricing.
- Do not entertain request for proposals (RFPs) that come in where you are just one of the participants and have not developed the necessary relationships with the prospect to leverage your opportunity.

Having passed that acid test … now an *opportunity* is moved up in status to a *prospect*.

In the numbers game … I think you need a certain number of serious prospects in the pipeline to close a certain number of deals to eventually meet your strategy and your ultimate sales and growth goals.

Many factors will determine what this magic number is: the nature of your sale, the exclusivity of what you have to offer, the rareness of what you can do for the client, and your competitive pricing.

In many industry verticals, for the average salesperson … this might mean anywhere from a low of 10 to as much as 30 companies who have been vetted and can be considered a serious prospect.

This number in the pipeline over the course of time and experience … will equate to a track record of closed deals.

Management needs to know what these ratios are and hold their personnel accountable to achieve certain results.

Many companies would be very happy with closing ratios of 10%. Others have been successful in moving the numbers to 50% or higher.

Eventually a number will be determined that fits your business model. I would stress here that the more quality of the vetting process … will enhance the opportunity for a higher percentage-closing ratio.

The higher the ratio … means more closed deals against the sales strategy …, which is a wonderful occurrence.

Moving prospects into more closed deals also is an art all by itself outlined in the following:

Closing More Deals

Every salesperson and those in senior management would like to see more deals closed. What a great place to live in with a *Nirvana* of all our solicitations being successful. I think the last time we saw that was when Viagra first came out … and was the only erectile dysfunction solution in tablet form! Being a Pfizer sales person, back then … was probably a pretty good gig!

But reality smacks us in the face, and we all live with a ratio that falls in less than we would like.

But we can take steps to increase our odds of closing more deals and here are some thoughts to make that happen:

Price

Steer away from opportunities that are only driven by price. If they come to you for $.50 less a kilo today … tomorrow they will leave you for $.50 less when the next salesperson comes along and offers a better price.

Offering a competitive price is a very different approach than offering the lowest price.

Do not allow your service to be a *commodity*. If you do, you will become a market driven product and unless you can always produce the best price … you will always be struggling to maintain your accounts and obtain new ones.

In vetting the price, discuss with the opportunity of how they go about making their purchasing decisions. Stay away from those that tell you price is the only or highly important factor in their decision-making process.

And you must be able to sell a price where your company's margin requirements are minimally met and hopefully surpassed. This will make you a great salesperson versus one that is mediocre.

NO one wants to lose an opportunity. But it is okay to walk away from opportunities that will not allow your company to earn a responsible living.

Learning when to move on to the next and the next better opportunity is part of the maturing process of quality sales personnel.

Customer Service

We all talk a good story and say we offer great service … but do we really? And how do we know?

Many unhappy clients never complain first … they just move on quietly one day.

> Quarterly Business Review in Sales Management and Customer Service

Thoughts on a great customer service program in most industry verticals:

- We need to continually assess how we are doing. Client surveys and outreach are good ways along with quarterly business review meetings where this subject gets discussed directly and openly.
- Are our customer service representatives out seeing our larger and more important clients?
  Face to face with operations personnel is a great way to *bond and further develop* client relationships.
- Can our customer service team offer the scope of services, skill sets, and capabilities to satisfy the client's needs?
- Are our customer service representatives being trained with contemporary tools, skill sets, and education to ensure their performance?
- Are we adding value to the client relationship that differentiates us from the competition?
- Do we have the technology in place in our relationship with our clients that is contemporary and offers real value?

Specific Sales Strategy

- Does the salesperson have the necessary relationships with the prospect and are they senior enough to approach this size client or complexity of the deal?
- Are you offering a *compelling* story to the prospect? Did you qualify upfront what you needed to do to get the business and are you now there?
- Can you offer enough intelligence, serious rationale, and business process improvements to overcome the cost of airfreight versus other modes of transit?
- How is your ability to negotiate overall? When is the last time you received training in negotiation skill sets?
- Have you mined and dug for information valuable about your prospect that will help close the deal?
- Are you offering leveraged points of engagement that differentiate you from the competition?
- Are you able to minimize the importance of being the *least expensive* with the balance of a higher value added and service portfolio?
- What is the quality of how you are presenting your story? Utilizing a PowerPoint … is it mind boggling or just ho hum? Who is making the presentation? Is your best foot moving forward?
- Do you have the resilience and stamina necessary to work on the prospect until it closes into a client?

Concluding Remarks

If we as members of a global business community are searching out our best options to grow our business, than we must bring organic sales into the picture to some extent.

Following the earlier recommendations and allowing ourselves to be challenged with all the questions being asked and thought out … gives us the best opportunity to grow our businesses and increase margins and long-term sustainability.

OPERATIONS

The backbone of any organization is in its operational profile and business model.

Operations drive the organization in support of sales and business development activities.

Operations might include any of the following silos:

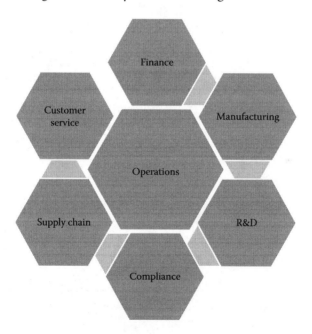

Every company and business model has varied structures and reporting mechanisms. The previous pictorial is one that is commonly found in many organizations.

Keep in mind that these silos can also be further broken down into more specific areas or responsibility and discipline.

Executives in a global profile must understand the importance of silo structure and the various responsibilities, activities, and operational needs of each one.

Supply chain	Manufacturing	R&D
• Sourcing • Purchasing • Logistics • Inventory management • Demand planning	• Supply • Raw materials and components • Locations and sites • Regulatory issues • Vendor management	• New products • Applied research • Technology • Resources • Contract manufacturing

Finance	Compliance	Customer service
• Capital requirements • Cash flow • Payables and receivables • Accountins	• OSHA • HR • Trade • Safety • Hazardous materials	• National accounts • Client interface • Returns • Technology interface

Management and leadership in the international business model require significant expertise, all of which is outlined in this book. The comprehensiveness of knowledge in managing all these company silos and their numerous subdivisions create an enormous challenge.

The key is having an exposure to and information flow that keeps you in the loop in all these areas of concerns.

Weekly management reports such as the one outlined in the following …
help keep busy executives in current events and status within all operating silos in their company:

BTI Monthly Management Report

Division: Supply Chain

Date: 7 October 2017

Manager: John R.

New business: 4 new accounts: Apex, Demon Industries, Spelin and Quicken … approx. revenue … 1.2 m

Lost business: 0

Key issues: Waiting for IT to install new CSR system, Creating new program for client returns week of 11/7

Personnel: Terminated Tom L, as agreed and hired two new admins starting next week

Technology: Installed all new terminals in the warehouse and that will complete IT requirements for this year

Senior management needs: Awaiting authorization on expenditure for managing a logistics RFP for all our inbound freight

Reports like earlier set up a consistent information flow into senior management. It also creates a line of accountability and responsibility between interested and vested parties within an organization.

Larger companies with numerous silos and subdivisions are best managed with a tool like this management report accomplished each month and reviewed at least quarterly.

From a financial basis, operational costs need to fall in line with industry related percentages against revenue.

The percentages must be managed tightly and are often areas where companies can impact overall costs and spending with the organization.

When business and the economy are good … operational expenses typical grow exponentially and out proportion acceptable ratios.

Mangers need to watch the ratios closely and practice lean operations to keep costs down.

Each industry and business model has to be aware of what the acceptable ratio parameters are.

The operating ratio can be used to determine the efficiency of a company's management by comparing operating expenses to net sales. It is calculated by dividing the operating expenses by the net sales. The smaller the ratio, the greater the organization's ability to generate profit.

Keep in mind the ultimate goal is to enhance margins, grow profits, and build the business larger.

Controlling operating costs is a centric component of that formula.

> The operating expense is a measure of what it costs to operate a piece of property compared to the income that the property brings in. The operating expense ratio is calculated by dividing a property's operating expense by its gross operating income and used for comparing the expenses of similar properties.

STRATEGIC PLANNING AS AN OPERATIONAL RESPONSIBILITY

Thinking through the planning process as an operating function requires a number of steps:

Strategic Planning Considerations

Mantra

An important and necessary step in strategic planning is for a company, senior executives, the board, and the owners to define who they are.

This is often accomplished in a mission or vision statement or what is often referred to as the *mantra*.

This sets the tone for the company at a *mile high* perspective. All else follows what the mantra is.

Goals and Deliverables

Goals and deliverables are best created by following a very established strategic thinking process called *SMART-C.*

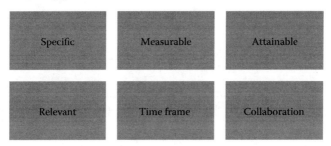

Specific

The goal cannot be set up rhetorically. We must make progress, do our very best, and grow the business.

Specific means ... grow by 6%. Increase sales by 1 million dollars annually, finish the job by 12 noon tomorrow.

Specific eliminates or reduces the opportunity for any subjectiveness which then becomes interpretative.

Measurable

When we establish a goal, we must have a capability to measure if that goal has been achieved.

Goals need to have a reference point and a time frame!!!

Therefore, a starting point of constant must be first identified, along with the system utilized and time frame for measuring.

Keep in mind all goals are just not reference points, but are reference points within a given time frame.

Attainable

Goals and deliverables, when established, must have a determination of having to be attainable. Having goals that are too high or too low will only create grief, disappointment, and potential disruption.

Relevant

Goals must have a relevance to contemporary circumstances that will emanate from political, economic, industry, and other demographic reference points.

Time Frame

The goals and deliverables need to be framed within an agreed time line. The time line brings attainability and relevance into the overall formula for establishing a goal and really ties the five foundation points into one another.

This means that they are interwoven and connected to one another in the overall thought process when establishing a goal.

Collaboration

Most professionals only utilize *SMART* in goal setting. Over the years I have expanded this concept to include an element of *collaboration*.

This means that goals typically require in a business setting to be a function of input and team initiative to produce a set of goals that everyone will follow or attempt to achieve.

The collaborative process creates:

- Camaraderie
- Input from others which is both appreciated and can provide value
- Makes eventual implementation easier, when everyone participates in the goal setting process
- Creates a stronger sense of relevance

Goal setting following SMART-C structure creates the best opportunity for goals to be constructed intelligently and for their eventual achievement to be gained.

3

Financial Considerations

A critical management skill set, no matter what your title or scope of responsibility ... all executives need to have a granular understanding of how the decisions they make have a huge impact in the financial status of the organizations they are engaged with.

The better they know financial impact, the better they can manage their overall responsibilities. This chapter looks at the basic financial considerations that all executives need to comprehend.

FINANCIAL CONTROLS

Every executive with a desire to lead and manage an organization has to have the basic working knowledge of the financial operations in their company.

The primary purpose of business is to return dividends and growth to the shareholders.

Senior managers who understand how the numbers work will be in a better position to make more quality decisions that impact financial results.

This does not mean that every decision has a financial incentive ..., but most do.

Some areas that I recommend every executive learns the basics:

- Revenue and expenses
- Payables
- Receivables
- Profit and loss statement

Accounting 101

- Assets and liabilities
- Balance sheet
- Cash flow
- Financial reporting
- Banking and creditor relationships
- Financial exposures and risks
- Insurance considerations
- Budgeting
- Inventory
- Employee costs/payroll
- Taxes
- Technology in accounting

Revenue and expenses: Making sure you have the basic knowledge of money in and money out, on a micro, transactional, macro, yearly, and budgeted basis. This includes both planned and actual.

Payables: Knowing exactly what is owed, how much, by when, to whom, and how was it reconciled and audited.

Receivables: Knowing exactly how much you are owed, by whom, and when and how was it reconciled and audited. Additionally, margin intelligence would be a subtopic of serious concern in this regard.

Profit and loss statement: A snapshot of a company's position in an agreed time frame (quarterly, annually, etc.) also referred to as an *income statement* shows the profit and loss or the financial performance of that company.

Assets and liabilities: The assets are resources, owned things, such as, but not limited to: cash, receivables, inventory, fixtures, land, buildings, investments, etc.

Liabilities are the obligations … or the future sacrifices that are obligated for the use of the assets … loans, wages, payables, etc.

One must also understand the differences between liability and debt and *current versus long-term*.

Balance sheet: The balance sheet is a snapshot of the assets and liabilities in a formal generally accepted accounting format. It details the balance of income and expenditure over the preceding period.

Cash flow: Refers to the total amount of monies that move in and out of a business, which will help determine liquidity, as well as any borrowing needs.

Financial reporting: Financial reporting is a procedure of producing certain types of statements that review and disclose a company's financial status to shareholders, business owners, managers, and various government agencies.

Banking and creditor relationships: Your company will have banking and creditor relationships that are a key to a company's well being. It is critical as a senior executive to develop relationships with the key executives to make sure these financial needs are taken care of as comprehensively and professionally, as possible.

Financial exposures and risks: A company will have financial exposures and risks … such as, but not limited to: not being able to fund cash flow requirements, capital expenditure funds, operating expense requirements, etc.

Management needs to understand to what extent these risks are valid and to what extent they may impact operational needs, thereby creating strategies and action plans to transfer, mitigate, or assume these risks.

Insurance considerations: Risks that a company faces go way beyond just financial, and a company must evaluate these exposures and arrange for risk transfer mechanisms in some of the following areas:

- Property and asset protections
- Liability
- Product liability
- Errors and omissions
- Transportation, storage, and warehousing
- Receivable protections

- Cargo risks
- Fiduciary
- Surety and bond exposures
- Cyber risks
- Workers compensation
- Directors and officers
- Employee benefits
- Automobile
- Umbrella and excess
- Political risk
- War, strikes, riots, and civil commotions

Budgeting: Part of an overall strategic plan is the budgeting process, which is a predictive structure that allows a forecast of what the financial picture and needs of the company will need to be in order to operate in.
  It becomes the basis of defining what the financial picture will look like at some point down the road.

Inventory: The comprehensive list of items in a company, such as, but not limited to: property, goods in stock, and other related assets.

Employee costs/payroll: The primary list of employees and what they are to be paid is the payroll ledger.
  Other costs might be social security, disability, state fees, employee benefits, health insurance, retirement accounts, 401k, etc.

Taxes: A company will have a host of tax obligations that they have to accrue for and ultimately pay out on a regular and timely basis. The government requires its money timely.

- Federal
- State
- Local
- Payroll
- Withholding
- Sales
- Income
- Property
- Excise
- Gross receipts
- Franchise

Technology in accounting: Most companies will require a technology solution to manage their accounting needs.

The basic systems record all expenses and revenue on a transactional level and from that basis will be able to accommodate all financial reporting requirements ... payables, receivables, cash position, profit and loss (P&L), balance sheets, banking reconciliations, etc.

Managers operating in all verticals need to be fully aware of the technology capability, and how the information in the system can help them manage their responsibilities.

The technology is a starting point on how the company is doing, what is going right, and where adjustments need to be made.

CONTROLLING SPEND THROUGH PROCUREMENT MANAGEMENT

Senior Management's Role in Procurement

Overview

A critical area of any organizations *spend* and ultimately its ability to operate successfully ... is in the area of procurement management.

The larger a company is and as it grows ... procurement is a critical area that will increasingly become an integral component of managing and controlling costs and the sustainability of its operation, in the long term.

As most companies mature, so does their structure of a fixed and robust purchasing management functioning department.

This department will focus on developing and managing supplier relationships. Keep in mind, suppliers can be a very important ingredient to your company's overall business model and therefore greatly impact both adversely and positively your sustainability, growth, and profitability potentials.

Most companies have a *supply chain* that is a foundation for their operational profile. Typically, procurement runs in tandem with the supply chain and is sometimes the most important aspect in a supply chain and in particular ... organizations that have a global presence, where products and services are sourced, manufactured, or operated in ... overseas.

Procurement primarily impacts risk, spend, and business processes. Depending upon a company's gross sales volume ..., a 5% reduction in spend can be compared to several million dollars in sales ($$$$).

Procurement is an internal servicing function that works on behalf of business owners and stakeholders who utilize the materials, products, components, and services purchased by the procurement group.

A robust procurement initiative keeps the supply chain open and the business model working successfully. Conversely, a poorly managed procurement operation causes delays, disruption, and additional expense to a company's operation.

The best run procurement operations not only keep the supply chain running, but they continually add value and benefit through their sourcing, purchasing, and supplier/vendor management practices.

Procurement can be divided into three separate functions: sourcing, purchasing, and vendor management.

Sourcing

Sourcing is the function that finds supplier and vendor options, both reactively and proactively, to the internal needs of business owners and stakeholders in a corporation.

The successful sourcing manager has a corral of business contacts and will know who to call when an internal purchasing need is required.

Sourcing managers are responsive to internal *fires* when they ignite and often *come to the rescue* on and as imminent supply needs develop.

Great sourcing managers are engaged in the strategic planning process in an organization and will often proactively find sourcing options before that are actually called for. Then … they will be ready as needed.

Sourcing managers are *state of the art*, contemporary and utilize leading edge technologies and business processes to find and develop raw material, product, components, and services, anticipating future demand and need.

Often, they can add significant value in a number of ways:

- Lowering acquisition costs
- Negotiating better supply deals
- Finding supply options that offer competitive advantages
- Develop vendor/supplier relationships that assist your operations to be viable, productive, and sustainable

Purchasing

Once sourcing options are found, it is the responsibility of purchasing personnel to transition the vendor/supplier into the organization.

This transition process can often be convoluted and arduous and will often determine the outcome of a successful vendor relationship.

Purchasing managers need to be excellent negotiators, as they will be the front line in finalizing a vendor/supplier relationship.

Some of the negotiated areas are:

- Price
- Payment terms
- Contract period or tenure
- Scope of work
- Agreed deliverables
- Performance specifications
- Warranty and return policies
- Insurance requirements
- Dispute resolution
- Cancellation wording
- Responsible parties
- Signing officers

These relevant and salient points get transferred into a statement of work, master services agreement, or just a service agreement or contract between the parties.

This dimension of responsibility for the purchasing officer adds another required skill set ... legal prowess. An attorney still may be required to review and finalize any contracts, but the purchasing officer must be able to negotiate the basic terms and bring it all the way past *third base.*

This brings us to an interesting and important aspect of the purchasing function ... it requires an array of management skill sets:

- Ability to communicate well ... writing, speaking
- Be organized
- Prioritize
- Negotiation
- Legal
- Insurance
- Product knowledge(s) in the company's verticals
- Team and project management
- Conflict resolution
- Finance
- Understanding people's behavior
- Leadership

The purchasing manager is a conduit between all operations in a company to organize and execute their *spend*

Primary responsibilities are:

- Reducing risk
- Reducing spend
- Business process improvements

Secondary responsibilities include:

- Creating internal controls on procurement
- Creating standard operating procedures and protocols in the purchasing functions
- Internal resource for all operating and business owners in an organization
- Vendor management
- Strategic planning for future purchasing needs
- Managing requests for proposals (RFPs)
- Developing long-term sourcing options
- Market intelligence
- Budgeting
- Collaborating with demand planning initiatives
- Managing various projects
- Both transactional and enterprise solutions
- Technology and its utilization throughout an organization
- Compliance
- Diversity inclusions
- Sustainable practices

The purchasing manager has numerous challenges while making an attempt to bring responsible procurement practices into their organization, namely:

- Silo protectionism
- Resistance to change and betterments
- Personalities
- Disbelief and suspicious motivations
- Internal leadership and cultural issues
- Lack of effective working relationships

All these challenges must be overcome and managed successfully if the purchasing manager will have any opportunity to move forward triumphantly with any procurement initiatives and betterments.

Relationship building with business owners and company stakeholders will go a long way in creating more effective opportunities for successful collaboration.

Mutual respect and trust are paramount and foundation characteristics of good working relationships within an organization.

Trust will help a purchasing manager move company personnel into a better scenario for procurement initiatives and betterments.

Though ultimately, trust only goes so far ... performance that delivers consistent and frequent successes will also greatly help relationships build and sustain.

Vendor Management

Once a new supplier/vendor is on-boarded into an organization the concept of *vendor management* is that the following matters are cared for:

- Transitioning successfully the new vendor/supplier into the organization
- Taking ownership of the maintenance of that vendor/supplier and their well being from an oversight perspective
- Taking responsibility for the vendors/supplier's performance in the delivery of their product or service into the organization ... to the benefit of senior management, business owners, stakeholders, or any of the other business beneficiaries
- Coordinating with internal stakeholders any activity with the vendors/suppliers that may impact on operations now or in the future
- Conducting vendor risk assessments and managing any areas of risk to mitigate or transfer
- Managing the system that *tiers* vendors by amount of spend or the critical nature of the product or service they provide to your organization
- Maintaining a robust relationship with the vendors and suppliers, so they continually add value to the alliance between both organizations
- Continually benchmarking price and costing to make sure that your *spend* is *in order* and continually receiving value for your spend
- Handling a proactive system for renewing vendors, as their contracts and agreements reach expiration

The RFP Tool in Managing the Purchasing Function

A lucrative tool for those in sourcing, purchasing, and vendor management is the request for proposal (RFP). Often also referred to as request for interest (RFI), request for quote (RFQ), and so on ... this business concept allows those in procurement to create a process to:

- Identify potential vendors and suppliers
- Keep favored incumbents *sharp*
- Vet potential providers
- Maximize favorable results in any bid initiative
- Establish a consistent and responsible means of managing spend with both existing and potential providers, vendors, and suppliers.
- Develop a favored and professional relationship both within your organization and with outside vendors/suppliers, of which will establish better working relationships and a greater opportunity for successful and consistent procurement

The management of RFPs is both an art and science. Managing successful RFPs can be learned, schools inside of organizations include AMA (amanet.org), NIWT (niwt.org), or ISM (ismny.org).

Continual learning is the key to mastering the management of RFPs and being a *top-notch* procurement professional, well respected, and with a robust career ... and accomplishing successful purchasing for your organization's benefit.

Risk Management in Procurement

Purchasing managers need to understand that vendors and suppliers, just as any aspect, activity, or person in your organization ... can cause *risk*.

These vendor risks must be evaluated, assessed, and a determination made on one of the three options to manage same:

- Assume the risk and set up a contingent liability
- Transfer the risk to a third party, such as a surety or insurance company
- Mitigate the risk through actions sometimes referred to as loss control, loss prevention, and other related options

Managing the risks of vendors and suppliers can be a heavy percentage of work hours of those engaged in vendor management. But it is considered a necessary component of a successful vendor management program. This initiative will prevent occurrences from causing damage and financial losses within or to your supply chain, when the vendor fails to perform.

Some of the risks might be:

- Financial failure of the vendor/supplier
- Missed deliveries or delays
- Quality control issues
- Nonperformance
- Intellectual property rights concerns
- Inability to compete

In vendors/suppliers that provide *critical* raw materials, parts, components, finished products, or services, their failure in anyone of these earlier outlined sample risks could cause a serious blow to your operations and even be catastrophic.

In the overall risk management concept with vendors and suppliers, those engaged in vendor management need to coordinate a continual search with those responsible for sourcing ... to always have options in the pipeline and creating *plan B's* with alternate vendors and suppliers.

In the world of procurement, this ties into the debate about *single source* versus *multiple source* strategies utilized by various companies to leverage spend and at the same time reduce risk. Some would argue that multiple options clearly reduce vendor/supplier risk. Others would argue that single sourcing allows you to focus spend in one entity to leverage your purchasing power.

Both are correct strategies. A purchasing manager should always be assessing the risks in both options and making decisions where consensus and compromise provide viable choices.

This must be done in concert with senior management to understand their tolerance for acceptable risk levels.

SUMMARY

Procurement is clearly a vital and growing function of relevance and importance in every organization. Senior management must consciously recognize this fact and allocate funds and resources to the procurement structure within their organization.

They must give the authority to procurement managers who will set up standard operating procedures, protocols, and business processes in the sourcing, purchasing, and vendor management verticals to assure that both risk and spend are completely managed on all goods and services acquired from third party entities.

Senior management must create a *culture* within the organization that brings both the quantitative and qualitative disciplines of procurement into every *nook and cranny* of your business model and the organization overall.

There are no secrets to success. It is the result of preparation, hard work, and learning from failure.

Colin Powell

4

Going Global—The Business Case to Go Global: Foreign Purchasing and Export Sales

International business will typically take three forms: ownership of overseas assets, purchasing goods and services from foreign markets, or sales of domestic product into global markets.

This chapter explores these three primary options and will offer the reader a comprehensive overview and a *best practice* panorama of advice and counsel.

- The case to go global
- Overseas expansion
- Foreign purchasing
- Export sales
- Developing the skill sets of global business
- Global operational, trade compliance, and regulatory responsibilities

THE "CASE" TO GO GLOBAL

95% of the world's population lives outside the United States. And 60% of the world's wealth is also outside the United States. From a business development perspective, there is no reason not to approach foreign markets from a business opportunity perspective.

The goal of all businesses should be the following:

- Growth exceeding 10% annually
- Profitable operations (minimum 5% annually)
- Sustainable operations
- Exciting business development and ... expansion into new areas, products, and services
- Margin protection
- A great place to work from an employee perspective
- Diversity
- Responsible cost controls
- Connectivity to the community

These goals outlined earlier can best be achieved when a company decides to go global, approached in three distinct, but connected ways:

1. Export sales
2. Global sourcing
3. Foreign asset expansion

Export Sales

This concept expands domestic marketing and sales into foreign markets, where opportunity could be greater than here in the United States.

American made products, contrary to public beliefs are in huge demand in many overseas markets. It is prestigious to utilize American consumer brand names.

Additionally, we produce numerous manufactured products, grow various products, and have varied natural resources that are in high demand in numerous and extensive foreign markets.

Export sales from the United States exceed 50 billion dollars monthly and represent more than 10% of our annual GDP.

In some companies, exports can represent over 30% of total sales volume.

With over 95% of the consumer market and over 70% of the commercial market located outside the United States ... exports is a certainty for companies looking to grow and expand.

Sound reasons for exporting:

- Market share
- Diversification and risk management
- Meeting competitive pressures
- Margin expansion
- Participation in globalizing your company

FOR NEW EXPORTERS

Following are 11 questions the department of commerce (DOC) advises you should answer in developing an export plan:

1. Which products are selected for export development, and what modifications, if any, must be made to adapt them for overseas markets?
2. Is an export license needed?
3. Which countries are targeted for sales development?
4. In each country, what are the basic customer profiles, and what marketing and distribution channels should be used to reach customers?
5. What special challenges pertain to each market (e.g., competition, cultural differences, and import and export controls), and what is the strategy to address them?
6. How will your product's export sales price be determined?
7. What specific operational steps must be taken and when?
8. What will be the time frame for implementing each element of the plan?
9. What personnel and company resources will be dedicated to exporting?
10. What will be the cost in time and money for each element?
11. How will results be evaluated and used to modify the plan?

Exporters that are more seasoned need to pay attention to the following areas:

- Choice of international commercial term of purchase or sale (INCO) terms
- Utilization of freight forwarders
- Landed costs
- Competitive pressures
- Trade compliance issues
- Use of distributors and agents
- Global expansion

All the export issues are connected to one another and have to be managed mutually to obtain the maximum benefit of any export initiative.

Choice of INCO Terms

Exporters need to be careful and utilize INCO terms that leverage sales opportunity, keep costs minimized, and maintain trade compliance responsibilities.

Ex works and DDP are not preferred terms. Free alongside ship (FAS)/ free on board (FOB)/free carrier (FCA) are okay options. We prefer the other six terms, which from a trade compliance and freight logistics basis ... provide more beneficial options to the exporter.

Those terms are: cost, insurance, and freight (CIF), carriage and insurance paid (CIP), cost and freight (CFR), carriage paid to (CPT), delivered at terminal (DAT), and delivered at place (DAP) provide options that more closely control shipping to a specific country, destination, and end-user, which protect trade compliance risks.

DDP is a good customer service option, but handling foreign customs responsibilities is fraught with risk and spend.

Ex works takes the exporter out of the functional responsibility, but not the compliance responsibilities. And is not so client-friendly.

Consult with your compliance expertise along with your freight forwarder to choose the best option.

Utilization of Freight Forwarders

Choosing a quality and expert service provider/freight forwarder could be one of the most important responsibilities of an exporter to assure successful export sales.

The freight forwarder becomes the traffic department for an exporter in moving the goods from your site to your customer located overseas.

The forwarder handles:

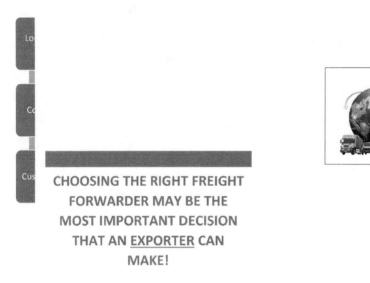

Lo...

Co...

Cus...

CHOOSING THE RIGHT FREIGHT FORWARDER MAY BE THE MOST IMPORTANT DECISION THAT AN <u>EXPORTER</u> CAN MAKE!

Freight forwarders should be chosen on a number of key factors:

- *Price*: The shipping costs must be competitive and at the same time get the job done.
- *Customer service*: The forwarder charges fees for their services and expertise in all the areas outlined earlier. They must be user-friendly, 24/7/365 operational, and offer comprehensive service all over the world.
- *Trade compliant*: The forwarder needs to be trade compliant and assist you, as the exporter be trade compliant.
- *Global scope*: The forwarder needs to have a *global reach* with offices and/or agents in the cities and countries you are exporting to.
- *Technology*: In 2018, technology is driving the export supply chain. Compliance, logistics, communications, regulations, tracking and tracing, and management reports are a few of the areas that technology provides efficiency and prowess.

- *Carrier interface*: The forwarders value to the exporter is also determined by their reach into trucking, air, rail, and vessel carriers to obtain space when needed and pricing that is competitive.

> Choosing the right Freight Forwarder may be the most important decision that an *exporter* can make!

Landed Costs

The landed costs are the accumulation of costs (reviewed in the appendix) that makes up the total cost of shipping the product from origin to destination. The exporter needs to price their product in consideration of all the other costs … freight, duties, taxes, handling, and so on … to assure the competitiveness of its export sale.

Competitive Pressures

The exporter needs to consider that companies within the United States and from overseas are competing for the same markets and customers that we are, as well. Many countries because of free trade agreements, government incentives, and tax rebates can be more competitive then we can be shipping from the United States.

We need to be cognizant of these competitive pressures when marketing and pricing out our products and services. Additionally, we also may have certain advantages, as well.

Trade Compliance Issues

As an exporter, we have to follow numerous regulatory concerns mostly governed by the Departments of: Commerce, Treasury, State, and Homeland Security.

Failure to comply:

- We can lose our right to export.
- Incur shipping delays.
- Have dissatisfied overseas customers.
- Incur fines and penalties.
- Potential criminal prosecution.

Use of Distributors and Agents

Exporters can sell direct or through distributors and agents. Many companies approach foreign markets through agents or distributors in their initial strategy, as it presents less risk and cost to the overall export initiative.

Managing these agents then becomes an important part of your export program. Also, having comprehensive contracts in place, reviewed by international and local legal expertise, is a prudent measure.

Global Expansion

Exporters best interests, in the long-term, are best protected by an initiative that expands into numerous countries in the other six continents where commercial and consumer sales offer options.

This diversifies country and economic risk and builds a larger market to sell to.

Economies of scale are best achieved when you have more to sell and more places to sell to.

Executives, leaders, and managers must bring exporting into their business models, as there is so great a market outside the United States. However, this takes developing the necessary skill sets outlined in the various chapters of this book in mastering globalization and the distinct activities and capabilities required to export well.

Global Sourcing

The big advantage to global sourcing is access to finished products, components, and materials at a lower cost than available if acquired here in the United States.

This obviously lowers costs to the American company, retailer, distributor, or consumer, which makes importing both a competitive and lucrative option.

Foreign Asset Expansion

This is neither exporting nor global sourcing, but relates to U.S. companies acquiring or developing assets on foreign shores.

- This might include the building of factories and manufacturing sites.
- Acquiring foreign companies.
- Making both direct and indirect investment in foreign entities.
- Developing resources located in overseas markets.

A major reason for foreign asset expansion is that it becomes a risk management tool in diversifying your assets over a larger geographical, economic, and political demographic.

It is also a way of leveraging overall corporate growth, gaining access to overseas markets, and obtaining potentially enhanced sales, profits, and margins.

And it creates differentiation from other companies who may shy away from foreign asset development.

DEVELOPING THE SKILL SETS OF GLOBAL BUSINESS

For a company to succeed and for an executive to navigate successfully through the maze of international complexity ... one needs to develop the necessary skill sets of international business and global trade.

The critical skill sets fit into the following areas:

- Understanding foreign cultures
- Understanding import and export operations, regulations, and procedures
- Global supply chain
- International legal, accounting, and finance issues
- International marketing, sales, and customer service
- Technology on a global scale
- International purchasing

Mastering the skill sets secures the best opportunity to succeed in handling your management responsibilities in global trade. Some thoughts in each of these areas:

Understanding Foreign Cultures

If you are going to operate globally, then you need to take the time and initiative to learn the basics of all the cultures you are working with.

This is not only a *best practice*, but will maximize your effectiveness in those markets. The more you understand who and what the people are, who you are dealing with … the better you can have successful business relationships.

Every country around the world presents challenges in navigating the differences of their culture from ours.

We must be respectful of those foreign cultures. Understanding those cultures creates the best path to being respectful. It is always appreciated from a foreign business partner when we show them the respect by demonstrating our knowledge and respect for those cultural differences.

Understanding Import and Export Operations, Regulations, and Procedures

There is a very foundational uniqueness surrounding the world of importing and exporting. Skill sets are required, but not often had. One must acquire it through a difficult and long-term learning curve.

There are very few institutions that teach *hands-on* functional skill set capability in import and export operations.

One such training center … The American Management Association, based in NYC (amanet.org) has a global supply chain class run in various cities like NY, Atlanta, Chicago, and San Francisco several times a year. National Institute for World Trade (niwt.org) is also another option.

Import and export operations require the knowledge of what it takes to move goods through the border outbound and inbound.

It requires knowledge of documentation, packing, marking, and labeling along with any regulatory requirements.

It requires domain over the creation of operating procedures, protocols, and business process where all aspects of the import and export process is documented and in order.

Global Supply Chain

Operating in the global supply chain means mastering cost effective and comprehensive logistics, warehousing, and distribution.

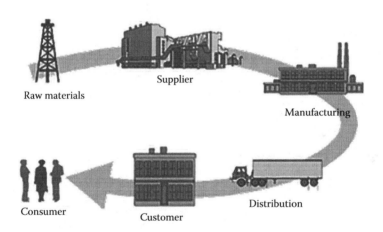

Goods must move through the supply chain internationally: timely, safely, and cost effectively.

Well-managed supply chains accomplish the necessary balance between all three requirements.

Favoring any one over the other two will jeopardize the shipment from completing successfully.

Global supply chain managers successful strategic planning:

- They foster successful partnerships with service providers, freight forwarders, and customhouse brokers who assist them in managing global logistics

- They operate in a close connection to all the operating fiefdoms in their organization who are impacted by their actions: finance, legal, purchasing, sales, customer service, demand planning, etc.
- They master the use of technology in their global supply chain operations: order processing, government interface, carrier interface, regulatory compliance, management data, tracking, and tracing, etc.

International Legal, Accounting, and Finance Issues

These subjects are outlined in various chapters throughout the book, where appropriate to the material presented.

It is covered in basic detail because all international executives irrespective of their primary responsibilities must be paying attention to legal and accounting issues.

These legal and financial matters are important to any aspect of the running of an organization and assuring its profitability and sustainability.

The point we make in Chapter ____ is that the financial and legal aspect of any business touches every division and segment of any business model. Therefore, executives running various fiefdoms need to have a basic understanding of all legal and financial matters so the methods, practices, and operational steps they take to run the company are in sync with what is necessary from a legal and financial perspective.

International Marketing, Sales, and Customer Service

All businesses are built on how well it markets, sells, and services its prospects and customers.

I believe that the corporations that have a *mind-set* that they are a sales organization first … are the ones with the larger success in growth, business development, and expansion.

Selling to foreign markets requires paying attention to a number of key areas of opportunity:

- Understanding that each country of the world is a unique market and must be approached with total customization from how other markets are approached.

- Training business development and sales teams in foreign cultures and business practices is a vital component of any business development strategy.
- Though typically sales have a *broad brush* approach ... in foreign business development ... paying attention to detail is an important differentiation that impacts success favorably.
- Paying attention to costs and more specifically ... *landed costs* ... will create competitive advantage.
- Learn all the regulatory requirements so *staying out of trouble* ... is accomplished proactively.
- Work tightly and cohesively with supply chain and logistics ... as getting the products to customers makes sure of good will, future orders, and sustainable longer-term relationships.
- Make sure you are paying attention to the issues around getting paid.
- Understand the resources and support provided by various government agencies ... Department of Commerce, International Trade Administration, The Export Import Bank, etc.
- Make sure all risks are analyzed and steps are taken to either: assume, transfer, or mitigate the exposures. Insurance is an attractive option and always must be weighed and considered.
- Learn to pay attention to the economics and politics of the world. Both areas can often impact business development opportunities both negatively and positively.
- Paying attention might allow you time to take steps to proactively mitigate exposure or reduce the opportunity for any potential loss. Additionally, it might point you to an opportunity.
- Research the opportunities to leverage areas, such as, but not limited to bonded warehouses, foreign trade zones, and free trade agreements.
- Develop professional resources in all operational areas:
  - Legal
  - Accounting
  - Banking
  - Supply chain and logistics
  - Government resources
  - Insurance and risk management
  - Business development

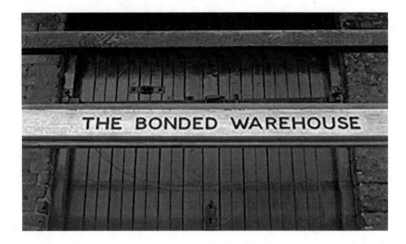

Another concern that enters the world of both legal and marketing consid-erations is in the area of branding and intellectual property rights (IPR).

There have been numerous cases around the world ... TESLA in China, Nike in Spain, Aqua Products/Spain in the USA ... to name a few of the hundreds of cases presented each year.

Companies looking to expand the sale of their products overseas must work with professional expertise to avoid the headaches, costs, and risks associated with an attempt to *brand* their product outside of their host country and enter a new market.

Keep in mind, we are referring to three very distinct, but related, legal areas: patents, trademarks, and copyrights.

Additionally, be reminded that the laws in every country around the world vary greatly from the United States statutes and court precedence established over 300 years of case law and legislation.

In some developing countries, these laws have little meaning. And in a country that is second to the United States in global trade ... China ... they are only beginning to take this area of law more seriously.

Many companies and executives have been quite frustrated at the slow progress in China to be more severe in IPR cases. Recently, Michael Jordan won a large case in China granting him ownership of his name translated in Mandarin.

It was a surprise and huge victory for the *West* in having been unsuc-cessful in so many other legal pursuits that take place in China every year.

Most professionals see this as a turning point in China to begin establishing a more *westernized* approach to protecting foreign IPR issues. Many companies have resisted growth of investment and sourcing in China because of the IPR concern.

This win will go far in establishing a higher level of trust with the Chinese-based legal system.

Most examples of IPR problems emanate from either:

- A lack of knowledge
- A lack of due diligence
- Or a rush to sell and *cutting corners* to move forward quickly

The international marketing executive must have some basic working knowledge of IPR issues in order to protect the company's brand and also mitigate any financial exposures, typically, which are not budgeted for.

You also must establish access internally or externally to legal expertise in IPR's containing copyright, trademark, and patent areas.

The costs and financial exposures for not addressing these IPR concerns proactively are huge. By being proactive upfront and incurring a budgetable expense exercising due diligence and working with legal expertise can avoid large unbudgeted expenses down the road.

Technology on a Global Scale

Technology is driving business expansion and operation in every vertical and corner of the world.

Another *hat* the international executive and business manager must wear is that of a *technology guru*. This does not mean you have to know how to *program*, but you need to understand how technology can be utilized to:

- Make for more efficient operations
- Reduce human error
- Lower costs
- Reduce risks
- Help manage companies to run better
- Afford interface between all operating divisions and connecting operations on a global scale

Technology is moving at the *speed of sound* and must be kept up with time. Most business models will only succeed when they are fully engaged utilizing technology to gain leverage and efficiency in their business models.

International Purchasing

Global sourcing can provide some of the following benefits:

- Lower costs of raw materials, components, and finished products
- Diversify sourcing to a broader and more diverse selection of suppliers and vendors
- As a risk management technique
- Gain access to sales in certain foreign markets where you are sourcing from
- Gain access to foreign technology, talent, and resources
- Creates a much broader view of global markets and globalization in general for your company

Global sourcing can take three forms:

1. Purchasing from a third-party supplier who sells to other companies as well
2. Purchasing from a third-party supplier where you have an exclusive contract for manufacturing
3. Own or joint venture the manufacturing site overseas

In many situations when a company first begins to source overseas it will chose option 1, as it is the less costly of the three and allows a *testing period* to take place before longer-term strategies need to be secure.

This is then followed by option 2, where a more exclusive arrangement is made. This provides a greater degree of influence and control over production and quality control. It becomes more like a *strategic partnership* between the buyer and the supplier.

The option 3 creates a longer more sustainable choice where an *investment* is made via ownership, acquisition, or building.

The third option has a greater expense, possibly presents a greater risk, as well. However, control and influence become your own destiny. Most companies at some point mature into option 3, as a well-managed scenario creates the best opportunity to reduce risk and spend in the overall global supply chain.

In this third option some of the risks are:

- Economic and political failures and complications in the host country.
- Business failures in the strategic plan of ownership.
- The business model changes, and in this host country, change does not occur quickly or comprehensively.
- Supply chain issues develop that are not easily remedied.
- Confiscation, nationalization, expropriation and deprivation occur … Cuba, Peru, Iran, and Argentina are all examples where foreign assets were seized by host countries.
- Standard risk management concerns of ownership … loss, damage, liability, exposures, force maneuvers, and so on.

Having identified the risks of option 3, the attributes are:

- Control over production, manufacturing, quality control, and distribution
- Control over materials and components supply
- Potential lower cost of operations
- Less exposure to IPR concerns
- Control supplier selling price to parent entity in the United States
- Potential benefits of access local employees, talents, and resources

Benefits to Americans and the World

Foreign investment in overseas markets has proven to be a very valuable attribute for reducing the risks of war between the trading countries.

Robust trading relationships such as we have with most countries of the world help maintain business ties that translate into political stability.

This does not mean that on certain issues both politically and economically that there is some discord, but the balance of trade and business rapport reduces the likelihood of any sort of escalation or elevation to strife or war.

The best example of this is the relationship between China and the United States. The countries are 180 degrees apart politically and 90 degrees economically, but we have strong ties on the business front.

China is a huge supplier to the United States and North America in general. China is also a larger market for U.S.-based manufacturers.

This business and trade relationship keeps the political discourse to more rhetorical then functional adversity.

Under the new administration, President Trump ran hard in his political effort during his campaign against China …, but since taking office and developing a relationship with China's leader Xi Jinping, the situation has settled down.

Additionally, it appears China has helped the United States navigate a difficult and tumultuous relationship with North Korea, which has tempered the rhetoric from President Trump towards the China Government.

The expression … "trade prevents war …" has much merit! This has been put forth by many historians, war writers, and economists over the years. Some credit is extended to Stanford Professor Matt Jackson.

FOREIGN PURCHASING

Sourcing Globally: Senior Managements Guide to "Twelve Key Best Practices"

Sourcing globally will continue to grow and expand into new markets as we enter the third decade of the new millennium.

Multinational companies down to smaller family-owned organizations are learning he critical importance of developing multiple and varied sources of raw materials, components, and finished products.

Traditional foreign sourcing such as China is being challenged for the first time in its 40-year tenure as the fastest and expansively growing foreign source of manufactured goods.

Senior management is best guided by setting up policies, protocols, and standard operating procedures (SOPs) in how their management teams and staff operate in their global sourcing opportunities and initiatives.

In public companies, these guidelines would help meet Sarbanes-Oxley regulations and in private companies ... *best practices*. The SOP's create a standard with the following benefits:

- Documented and written commitment to follow government regulations
- Consistent approach to regulatory adherence
- Foundation and resource for all global supply chain personnel to follow
- Creates training module to make sure everyone knows how to operate in their companies following all necessary regulations

Having said all of that ..., the following best practices, outlined in 12 steps offer the international executive a blueprint for either new or matured global sourcing initiatives:

1. Learn how to navigate the opportunities offered through the numerous free trade agreements that can be leveraged for economic advantage in the global sourcing arena.

   Utilizing free trade agreement's (FTA's) lower lands costs by reducing or eliminating duties and taxes.

2. Diversify sourcing into multiple countries so dependence on single sourcing is not relevant.

   This becomes a risk management concept in spreading the sourcing exposure over variable options.

3. Learn the culture of the countries you source from. This will maximize your opportunity to negotiate better deals and build stronger relationships.

   Keep in mind in overseas markets ... *relationship* drives the success of the business deal and the long-term partnership with the vendor/supplier.

4. Utilize specialized professional attorneys who can guide you through the maze of foreign regulations, laws, and policies that will influence sourcing options, agreements, and contracts.

   Legal expertise can be expensive, but it is a necessary expenditure that helps avoid pitfalls, mistakes, and serious financial consequences.

   Laws vary greatly in foreign countries, and companies that learn how to proactively avoid litigation and other legal issues will always minimize risk and maximize opportunity.

5. Develop sourcing reach into Mexico where maquiladora programs and near sourcing initiatives can prove to be valuable options as a sourcing alternative.

   Near sourcing can prove to significantly lower landed costs, reduce risk, and enhance demand planning sand lead-time reductions.

6. Utilize the service of specialized freight forwarders who can provide local support in the sourcing countries in arranging local freight needs, outbound logistics requirements, handle export specifics, and the inbound process into the United States.

   The freight forwarder or customhouse broker can be a valuable partner in impacting risk and cost along with huge benefits in managing inbound supply chain needs.

7. Tread cautiously through all IPRs that can happen once you start to trade in foreign markets, share business models (trade secrets and confidential manufacturing data).

   Managing IPR issues needs to always be addressed proactively when forming relationships in global sourcing models. The headaches and costs in chasing and dealing with IPR breaches can be costly, aggravating, and a waste of time and effort. And litigation in markets such as China typically creates less than robust results ... leaving both parties dissatisfied and filled with angst.

8. Pay close attention to the choice of INCO term. The choice impacts risk and cost between the supplier and the buyer.

   There are 11 INCO term options: Ex works, FAS, FCA, FOB, CIF, CIP, CPT, CFR, DAT, DAP, and DDP. This is supported by additional material in the appendix.

   Importers need to choose a term where they typically control the international freight inbound, the customers clearance process, and delivery to the ultimate consigned.

Incoterms

This helps reduce both cost and risk and typically will offer better options and performance on the inbound logistics.

9. Make sure you:
   a. Understand all the regulatory issues with customs and other regulatory agencies.
   b. Make sure you have a *point person* who takes ownership of regulatory concerns ... typically referred to as the *trade compliance manager.*
   c. Develop SOP's to integrate into the sourcing business model.
   d. Train all stakeholders in the global supply chain on all the aspects of regulatory controls and just how it related to their specific responsibilities.

10. Always make sure you have supported your sourcing decision by working up *landed cost modeling* to affirm the purchasing decision utilizing specific metrics as outlined in Chapter _____.

    Landed cost modeling creates a metric to do comparison shopping and to evaluate options or choices by adding up all the direct, indirect, and ancillary costs added to the origin purchase or acquisition cost.

    Landed cost modeling creates a comprehensive formula to measure the method and process in making a sourcing decision on foreign shores.

11. Document these protocols in written SOP's, to evidence adherence to government regulations and best practices. This provides clear and concise senior management influence on managing with good intent, behavior, due diligence, and reasonable care.

12. Create internal training programs for your management teams and your operating staff in all these guidelines and best practices. Solid training initiatives are an excellent and proven method to make sure everyone has comprehensive information flow, know what is expected, and how best to execute.

The role of senior management is to lead. Following these thoughts and turning them into effective actions within your business models is the best way to assure the opportunities to minimize risks and maximize profits within your global sourcing business models.

Senior management is best off by leading their teams into best practices and always exercising due diligence in their business behavior patterns. Any short-term costs and inconvenience will be outweighed by long-term benefits to any organization.

Benefits will include: reduction in risk and cost, business process improvement, more efficient operations, sustainability, and significant growth potentials.

TRADE COMPLIANCE AND REGULATORY RESPONSIBILITIES

Trade compliance in international business is managing the responsibilities associated with shipping freight as an importer and exporter to and from the United States.

Governing agencies are not limited to, but primarily:

- Department of Commerce/Bureau of Industry and Security (BIS)
- Department of State/ITAR
- Department of Treasury/Office of Foreign Asset Controls (OFAC)
- Department of Homeland Security/Customs and Border Protection (CBP)
- And the Census Bureau

U.S. Customs and
Border Protection

Managers of global trade have to learn the basics of trade compliance because the consequences are potentially severe:

- Shipment delays
- Fines and penalties
- Dissatisfied suppliers and customers
- More expensive shipping
- Loss of access to foreign sourcing and markets
- Potential criminal exposure

Most companies either have a person on site with this responsibility or they outsource the function to companies such as Blue Tiger International, www.bluetigerintl.com.

Senior executives are best off in demonstrating leadership skills in making sure that company policy mandates trade compliance adherence.

They act as follows:

- Assess where they need change
- Appoint a point person or outsource the responsibility
- Create SOP's in compliance
- Train their staff
- Access technology that can offer compliance services
- Continually audit the global supply chain for process betterments in trade compliance and logistics

A summary of the more important regulatory controls in imports and exports are outlined below:

Buying Internationally: Import Supply Chain

The United States imports over $200 billion a month, which represents over 70% of the global supply chain. The inbound supply chain may consist of purchasing components, raw materials, finished goods, as well as returned merchandise and receiving samples. Many importers focus on the landed cost of a product, typically what are my duties and costs to clear my shipment and deliver, without taking into account other factors that present risk in the inbound supply chain, such as partnering with a customs broker who will help the importer be compliant, making certain goods are properly marked with the country of origin, avoiding copyright infringement, and so on. Understanding the U.S. import regulations and working with a knowledgeable customs broker can reduce the risks of importing.

Duties and Fees

The amount of duty to be paid on an import shipment is determined by a number of factors including, the country of origin, the harmonized tariff number, the circumstances of import, and the use of the goods.

Most duty is paid ad valorem, based on the value of the goods. However, in some instances, there may be compound duties paid, such as with shoes. There is a tariff rate paid on the value of the import shipment and an additional charge per pair of shoes.

In addition to duties there are merchandise processing fees, which are assessed by customs as a document fee, and harbor maintenance fees, which are assessed on ocean shipments.

These duties and fees are the more obvious part of landed cost and somewhat easier to nail down provided the importer can properly classify their product to obtain the correct duty rate. Tariff classification can be a bit tricky though and what may seem obvious may not be as clear as first thought in reviewing the 99 chapters of the Harmonized Tariff Schedule of the United States (HTSUS).

Harmonized Tariff Classification

Importers are responsible to provide customs with the correct harmonized tariff classification for each item entered on the import declaration. This is done through the guidelines established in the HTSUS. Importers are also responsible to understand the principles of classification, so they can oversee the advice offered by their customs brokers.

Many importers rely on their internal experts to take a look at the HTSUS and make a determination as to the correct classification. This is usually done by an online search resulting in jumping directly to the classification, choosing a number closest to the product, and following through with the applicable tariff rate.

While this makes sense in using internal experts who have the best understanding of the properties of a product, those internal experts may not understand there are specific rules to follow in classification. The General Rules of Interpretation, section notes, and chapter notes are the map legend for the HTSUS.

Arriving to the classification, which makes the most common sense, is actually a noncompliant practice and represents a failure to meet reasonable care, which will be discussed later in this chapter.

An importer has a shipment of relief maps, which is a flat map that has raised surfaces. A quick look at the alphabetical index will easily identify maps in Chapter 49 under printed maps. However, a closer look at the Chapter 49's chapter notes will identify that relief maps are specifically excluded from Chapter 49 (printed books, newspapers, pictures, and other products of the printing industry; manuscripts, typescripts, and plans) and should be classified in Chapter 90 (optical, photographic, cinematographic, measuring, checking, precision, medical or surgical instruments and apparatus, clocks, and watches …). While the duty rate is free for either tariff classification, the tariff classification is still incorrect.

Failure to properly supervise the classification process can result in false information being tendered to customs. This false information is legally viewed as a false statement.

Country of Origin Marking

Importers are responsible to ensure that all merchandise is properly marked with the country of origin upon entry into the United States. Import documentation must also indicate the proper country of origin on all shipments, as a separate invoice requirement.

Many importers are not aware of the specific requirements for marking goods imported into the United States. Imported goods must be marked to indicate the country of origin to the ultimate purchaser of the goods. For most articles, with the exception of textile apparel products, the country of origin is the country of growth, manufacture, or production.

Unless the product is exempt, permanent marking is required on every imported article. In cases where the item itself cannot be individually marked, customs may accept the marking on the outer carton.

For those instances in which customs believes imported merchandise does not comply with the legal requirements, customs may issue a redelivery notice, requiring the importer to redeliver all of the imported items, previously released, back to customs and may do so up to 30 days from the date of customs' release. As another option, customs may release the goods to the importer and require the importer to properly mark the goods and submit a sample of the item to customs to prove the marking was completed.

Trade Compliance with Customs

The Bureau of CBP operates under 19 Code of Federal Regulations (CFR). In addition to customs regulations, importers are required to follow the regulations of any other government agency that may be involved in the import clearance process. For example, an importer of retail household items may find itself responsible for Food & Drug Administration requirements in addition to CBP regulations for the appliances that may be sold in its stores.

Many importers use a customs broker to assist with the customs clearance process. While an importer is permitted to clear their own goods into the United States, the customs broker provides a level of expertise in communicating with CBP electronically, as well as in their understanding of tariff classification, valuation, and country of origin determination and other factors involved in the customs process. The customs broker facilitates the import process, and a knowledgeable and qualified broker can be an importer's best asset in navigating the import clearance process.

Customs requires importers and their service providers to exercise reasonable care in the clearance process. Failure to do so may result in fines, penalties, and other consequences including shipment delays.

Reasonable Care Standard

Under the reasonable care standard an importer:

- Should seek guidance from customs for proper compliance using the formal rulings program
- Should consult with *qualified experts* like a customs broker or attorney or a consultant specializing in customs law
- If using a broker, must provide such broker with full and complete information sufficient enough for the broker to properly make an entry (import declaration) or for the broker to provide advice as how to make entry
- When appropriate, obtain analyses from accredited labs to determine technical qualities of an imported product
- Use in-house employees like counsel, a customs administrator, or if valuation is an issue, a corporate controller, who has experience and knowledge of customs laws, regulations, and procedures
- Must follow any binding ruling requested and received from customs

- If importing any textile or apparel product, ensure that the products are accompanied by documentation, packaging, and labeling that are accurate as to its origin
- Cannot classify own identical merchandise or value own identical transactions in different ways
- Must notify customs when receiving different treatment by customs for the same goods in different transactions or at different ports
- Must examine entries (import declarations prepared by the broker to determine accuracy in classification and valuation)

Failure to exercise reasonable care may result in:

2xs the loss of duties for negligence
4xs the loss of duties for gross negligence
20% of the entered value of the shipment for nonrevenue loss
40% of the entered value of the shipment for nonrevenue loss

The concept of reasonable care means the importer must be able to evidence to customs how they have implemented reasonable care into the clearance process. This may be through documented and verifiable procedures on the import process, training presentations including training rosters, recordkeeping checklists, and a review of entry files.

Should seek guidance from customs for proper compliance using the formal rulings program. Should consult with *qualified experts* like a customs broker or attorney or a consultant specializing in customs law.

Typical questions that an importer may have regarding an import shipment may range from classification of one or multiple items; how to treat specific circumstances of import, such as an item returned after having been repaired or an item being temporarily imported into the United States; whether an import meets the preference criteria of a specific trade agreement or is eligible for special tariff treatment; and how to value a product correctly.

An importer will be meeting their reasonable care responsibility by contacting customs or a qualified expert to assist with researching these questions and applying the information as part of the entry process.

Customs publishes informed compliance manuals which cover a number of different aspects of the customs clearance process, as well as how to classify specific commodities. Topics of these publications include valuation, classification of aircraft parts, tariff classification, country of origin marking, and children's wearing apparel.

If using a broker, must provide such broker with full and complete information sufficient enough for the broker to properly make an entry (import declaration) or for the broker to provide advice as how to make entry.

Importers are not required to use a customs broker. If a customs broker is used, the importer must provide sufficient information to the broker so the broker can properly advise the importer. It should be noted this also helps the broker fulfill their requirement to meet reasonable care as well. The importer should disclose full information to the broker, as what the broker does not know may prevent the broker from providing a complete picture to the importer and this may be detrimental to the importer.

For example, an importer advises the broker that the product being imported was previously imported to the United States and subsequently returned for repair to the foreign supplier. Under import regulations, the importer need only pay duty on the value of the repair made to the product and not on the full value of the import. If the importer fails to notify the broker of this, and the broker does not know these circumstances, the importer will be paying additional duties to customs unnecessarily. However, if an importer advises the broker that the product being imported was previously imported to the United States and was subsequently returned for repair to the foreign supplier, but the foreign supplier was unable to repair the item and replaced it for free with a new product, this is a different declaration.

If the broker is not made aware the item being imported is actually a replacement, the importer may end up with a false declaration stating the goods are returned after repair and subject to reduced duty, when in fact the item is subject to duty based on the full value of the new imported item.

When appropriate, obtain analyses from accredited labs to determine technical qualities of an imported product.

If an importer is not sure of the actual make-up of a product, the importer has an option to obtain an analysis from their internal experts or outside experts to correctly determine the technical qualities of the product. This is especially important for tariff classification whether or not the duty rate for the imported item is free. In addition to collecting revenue through duties and fees, customs is also collating statistical data for census. Failure to provide customs with the correct tariff classification and other statistical information is a lack of reasonable care and may result in a penalty.

Use in-house employees like counsel, a customs administrator, or, if valuation is an issue, a corporate controller, who has experience and knowledge of customs laws, regulations, and procedures.

In order for in-house employees to be knowledgeable about customs regulations and procedures, they need training and access to resources to expand their knowledge, keep current, and network with fellow importers. This can be done through webinars, on-site or off-site training, membership in local and national associations focusing on compliance, and attending government-sponsored seminars. The National Institute for World Trade (niwt.org) is an excellent option.

Shippers must follow any binding ruling requested and received from custom.

There is a process for obtaining official advice from customs called the binding ruling process. If an importer requests such advice and receives a binding ruling from CBP, they are obligated to follow this advice even if the importer believes the advice to be incorrect. While a binding ruling is an option for an importer, the first step for advice is usually better off being the customs broker or a customs attorney.

If importing any textile or apparel product, ensure that the products are accompanied by documentation, packaging, and labeling that are accurate as to its origin.

Textiles and wearing apparel have very specific requirements as to the packaging and labeling of these commodities. A textile declaration, which details the weight, fabric weave, and many other details, may also be required to accompany the customs entry. The country of origin for textile items also carries its own rules; for example, a shirt that is cut to shape in Denmark, but sewn in the Dominican Republic. The country of origin may appear to be Dominican Republic, but country of origin for shirts is determined by where the article is cut to shape.

It should be noted that while this reasonable care requirement is targeted for textiles and wearing apparel, it is an import requirement that all imported items must declare the correct country of origin on the product itself (with a few exceptions) and the documentation presented to customs must be in accordance with customs regulations, as we will discuss further on.

Cannot classify own identical merchandise or value own identical transactions in different ways.

Must notify customs when receiving different treatment by customs for the same goods in different transactions or at different ports.

Importers must be consistent in the declarations they make to customs. A leather wallet imported into the port of San Francisco must be classified and valued in an identical manner to the same wallet being imported at the port of Newark.

Customs also requires importers to notify customs if they are receiving different treatment by customs in different ports. If the leather wallets are being pulled for examine each time they are imported in San Francisco, but cleared paperless each time in Newark, importers are required to advise customs. This is swift water to navigate, as the importer does run the risk that customs management may approach Newark for their lack of diligence rather than question San Francisco for being overly diligent.

Must examine entries (import declarations prepared by the broker to determine accuracy in classification and valuation).

While an importer may be providing the broker with the information to make entry, the importer is still required to make certain the broker is properly clearing the import. Many importers will just accept the broker's invoice, glance at the back-up paperwork, and hand the bill off to accounts payable for payment. This is a lack of reasonable care.

The importer must implement a process for reviewing the entry paperwork whether through reviewing Automated Commercial Environment (ACE) reports or examining the entry paperwork and ideally, the information being submitted to customs should be approved by the importer prior to entry submission and then verified again following entry.

The concept of reasonable care means the importer must be able to evidence to customs how they have implemented reasonable care into the clearance process. In addition to the aforementioned referenced steps, importers can also exercise reasonable care through documented and verifiable procedures on the import process, training presentations including training rosters, record-keeping checklists, and a review of entry files. Proactive management of the importer's relationship with the customs broker or customs brokers is another key to exercising reasonable care.

Customhouse Brokers

Customhouse brokers are licensed by customs to clear goods into the United States. Brokers are governed by customs regulations and may collect duty and taxes on behalf of customs.

In choosing a custom broker, it is important to find a broker that is a good match for the importer's size and needs. Friendly competitors, carriers, international trade organizations, and even customs in the local inbound gateway can all be sources used to assist in making the right selection.

Custom brokers are required to have a valid customs power of attorney on file from the importer in order to conduct customs business on behalf of the importer. The power of attorney legally authorizes the customhouse broker to act on behalf of the importer, which legally binds the importer to its obligations to customs.

Extreme care needs to be exercised in this selection process. Unfortunately, many brokers operate at a level below the reasonable care and compliance standard that is legally required of them. This lack of reasonable care and compliance equates to fines and penalties for the importer and broker.

As previously mentioned, a customs broker does not have to be used in clearing an importer's goods. Customs brokers are not only familiar with customs and other government regulatory agencies, but they also have tremendous experience in logistics and coordinating the movement of goods once they have been cleared by working with freight forwarders, warehouses, and trucking companies. Importers who partner with a knowledgeable and compliant customs broker will eliminate some of the risk involved in the import process.

Just as reasonable care is mandated for importers, customs brokers are required to follow customs regulations and to exercise reasonable care in managing their business, their employees, and their relationship with their importer clients.

Under the reasonable care standard, a broker:

- Must exercise due diligence to ascertain the correctness of information that is imparted to a client
- Shall not knowingly import false information to a client to any customs business
- Shall not withhold information from a client who is entitled to that information
- Shall establish internal procedures to limit advice being given by qualified licensed individuals
- Shall obtain and receive directly from importer complete and accurate information sufficient to make entry or to provide proper advice

The penalty for a broker not meeting reasonable care is up to $30,000 per violation.

Must exercise due diligence to ascertain the correctness of information that is imparted to a client.

Obtain and receive directly from importer complete and accurate information sufficient to make entry or to provide proper advice.

Customs brokers are required to have a valid power of attorney in place with their importer client. Most brokers require the importer to complete a questionnaire and broker letter of instruction as part of the entry process. Truly diligent brokers will go out of their way to ensure reasonable care by visiting their clients to gain a better understanding of their business.

Customs brokers must understand the use of a product, the circumstance of import, and make certain they receive accurate information from the importer. An importer may not know they should be sharing certain information with the customs broker that may change the advice being offered.

For example, an importer advises they have an import from their sister company overseas. If the broker does not request additional information from the importer, such as, is the relationship between the companies affecting the pricing, the importer may unknowingly declare the import under transaction value (the price paid or payable), which may not be an acceptable method of valuation if the price paid or payable by the importer is 90% below market value.

Shall not knowingly import false information to a client to any customs business.

Shall not withhold information from a client who is entitled to that information.

Customs brokers are considered experts and are required to provide truthful information as to the status of a clearance and correctness of information in the entry process.

Establish internal procedures to limit advice being given by qualified licensed individuals.

Customs brokers are required to have procedures in place as to how client information is dispersed and who is advising an importer client on proper marking and/or valuation. The circumstances surrounding specific commodities may designate a unique situation requiring a different set of marking, as we read with the wearing apparel example earlier. If an employee without much experience in the import process mistakenly advises a customer that marking is not required on a table because they are familiar only with the business of a client who imports hairnets which are exempt from marking, that employee may create a penalty situation for the importer and a reasonable care violation for the customs brokerage office.

In selecting a customhouse brokerage service, the following steps should be taken into consideration:

- Confirm the brokerage operation has qualified customs brokerage personnel with at least five years of operational experience in handling customs entries.
- Verify the number of license holders in the company and how they supervise the operations staff. A brokerage office consisting of ten employees with 1–2 licensed brokers supervising activity is certainly preferable over a brokerage office of 100 employees with 1–2 licensed brokers supervising activity.
- Confirm the operations staff receives training on a regular basis. Ask to see training records.
- Verify the operations staff has experience in valuation concepts, harmonized tariff classification, and country of origin determinations. Ask to speak with the operations staff and pose an assist question and see how well it is answered.
- Ask questions regarding compliance knowledge and value added services to importer clients including in-house training and webinars.
- Confirm how the broker will share clearance information including entry status and reports with clients.
- Ask for references and contact the references to discuss their experience with the broker.

Internal Supervision and Control

The importer of record is responsible for operating their inbound supply chain in compliance with U.S. import regulations. Written procedures encompassing compliance help mitigate the risk of being noncompliant with CBP regulations. Internal supervision and control represents a measure to control the correctness of information being provided to customs and any other government agency. These procedures should include monitoring all communications made on behalf of the importer to CBP or any other government agency by the broker on behalf of the importer.

It has been a common practice for the importer to outsource the day-to-day responsibilities of importing to their broker and allow the broker to handle the entire import process. Many importers continue to rely heavily on their broker, which is a noncompliant practice.

For example, the foreign vendor e-mails the import notification and importer security filing directly to the broker; the broker handles the clearance and advises the importer when the goods have cleared and are being delivered. The broker follows that up with an invoice. There are many decisions that need to be made prior to the entry, which requires feedback and instruction from the importer. This practice is not compliant on the part of the importer and the customs broker.

Importers who demonstrate supervision and control over the import process have established an import notification process to validate the shipment information, to match up purchase orders against the shipping documentation, and to ensure invoices are accurate. Brokerage providers do not typically have access to this depth of information and therefore cannot substantiate the validity of the overseas vendor or accompanying entry documentation.

If piece count is off due to a change made between the supplier and importer, the broker would not be a party to those communications and may submit entry declarations on behalf of the importer that are inaccurate. Failure to implement such a process could result in entry corrections and amendments being made after the fact, which is allowed, but is not a compliant practice if it is done as common practice.

Supply Chain Security

Supply chain security has become an integral part of global supply chains. CBP implemented the Customs-Trade Partnership against Terrorism (C-TPAT) in 2002 as a voluntary program open to importers, carriers, consolidators, brokers, and highway carriers. The program has matured to now include exporters as well.

The threat of terrorism in the supply chain is a global effort. CBP has established mutual recognition agreements with over a dozen countries that also have their own national supply chain security program.

Participation in the C-TPAT program has many benefits which reduce risk in the supply chain including:

- Reduced compliance exams.
- Reduced number of inspections.
- Reduced waiting time for cargo to be examined.
- If cargo is selected for exam, it will receive priority and be moved to the front of the exam line.
- Decreased transportation times.
- Assignment of CBP supply chain security specialist.
- Access to Free & Secure Trade (FAST) lanes at Mexican and Canadian borders.
- Invitation to participate in C-TPAT training seminars offered by CBP.
- Incorporation of security practices into existing logistical management methods.
- Greater supply chain integrity.
- Reduced freight surcharges, such as exam fees and demurrage.
- Meet C-TPAT customer requirements.
- Lower insurance costs.
- Reduced theft/loss of inventory.
- Mutual recognition allows freight exported from the United States to move faster through participating countries local customs.
- When another event occurs that closes the borders, C-TPAT member shipments will be prioritized when the borders reopen.
- Mitigation of fines and penalties for participants.
- Five to eight times fewer exams than non-CTPAT importers.

Companies considering participation in the program must review the eligibility requirements and the security criteria of the program. This is best completed through a security assessment to determine where security gaps exist in the supply chain between what *must* be in place to participate in the program and what should be in place, but is not mandatory. The individual security criteria has flexibility, as no single supply chain is identical. Additionally, the security criteria will differ depending on whether the company is entering the program as an importer, exporter, broker, and so on.

Supply chain security must include a review of the cargo from the point of origin overseas to the point of receipt here in the United States.

The foreign location and origin of shipments may also pose a geographical threat, which must be taken into consideration as well. There is a minimum requirement of container and trailer security for ocean and cross border shipments, how air shipments are packaged and screened, advanced shipment notification, product identification, shipping controls, photo identification of drivers, visitors and contractors, employee access controls, company badges, hiring practices, container inspection, tracking containers and shipments, surveillance cameras, alarm systems, lighting, physical security maintenance, separation policies, integrity of documentation, seal controls, visitor logs, resolving discrepancies in receiving of cargo, seal verification, protection of information, information technology controls, to name a few. Training employees on threat awareness to the supply chain will also be part of the threat assessment.

Supervision and control of where merchandise is sourced and background checks on overseas vendors will also be scrutinized. A detailed knowledge of the storage and handling of all imported cargo is the responsibility of the importer, even when delegating such services to outside service providers like freight forwarders and common carriers.

Invoice Requirements

The import invoice is the engine that drives the international shipment and clearance process. Incorrect statements of fact on an invoice can inadvertently lead to circumvention of governing authorities from properly exercising control and safety over imported goods.

Importers must understand there are actual requirements, which must be contained on an import invoice in order to be presented to CBP. It is a common practice to judge a complete invoice by the amount of information that is contained on the document rather than the quality and actual information. Submission of incomplete and inaccurate information is considered to be noncompliant and may result in clearance delays and/or a penalty. Penalties for this type of violation can be assessed at the value of the merchandise plus estimated duties.

Customs expectation is for the importer to review the contents of the invoice to affirm the correctness of information on a transactional basis. Random post entry audits by the importer do not meet the regulatory requirement of supervision and control. Most brokers use the foreign shipper's invoice as the key point of reference for the entry declaration. The information contained in each invoice must be properly reviewed prior to submission to the brokerage provider and prior to the customs entry declaration being submitted. While this may be viewed as a delay in the import process, it is actually a compliant practice and is a requirement.

For some types of commodities, there may be additional invoice requirements required. For most imports, the importer should ensure the following information is contained on the import invoice:

- The name and address of the foreign shipper or manufacturer.
- The name and address of the importer of record and consignee.
- A full and accurate description of the imported merchandise.
- Quantity of the merchandise being imported with net weights and measures included.
- The unit price of the imported commodity.
- Terms of sale associated with the international transaction.
- Invoice date.
- Invoice number and purchase order number.
- A detailed breakdown of any and all prepaid freight and insurance charges associated with the transaction of sale.
- All discounts offered and/or taken.
- Any commissions must be detailed on the invoice.
- Invoice must be in the English language or have an attached translation.
- Any royalties that exist must be indicated on the invoices.
- A complete invoice value.
- Country of origin of the imported merchandise.
- A name of a responsible person as the preparation party of the invoice.
- A statement of use is recommended to establish special entry procedure.

Bonds

Importers are required to have a bond on file with CBP. The first bond condition is for the importer to pay duties, fees, and taxes on a timely basis. It is the importers responsibility to establish and verify that all duties, fees, and taxes are being submitted in accordance with CBP regulations.

As a common practice, many importers use the services of the brokerage provider to layout the duty payment to customs on their behalf or pay the duty as part of the periodic monthly statement. The importer then reimburses the broker as part of their invoice or the importer pays the broker's invoice, including the duty, and the broker pays the duty on the next statement. It is important to note that the payment of duties, taxes, and fees to CBP is the obligation of the importer. Using a broker to pay duties on the behalf of the importer does not relieve the importer of their responsibility to pay duties, taxes, and fees owed to CBP. Copies of the receipts of payment need be reviewed and retained by the importer to ensure the broker is paying the duties on time.

In the customs audit process, an importer will be asked how they manage the duty payment process. It is an unacceptable answer to simply state, "my broker pays the duty for us." A system of accountability needs to be implemented to ensure that timely payment is being managed as part of supervision and control over the import process.

Copies of the final automated clearing house (ACH) statement copy will serve as proof of payment as will copies of checks with a receipted copy of the CBP 7501 Customs Entry summary or a copy of the ACE report reflecting payment was received. It should be noted a stamped copy of the CBP7501 is not proof of payment and only represents entry submission.

Record Retention

Importers are responsible to establish a record retention system that maintains all records relative to an import transaction for five years from the date of entry of the merchandise into the commerce of the United States. Many importers do not keep satisfactory records in accordance with the customs regulations.

In their regulatory audits, customs finds multiple errors associated with recordkeeping. Importers must be aware of all documents that they are responsible to maintain as outlined in the (a)1(a) listing of the customs regulations.

All records associated with the import transaction from the point of purchase inquiry, throughout the customs clearance process, up to the final disposition of the merchandise at the ultimate place of delivery needs to be retained. Once all of the required documents are identified, every importer needs to create a standard operating procedure to ensure that these documents are properly collected on a transactional basis.

Third party service providers, like brokers and freight forwarders, need to be a part of this process to ensure that all documents that are generated by their services are duly tendered to the importer. The importer is responsible to keep all of the aforementioned records. This obligation cannot be delegated to a third-party service provider.

Custom brokers have their own recordkeeping requirements, which are not necessarily the same requirements as the importer. Many brokers do not properly advise importers of the full obligation to maintain correct records. Importers who rely on their brokers to maintain their records also create risk in the event they change brokers and no longer have access to those records.

The importer is not only responsible to keep records, but they must also be able to retrieve their records in a reasonable amount of time. Records that are maintained, yet are not retrievable, do not meet the customs regulatory standard of compliance.

Selling Internationally: The Export Supply Chain

In 2016, the United States exported over $2.2 trillion in goods. There is tremendous opportunity for export sales for many businesses. It is important to understand the risks involved with exporting. These risks may include compliance risks, such as exporting to prohibited destinations or denied parties, exporting controlled items without prior government authorization, or financial risks, such as making sure receivables are protected. Managing risk in the export supply chain requires diligence, recurrent training, and the support of senior management.

Government Agencies Responsible for Exports

The export supply chain is subject to various government agencies regulating the export process. Minimally, exports require reporting to the Bureau of Census, knowing and screening business partners through the Consolidated Screening List, reviewing purchase orders and documentation for boycott language, and understanding to which country the goods will ultimately be shipped. Prior government authorization may be required for specific commodities.

Exporters may find themselves working with all or a few of the following government agencies:

Department of State: Defense Trade Controls
Department of Commerce: BIS
Department of Commerce: Bureau of Census
Department of Treasury: OFAC
Department of Homeland Security: Bureau of CBP

International Traffic in Arms Regulations

Exports falling under the international traffic in arms regulations (ITAR) require registration with Defense Trade Controls and the prior approval of a license for exports, temporary exports, and temporary import of United States Munitions List items. If an activity is controlled under the ITAR, it follows that most transactions require a license. This includes furnishing a defense service, as well as providing proposals to sell significant military equipment.

Defense services include furnishing assistance to foreign persons, whether in the United States or abroad, in the design, development, engineering, manufacture, production, assembly, testing, repair, maintenance, modification, operation, destruction, processing, or use of defense articles.

Violations of the ITAR can include policy of denial of export licenses, debarment, criminal fines up to one million dollars, imprisonment, as well as civil penalties up to just over one million dollars per violation.

Export Administration Regulations

Most exporters are not subject to the tighter controls of the ITAR, but will be subject to the Export Administration Regulations (EAR). The EARs are broad and cover exports from the United States, reexports of U.S. products, U.S. persons overseas, foreign subsidiaries of a U.S. parent, foreign made products of U.S. technology, and/or U.S. component parts and the transfer of information to a foreign national.

One of the key differences between the EAR and the ITAR is that most transactions under the EAR do not require an export license, provided the commodity is not controlled.

Commerce Control List

If a product is not controlled under the ITAR, then the product is subject to the EAR. Subject to the EAR requires the exporter to understand their export transaction, the parties to the transaction, the destination of the product, and how their product will be used. The EAR may define some products as being controlled for export. These items are identified under the Commerce Control List.

If an exporter determines that the product is subject to the Commerce Control List and falls under a specific Export Control Classification Number, then they must take the next step in determining whether government approval in the form of a license is required prior to export. The first step is to review the Reasons for Control, which are indicated at the beginning of the Commerce Control List. Once the Reasons for Control have been determined, the Commerce Country Chart must be examined.

The Commerce Country Chart is a matrix bringing together the Reasons for Control for all commodities listed on the Commerce Control List against all countries. The exporter need only to review the Reasons for Control for their particular commodity, as well as the destination country to which they are shipping. If there is an "x" in the box, the shipment requires export authorization. If there is not an "x" in the box, the shipment does not require export authorization based on the commodity.

Should an exporter determine their product is not listed on the Commerce Control List, then that product will be designated as EAR99. EAR99 means the product is subject to the Commerce Control List, but not specifically controlled for export based on the commodity.

The majority of products exported from the United States are EAR99. However, a product being EAR99 does not mean the product is not subject to additional regulations governing exports. Exporters must be aware of the additional compliance responsibilities they have under the EAR, as well as the Office of Foreign Asset Control Regulations and Foreign Trade Regulations, which also cover EAR99 items.

Electronic Export Information

The Department of Commerce, Bureau of Census requires the exporter to report information on their exports. This information is used to compile official trade statistics and is called the Electronic Export Information (EEI). The EEI serves an additional purpose as it is also used as a compliance tool by other government agencies such as the BIS, the Bureau of CBP, and Defense Trade Controls.

An EEI is required when merchandise is shipped from one United States principal party in interest (USPPI) to one consignee on the same flight/vessel to the same country on the same day and where the shipment is valued over $2500 per Schedule B or Harmonized Tariff Number or any dollar amount if a license is required.

The EEI may be filed by the exporter or the exporter may choose to have their freight forwarder file the EEI on their behalf. The transmission of information is done through the ACE, which is the same platform used for processing import entries.

Information contained on the EEI must be true, accurate, and complete. Late EEI filings and/or incorrect information (false statements) may lead to penalties. Any EEI record filed later than ten calendar days after the due date will be considered failure to file. Failure to file could result in a penalty up to $10,000.00. Late filing penalties can be $1100.00 per day up to $10,000.00. Filing false/misleading information carries a penalty up to $10,000.00 per violation. In addition to the previous listed penalties, any property involved in a violation is subject to forfeiture.

If the USPPI chooses to delegate the filing of the EEI to a freight forwarder, the USPPI will be held liable for these penalties in addition to the freight forwarder. This is one of the most important reasons to purposefully manage freight forwarders and for exporters to take the time to train their personnel if the exporter is filing their own EEI.

U.S. Principal Party in Interest

The Foreign Trade Regulations define the USPPI as the person or legal entity in the United States that receives the primary benefit, monetary or otherwise, from the export transaction. USPPI is the party who is responsible for filing the EEI and for complying with export regulations. The USPPI is generally the U.S. selling party, manufacturer, or order party. A foreign entity may only be the USPPI if they were in the United States when purchasing or obtaining the goods for export.

While the Incoterms note where risk and costs, responsibility, and liabilities shift from the seller to the buyer, it is important to keep in mind that the Foreign Trade Regulations apply to the USPPI, the foreign principal party in interest (FPPI), and the authorized agent in the United States regardless of the Incoterm.

Schedule B Number/Harmonized Tariff Number

One of the key data elements required in the reporting of the EEI is the Schedule B Number or Harmonized Tariff Number. The Schedule B Numbers are based on the same numbering system as the Harmonized Tariff Schedule issued by the U.S. International Trade Commission. The Harmonized Tariff Schedule identifies commodities by a 10-digit number. Globally, the first six digits are shared, but the last four digits can be different.

The Schedule B Numbers tend to be a bit broader in their description than the Harmonized Tariff Numbers, which are very specific. For example, other cattle are broken down into two categories "other" and "buffalo" under the Schedule B Numbers, but under similar Harmonized Tariff Numbers other cattle are broken down into several categories based primarily on weight.

Schedule B Numbers may only be used for EEI reporting, while Harmonized Tariff Numbers may be used for both EEI reporting and import entries. However, not all Harmonized Tariff Numbers may be used for EEI reporting.

Valuation

In capturing statistical data through the EEI reporting, the value must be accurately reported. For EEI reporting purposes, the value is the selling price (or the cost if the goods are not sold) in U.S. dollars, plus inland or domestic freight, insurance, and other charges to the U.S. seaport, airport, or land border port of export. The cost of goods is the sum of expenses incurred in the USPPI's acquisition or production of the goods.

Many exporters and their authorized agents fail to report the FOB/FCA value on the EEI, as they generally take the bottom line of the export invoice as the value of the shipment. For those exporters shipping samples or company material, values tend to be underreported and a minimum value declared which does not reflect the actual value.

The final area where value is incorrectly reported is the value of repair work performed in the United States. The actual cost of repair should be reported and if the repair was performed under warranty, then the value of what the repair cost would have been should be the value reported.

Recordkeeping Requirements

Export shipments are subject to a recordkeeping requirement of five years from the date of export. Records to be retained include notes, correspondence, contracts, memoranda, invitations to bid, books of account, financial records, restrictive trade practice reports and boycott documents, and documents created in support of shipment including bills of lading, commercial invoices, packing lists, and EEI transaction copies. Exporters are well advised to retain their own documentation and not rely on their service providers.

Denied Party Screening

While a product may not be specifically controlled for export, there may be other factors that come into play that must be addressed. Who is receiving, handling, buying my product? Where is my product transiting? What is the final destination country for my product?

The Bureau of Industry & Security maintains an electronic tool called the Consolidated Screening List on its website. This list should be consulted for all export transactions for all parties to the transaction including service providers, carriers, vessels, customers, end-users, foreign freight forwarders, financial institutions, and distributors. The names of the companies as well as individuals should be screened.

Embargoed Country Screening

While the Export Administration Regulations contain a list of countries for which specific products may be controlled for export, the BIS also maintains a list of countries that are considered terrorist supporting countries. These are Iran, North Korea, Sudan, and Syria.

The Department of Treasury, OFAC, administers and enforces economic trade sanctions. OFAC maintains a listing of Specially Designated Nationals, which can be found through the Consolidated Screening List. Additionally, OFAC also maintains a listing of countries with active sanctions programs. This listing is provided on the OFAC website.

Each of the sanction programs summarizes the reason for the sanction, the scope of the sanction, prohibitions under the sanction, the type of authorized activities and transactions permitted, if any, and if a general license exists or if a specific license must be applied for through OFAC.

Due to the scope of some of the sanction programs, some transactions may be allowed without any prior authorization, while other transactions may be permitted and other transactions may be prohibited.

Consularization and Legalization

Many countries require export documentation to be consularized and legalized. This process can add additional costs and time into the export process. In some instances, a visit to the local Chamber of Commerce is sufficient, but if documents need to be sent to a consulate office, there will be additional fees including messenger delivery fees and consularization charges, which can run between $125.00 and $500.00.

Exporters should have a discussion with the foreign customer to find out if the destination country has an import requirement regarding consularization. The answer can differ from country to country and may also differ depending on the commodity and value of the shipment. In the event a shipment is moved without proper documentation, there may be a custom hold at the destination resulting in additional storage fees, potential customs penalties, and a frustrated customer.

Solid Wood Packing Material Certificates

The International Plant Protection Convention (IPPC) is an international plant health agreement that focuses on prevention of the introduction and spread of pests into wild plants and the protection of natural flora. The convention recognizes the introduction of pests can be spread through vessels, containers, aircraft, storage facilities, and soil.

This convention affects exporters, as the materials used for packing and transporting shipments must meet the IPPC specifications as part of the import requirement in over 175 countries. These materials must be heat treated, fumigated, or special heated. Exporters must be certain the materials used to package their shipments meet the current standard. This is typically reflected by materials containing a certificate and/or marking indicating they meet the IPPC standards.

Preshipment Inspections

Depending on the commodity, value, and destination country, a prein-spection of goods prior to export may be required. This may also be a requirement within a letter of credit. There are a number of agencies that specialize in this inspection process, which can include verification of quantity, quality, price, customs classification, and import eligibility.

The surveying company will schedule a qualified inspector to certify the cargo is meeting the requirements of the foreign importer's purchase order. The preshipment inspection is usually paid for by the foreign customer. Additional time may need be built into the export process to accommodate the scheduling of the preshipment inspection.

Free Trade Affirmations

Special certificates may be requested by the foreign customer for countries with which the United States has free trade agreements. Some certificates of origin including those required by the North American Free Trade Agreement (FTA), and the FTAs with Israel and Jordan, are prepared by the exporter.

In order to issue a valid FTA affirmation, the exporter must know that the goods are eligible and qualify for the FTA. This can be done by reviewing the preference criterion for the product and following the rules of origin relevant to the product. The rules of origin may be found in the General Notes section of the Harmonized Tariff Schedule or through the trade.gov website.

It is important to keep in mind that creation of an FTA affirmation requires the exporter to retain documentation validating the facts contained within the document. Failure to retain this back-up documentation or completing the documentation incorrectly can result in a fine and penalty.

Many companies make the mistake of assuming these FTA affirmations are an import requirement, which they are not. They are merely the method of complying with the free trade agreement in place to access duty free status.

Getting Paid

An important function of export documentation is to assure the exporter receives payment according to the agreed terms of sale and payment. One of the methods of receiving payment is a letter of credit.

In a letter of credit transaction, the exporter anticipates receiving funds once the goods are shipped. While this may be true in theory, in practice, the exporter will only receive payment once the required documentation is received and approved by the confirming bank. This process can be difficult if errors are found, documents are incomplete, or documents are presented outside the agreed upon time frame.

The bank scrutinizes the documentation thoroughly and the primary reason for this is the bank never sees the freight. Discrepancies in documentation create extra expense, payment delays, and aggravation. Using letters of credit can create risk if the bank presentation is not handled by a freight forwarder or company that is knowledgeable in letters of credit.

CUSTOMS-TRADE PARTNERSHIP AGAINST TERRORISM BENEFITS

C-TPAT offers businesses an opportunity to play an active role in the war against terrorism. By participating in this first worldwide supply chain security initiative, companies will ensure a more secure supply chain for their employees, suppliers, and customers. In addition, CBP offers the following benefits to C-TPAT members:

- A reduced number of inspections and reduced border wait times.
- A C-TPAT supply chain specialist to serve as the CBP liaison for validations, security issues, procedural updates, communication, and training.
- Access to the C-TPAT members through the Status Verification Interface.
- Self-policing and self-monitoring of security activities.
- In the Automated Commercial System, C-TPAT certified importers receive reduced selection rate for compliance measurement

examinations (-3X in FY 2003) and exclusion from certain trade-related local and national criteria.

- C-TPAT certified importers receive targeting benefits (-7X in FY 2003) by receiving a *credit* via the CBP targeting system.
- Certified C-TPAT importers are eligible for access to the FAST lanes on the Canadian and Mexican borders.
- Certified C-TPAT importers are eligible for the Office of Strategic Trade's Importer Self-Assessment program and have been given priority access to participate in the ACE.
- C-TPAT certified highway carriers, on the Canadian and Mexican borders, benefit from their access to the expedited cargo processing at designated FAST lanes. These carriers are eligible to receive more favorable mitigation relief from monetary penalties.
- C-TPAT certified Mexican manufacturers benefit from their access to the expedited cargo processing at the designated FAST lanes.
- All certified C-TPAT companies are eligible to attend CBP-sponsored C-TPAT supply chain security training seminars.
- Maintaining open supply chain in the event of another 9/11 attack or terrorist initiative.

CBP-provided benefits are not the only benefits that companies realize by joining C-TPAT. Companies have found that joining C-TPAT often results in discovering outdated procedures and/or discovery of best practices, protocols, and SOP's in raising the bar of their overall global supply chain management responsibilities.

Blue Tiger is an excellent resource for companies to enter the C-TPAT program.

BACKGROUND

In direct response to 9/11, the U.S. Customs Service, now U.S. CBP, challenged the trade community to partner with CBP to design a new approach to supply chain security focused on protecting the United States against acts of terrorism by improving security, while simultaneously speeding the flow of compliant cargo and conveyances. The result was the C-TPA—an innovative, voluntary government/private sector partnership program.

C-TPAT builds on the best practices of CBP/industry partnerships to strengthen supply chain security, encourage cooperative relationships, and to better concentrate CBP resources on areas of greatest risk. It is a dynamic, flexible program designed to keep pace with the evolving nature of the terrorist threat and the changes in the international trade industry, thus ensuring the program's continued viability, effectiveness, and relevance. Flexibility and customization are important characteristics of C-TPAT.

This partnership between CBP and trade is built on customs border authority and cooperative relationships. It is built on the knowledge—that the trade partner has demonstrated a commitment to supply chain security, and trust—that the company will continue to do so with minimal CBP examination.

To uphold this relationship, accountability is required. The trade partner must be willing to assume responsibility for keeping his supply chain secure to certain agreed upon security standards through self-policing and implementing changes as needs arise.

The current security guidelines for C-TPAT program members address a broad range of topics including personnel, physical, and procedural security; access controls; education, training, and awareness; manifest procedures; conveyance security; threat awareness; and documentation processing. Companies that apply to C-TPAT must sign an agreement with CBP that commits their organization to the program's security guidelines. These guidelines offer a customized solution for the members, while providing a clear minimum standard that approved companies must meet.

CBP's ability to leverage its customs authority and C-TPAT's unprecedented innovation enables the United States government to positively impact security practices throughout the global supply chain on a broad scale. This influence on security behavior overseas goes well beyond the conventional expectations or the reach of United States regulators. This is because private companies operating in the global supply chain, that choose to participate in C-TPAT, agree to implement increased levels of security throughout their international supply chains in exchange for benefits that only CBP can provide.

In addition, C-TPAT members must agree to leverage their service providers and business partners to increase their security practices. This requirement enables C-TPAT to improve the security practices of thousands of companies located around the globe that are not enrolled in the program. In fact, many companies are demanding that their business partners enroll in C-TPAT or adhere to its security guidelines, and they are conditioning their business relationships on these requirements.

C-TPAT also enables trade by improving supply chain security and increasing supply chain performance.

The program helps companies optimize management of their assets and functions while enhancing security. Together, enhanced security practices and increased supply chain performance reduce the risk of loss, damage, and theft, and lessens the threat that terrorists will attack the global supply chain.

The successful integration of increased security and enhanced supply chain efficiency is one of the great successes of C-TPAT. Through the collaborative work of CBP and the trade community, C-TPAT has become the focal point for all United States government and private sector supply chain security efforts.

CUSTOMS-TRADE PARTNERSHIP AGAINST TERRORISM APPROACH AND GUIDING PRINCIPLES

C-TPAT is a supply chain security program for international cargo and conveyances. It increases security measures, practices, and procedures throughout all sectors of the international supply chain. Central to the security vision of C-TPAT is the core principle of increased facilitation for legitimate business entities that are compliant traders.

All C-TPAT benefits are privileges offered to only the most secure and compliant program participants.

The following three principles define the approach of the C-TPAT program. CBP will develop and implement the C-TPAT program of the future consistent with these principles.

Customs-Trade Partnership against Terrorism will continue to develop as a voluntary government/private sector partnership.

At times, mandatory requirements for security may be both necessary and efficient—but may not always be the most effective. For example, CBP has extensive experience and knowledge as to offering areas that need improved security and efficiency. While performing the required supply chain assessment for C-TPAT membership, companies are able to streamline their operations. C-TPAT aids companies in optimizing their internal and external management of assets and functions, while at the same time enhancing security.

When administered together, enhanced security practices and procedures and increased supply chain performance will mitigate the risk of loss, damage, and theft and reduce the likelihood of the introduction of potentially dangerous elements into the global supply chain.

Other benefits companies have realized by participating in C-TPAT include:

- The incorporation of good sound security practices and procedures into existing logistical management methods and processes
- Greater supply chain integrity
- Reduced risk mitigation
- Reduced cargo theft and pilferage
- Stronger brand equity
- Improved asset utilization
- Greater efficiency between internal and external functions
- Improved security for their workforce
- Improved marketability
- Understanding the end-to-end process, including knowing each entity along the supply chain

The successful integration and alignment of increased security and enhanced supply chain efficiency is one of the great successes of C-TPAT. Through the collaborative work of CBP and the trade community, C-TPAT enhances the security and efficiency of legitimate trade.

EXTERNAL FACTORS

C-TPAT continuously monitors how internal and external factors affect the achievement of goals and ultimately the success of the program. Monitoring these factors, and developing strategies for mitigating them, are accomplished through an analysis of stakeholders, as well as internal and external strengths, weaknesses, opportunities, and threats in the C-TPAT program and its operating environment.

These analyses served as the starting point for the C-TPAT strategic planning process and are addressed in the strategic plan.

Strengths identified in the C-TPAT program include the voluntary nature of the partnerships, shared CBP/industry responsibility for supply chain security, and the trust engendered by external stakeholders as a result of the partnerships. In addition, C-TPAT offers the ability to influence and leverage entities in the supply chain that regulations often can't reach and allows for customization of security needs by the trade community. Finally, the vast knowledge and experience of C-TPAT personnel, and the access to information not previously available to CBP, were also seen as program strengths.

Opportunities include the ability to enhance internal and external communication with stakeholders, to provide continuing education for supply chain specialists, and to hire additional highly qualified personnel.

CUSTOMS-TRADE PARTNERSHIP AGAINST TERRORISM FOR EXPORTERS

U.S. CBP listened to the recommendations made by the Advisory Committee on Commercial Operations, which encouraged the creation of the C-TPAT Exporter Entity. CBP is introducing an exporter entity to C-TPAT to support export growth and increase the competitiveness of the U.S. business community, as outlined by President Obama's National Export Initiative. CBP is also interested in providing the U.S. business community with benefits currently enjoyed by foreign importers through Mutual Recognition Arrangements, which are explained in the following. Finally, this is an opportunity to align with the programs of foreign customs under the World Customs Organization's Framework of Standards to Secure and Facilitate Global Trade (SAFE Framework).

ADDITIONAL CONSIDERATION: DRAWBACK, FREE TRADE AGREEMENTS, FOREIGN TRADE ZONES, AND BONDED WAREHOUSES

Companies seeking to leverage supply chain opportunities as outlined earlier would be in a stronger position in dealing with CBP and other government agencies as a C-TPAT member.

Happiness does not come from doing easy work, but from the afterglow of satisfaction that comes after the achievement of a difficult task that demanded our best.

Theodore Isaac Rubin

5

Mastering Business Development

Companies must grow to be sustainable. A business in *suspended animation* is a dying institution. This makes three areas of a business: marketing, sales, and customer service an integral part of strategy and execution to maintain long-term expansion, margin protection, and sustainable operations.

This chapter has a focus on all three areas and offers practical and contemporary guidelines to maximize strategy and action oriented tactics.

DEVELOPING AN INTERNATIONAL BUSINESS STRATEGY

Companies wanting to grow exponentially need to develop a strategy, which includes expansion into global markets.

Almost every major company in the Fortune 2000 World is either:

| Building operations in overseas locations | Sourcing products from foreign markets | Selling goods and services in export markets worldwide |

Building operations in overseas locations, sourcing product from foreign markets, and selling goods and services in export markets worldwide accomplish numerous benefits, namely:

- Diversifying the risks of being isolated to business only in one market
- Access to 95% of the world market
- Opportunity for lower cost manufacturing, lower cost labor, reduced government interference, and regulation
- Potential of higher margins
- More robust growth prospects
- Access to diversity in: innovation, technology, cultural exchanges, and variations in economic and political opportunities

Many leading academic and professional internationalists strongly believe that global trade is one of the best deterrents to war and political strife. The relationship between the United States and China is an excellent example of how mutual trade between two countries that are 180 degrees apart politically, does not allow any disagreement over policy to interfere and create a risk of war or major political conflict.

While tension always seems to *be in the air* between the two countries, since 1975, when trade really started to take off between the two economic super giants, no real conflict has ever caused a failure in the overall relationship.

This situation between China and the United States makes the case that strong global trade ties between trading countries is a strong elixir to reduce the exposure for political conflict.

Corporations that create business development opportunities in foreign markets can be assured to some extent that when trade is robust, political exposures can be seriously diminished. Allowing corporate management to be rest assured that their foreign interests will be protected from political discord so they can focus on continued foreign business development.

UNDERSTANDING THE CULTURES OF THE WORLD

Managers in international business will have more success when they pay attention to all the cultural issues they face in foreign business development.

Business Culture

Even in this time of advance technology, where businesses can connect with their consumers from thousands of miles away, face-to-face connection is still valuable. When it comes to export partners and business partners, this personal interaction is even more important. But before hopping on the next flight to another country to meet with potential or current partners, make sure you are aware of any nuances in their business culture. For more information on how to be prepared for your business travel abroad, watch this exporting basics video all about international business meetings.

Considering Cultural Factors

Businesspeople who hope to profit from their travel should learn about the history, culture, and customs of the countries they wish to visit. Flexibility and cultural adaptation should be the guiding principles for traveling abroad on business. Business manners and methods, religious customs, dietary practices, humor, and acceptable dress vary from country to country. You can prepare for your overseas visits by reading travel guides, which are located in the travel sections of most libraries and bookstores.

Some of the cultural differences U.S. companies most often face involve business styles, attitudes toward business relationships and punctuality, negotiating styles, gift-giving customs, greetings, significance of gestures, meanings of colors and numbers, and conventions regarding the use of titles.

The cultural anthropology literature has given us many insights into how other countries do business and how to avoid cultural blunders. To Thais, for example, being touched on the head is extremely offensive. Is this useful to know? Maybe. But it is hard to imagine in the United States or anywhere else businesspeople meeting for the first time or even after several times and engaging in head touching or hair messing. So by all means read the literature and talk with people who know the culture. But do not be intimidated and do not be reluctant to meet people. And do keep these general rules in mind.

Both understanding and heeding cultural differences are critical to success in international business. Lack of familiarity with the business practices, social customs, and etiquette of a country can weaken your company's position in the market,

> Understanding local culture can be the difference between making and losing a sale. And, who knows—you may end up loving the local food, movies, and sports teams!

Always answer queries politely and promptly. Do not delay when responding to e-mail, fax, and telephone requests for price lists, quotes, and other information. Build your own marketing list from the contacts. Ask for each customer's communication preferences. The query you ignore today might have been your next best source of future business.

Start with what you know. Try beginning with a business culture and system similar to your own. Canada and the United Kingdom are often good markets for beginners.

Learn from your domestic customers. Apply cultural knowledge you gain from selling to customers from different social and ethnic backgrounds than yourself. Preferences, product usage, and business protocol may not translate perfectly to international customers, but helpful information can be harvested here in the United States and applied to market entry efforts abroad. Be patient. Different cultures have different concepts of time. Few markets have a faster business pace than the United States; many are slower.

Take time to develop personal relationships—especially with distributors or large-volume buyers. Remembering birthdays and other important events is a good intercultural business practice. It is generally not difficult for Americans to be warm, welcoming, respectful, and thoughtful. Be yourself—or even a little more. If you cannot, or if the self you know does not fit this profile, consider making a trusted employee the primary business contact. Learn the language. A few words of the native language of your buyers or business associates will go a long way. They will appreciate the effort. Words of welcome on your website, and maybe a currency converter, will further demonstrate your interest in doing business in ways that are mutually respectful.

> Something as simple and commonplace as a *thumbs up* may be meaningless—or even offensive—in some cultures.

Get an intern or hire a new employee. As business develops with overseas customers, consider recruiting a student intern or recent college graduate who speaks the language and understands the business culture. Investing in company staffing resources is especially valuable when doing business with customers in Japan, China, and countries in which Arabic is spoken. Attend a U.S. trade show. Find one in your industry that is attended by foreign buyers. You can make good contacts—even sales—and test the waters before heading overseas.

Attend an international trade show in your industry. U.S. embassies abroad often staff a national pavilion where U.S. sellers and foreign buyers, often from many countries in a region, meet. A great way to understand a different business culture is to do business, not read about how others do it.

Get help. Before you head overseas on a business development trip, contact the U.S. embassy and the U.S. Commercial Service. They'll line up qualified buyers for you to meet, and they'll counsel you on business protocol, market intelligence, regulatory issues, and much more, prevent you from accomplishing your objectives, and ultimately lead to the failure of your exporting effort.

Americans must pay close attention to different styles of doing business and the degree of importance placed on developing business relationships. In some countries, business people have a very direct style, while in others they are subtler and value personal relationships more than is customary in most U.S. business relationships. For example, in the Middle East, indulging in small talk before engaging in the business at hand is standard practice.

Gift giving is an important part of doing business in Japan, where gifts are usually exchanged at the first meeting. In sharp contrast, gifts are rarely exchanged in Germany and are usually not appropriate. Gift giving is not customary in Belgium or the United Kingdom either, although in both countries it is suitable to bring flowers when you are invited to someone's home. Customs concerning the exchange of business cards also vary.

Although this point may seem of minor importance, card giving is a key part of business protocol. In Japan, for example, the Western practice of accepting a business card and pocketing it immediately is considered rude. The proper approach is to carefully look at the card after accepting it, observe the title and organization, acknowledge with a nod that the information has been digested, and perhaps make a relevant comment or ask a polite question.

Negotiating is a complex process even between parties from the same nation. It is even more complicated in international transactions because of the potential for misunderstandings that stem from cultural differences. It is essential to understand the importance of rank in the other country and to know who the decision makers are. It is important to be familiar with the business style of the foreign company, to understand the nature of agreements there, and to know the significance of gestures, and negotiating etiquette.

Through research or training, you can acquire a working knowledge of the business culture, management attitudes, business methods, and consumer habits before you travel abroad. That knowledge is very likely to have a positive effect on your overseas travel. Your local U.S. Commercial Service office can provide what you need to make a strong first impression.

Attitudes toward punctuality vary greatly from one culture to another, and misunderstanding those attitudes may cause confusion. Romanians, Japanese, and Germans are very punctual, whereas people in many of the

Latin countries have a more relaxed attitude toward time. The Japanese consider it rude to be late for a business meeting, but acceptable—even fashionable—to be late for a social occasion. In Guatemala, though, people will arrive from 10 minutes early to 45 minutes late for a luncheon appointment.

> Attention to detail can go a long way in making you stand out among the competition.

When cultural lines are being crossed, something as simple as a greeting can be misunderstood. Traditional greetings include shaking hands, hugging, kissing, and placing the hands in a praying position. The *wrong* greeting can lead to an awkward encounter.

People around the world use body movements and gestures to convey specific messages. Misunderstandings over gestures are common occurrences in intercultural communication and can lead to business complications and social embarrassment.

Proper use of names and titles is often a source of confusion in international business relations. In many countries (including Denmark, France, and the United Kingdom), it is appropriate to use titles until use of first names is suggested. First names are seldom used by those doing business in Germany. Visiting business people should use the surname preceded by the title. Titles such as *Herr Direktor* are sometimes used to indicate prestige, status, and rank. Thais, however, address one another by first names and reserve last names for very formal occasions and written communications. In Belgium, it is important to address French-speaking business contacts as "Monsieur" or "Madame," whereas Flemish-speaking contacts should be addressed as "Mr." or "Mrs." To misuse these titles is a great faux pas.

Understanding gift-giving customs is also important. In some cultures, gifts are expected and failure to present them is considered an insult. In other countries, though, the presentation of a gift is viewed as an offense. Business executives also need to know when to present a gift (e.g., on the initial visit or afterward); where to present the gift (in public or privately); what type of gift to present; what color the gift should be; and how many gifts are appropriate.

Gift giving is an important part of doing business in Japan, where gifts are usually exchanged at the first meeting. In sharp contrast, gifts are rarely exchanged in Germany and are usually not appropriate. Gift giving is not customary in Belgium or the United Kingdom either, although in both countries it is suitable to bring flowers when you are invited to someone's home.

Customs concerning the exchange of business cards also vary. Although this point may seem of minor importance, card giving is a key part of business protocol. In Japan, for example, the Western practice of accepting a business card and pocketing it immediately is considered rude. The proper approach is to carefully look at the card after accepting it, observe the title and organization, acknowledge with a nod that the information has been digested, and perhaps make a relevant comment or ask a polite question.

Negotiating is a complex process even between parties from the same nation. It is even more complicated in international transactions because of the potential for misunderstandings that stem from cultural differences. It is essential to understand the importance of rank in the other country and to know who the decision makers are. It is important to be familiar with the business style of the foreign company, to understand the nature of agreements there, and to know the significance of gestures and negotiating etiquette.

Through research or training, you can acquire a working knowledge of the business culture, management attitudes, business methods, and consumer habits before you travel abroad. That knowledge is very likely to have a positive effect on your overseas travel. Your local U.S. Commercial Service office can provide what you need to make a strong first impression.

Paying attention to detail is a critical component of global business development.

Twelve Steps to Building a Successful International Business Model

We have outlined ten steps a company can follow in considering entering into an international business model:

1. Global mind-set
2. Mine heavily
3. Develop third party resources
4. Our government can assist
5. Develop multicultural basics
6. Understand the costs involved
7. Take the time to understand local economic and political factors
8. Learn what total cost of development, acquisition, and sale are

9. Develop global negotiation skill sets
10. Master financial, legal, and insurance issues
11. Hire locally … manage globally
12. Leverage technology

Global mind-set	Mine heavily	Develop third party resources
• Think on a global basis • Become multi-cultural	• Obtain information • Make numerous business contacts	• Business Brokers • Lawyers, accountants, bankers, and consultants

Our government can assist	Develop multicultural basics	Understand the costs involved
• Department of commerce/international trade administration • Customs and border protection (CBP)	• Basic language skills • Taking the time to learn and understand basic cultural issues	• Landed cost modeling • Lower cost options • Free trade agreements

Understand local economic and political factors	Total cost of development, acquisition, and sale	Global negotiation skill sets
• U.S. economic dominance • World political events • Terrorism	• Foreign Research and Development (R&D) • Foreign asset acquisition • Foreign channel partners	• Compromise • Multicultural • Combating indifference

Master financial, legal and insurance issues	Hire locally … manage globally	Leverage technology
• A muscle is to make sure you protect all the related functions and responsibilities of finance, risk management and regulatory and contract concerns • Identify specialists in finance, banking, insurance, accounting, and law who can operate locally on a global scale • (Text)	• Hire local talent • But manage considering you are a global company, bringing in the talent from wherever to wherever, as the situation requires	• Connects the business units on all the continents • Reduces risk and spend • Adds value • Allows sourcing, sales, and operations to be managed more successfully

E-COMMERCE IN GLOBAL TRADE

Thomas Cook, Blue Tiger International, December 2014

The growth of e-commerce through the past ten years has been nothing less than phenomenal.

E-commerce is now dominating consumer sales here in the United States and is working its way into most countries on all six continents.

E-commerce in the United States has both replaced and supplemented retail sales distribution outlets, which have been the main place where consumers find and buy everything they need.

E-commerce has always been in the 5%–10% range of sales for most companies, but it has now grown in some industry verticals to more than 50% of overall sales volume ... and it is still growing.

Any companies not thinking about e-commerce as a factor in overall sales both at the consumer and commercial levels will be left behind.

The following recommendations are based upon our experiences in helping companies enter into or further develop e-commerce markets globally.

E-commerce is expanding globally and becoming an integral part of every company's global strategy

1. Determine the viability of your product sales country by country before committing to any larger initiative. Test marketing and local resources can assist you in this evaluation stage.

   International e-commerce sales are very different than U.S. Domestic e-commerce sales.

2. Determine whether your web site can be accessed on a local basis. In many countries, the population has none or limited access to external Internet resources.

Additionally, in many countries, the best access may be through Internet trading platforms such as Amazon, Alibaba, Newegg, and Overstock.

3. You need to investigate an array of issues when selling into a new market overseas:
   - Competitive products and their approach to sales in that country
   - Legal issues regarding your products' sale in that country
   - Any intellectual property rights (IPRs) issues of concern
   - Import documentation requirements
   - Other government agency requirements, such as their equivalent to our United States Department of Agriculture (USDA), Food and Drug Administration (FDA), Federal Communications Commission (FCC), Bureau of Alcohol, Tobacco and Firearms (BATF), etc.
   - Packing, marking, and labeling requirements
   - Denied Party Listing review
   - Web site entry … your own or third party

4. In the United States, we have a mature and competitively based infrastructure for domestic distribution of products to consumers in home deliveries.

   While this system in the United States works well … it is a huge component of the overall costing model, and e-commerce sellers are always looking for less expensive and more timely options.

   Amazon has made this very clear with its potential use of drones as a delivery mode. Testing began in 2015 and continues into 2017.

Amazon drone in testing mode

Internationally, this has become more of a challenge, as many countries do not have a mature domestic infrastructure for sales and deliveries to consumers and their homes.

The importance of resolving this issue is cost. E-commerce sales only work when the cost of shipping from origin to destination is significantly minimized.

Some companies in North America are looking at driverless vehicles, and, in 2016, Budweiser successfully tested commercial driverless vehicles on routes in Colorado.

Budweiser driverless test vehicle in Colorado

5. Globally, those companies who have been successful in e-commerce sales in an array of foreign countries have mastered the cost of logistics and distribution.

This is best obtained following this outline of action steps:

- Partner with service providers who have defined expertise in e-commerce sales and distribution.
- Consolidate shipments in the United Sates and ship overseas in larger bulk orders. This will reduce the cost of the international leg.
- Obtain all the necessary information proactively on packing, marking, labeling, and documentation requirements.
- Make sure the websites you are utilizing contain all the necessary shipping information and costs relative to the buyers' needs to be made aware of.
- Arrange for competitively priced customs clearance along with the *last mile* delivery requirements.

This is much easier said than can be accomplished. Customs clearance costs and home deliveries are typically an expensive component of the overall sale or purchase.

E-commerce companies have had to be very creative to resolve these costing and business process concerns for low cost consumer items typically handled individually.

Those companies like Amazon and Alibaba in countries such as China have been successful in developing low cost and expedient processes to handle this area successfully for their e-commerce clients.

amazon

- Structure systems for return shipping needs proactively, as they will be potentially cumbersome and add cost to your e-commerce global supply chain.
- When starting e-commerce capabilities ... do *beta testing* in every foreign market, before committing to a final deployment of resources and capabilities.

    This helps to:
    - Work out the *bugs* in advance
    - Reduces initial cost if the process does not work
    - Creates a better foundation before diving in fully
- Make sure payment options are addressed in advance and tested before offering product for sale.
- Trade compliance concerns for all export and import regulations still apply in e-commerce sales as it does in all commercial transactions. Areas such as, but not limited to, in the following all need to be addressed:
    - Denied parties search
    - Harmonized Tariff System of the United States (HTSUS) and schedule B numbers
    - Documentation
    - Recordkeeping
    - Origin determination
    - Export license requirements

- Assuring the *Collecting Order Information* electronically.

    When you're ready to sell internationally, make sure that essential customer information does not fall through the cracks. Use these tips to create clear, customer-friendly payment descriptions:
    - Label your fields as clearly as possible and provide alternatives to help customers who do not speak English (or for whom it is not the primary language). For example, "First" could be displayed as "First Name/Given Name" and "Last" as "Last/Family Name/Surname"
    - Add a third or even fourth line to the address field to accommodate longer international addresses
    - Add a field for "Country"
    - Insert a "Country Code" field above or to the left of the "Telephone Number" field
    - Ask for "State/Territory/Province" rather than just "State"
    - Request "ZIP/Postal Code" rather than just "ZIP Code." Also, if your system uses the "ZIP Code" entry to automatically fill in the "City" and "State" fields, you might want to offer separate fields for "ZIP Code" and "Postal Code"—many other countries use 5-digit postal codes, and a postal code keyed into the "ZIP Code" field could gum up the customer's address
- Act with due diligence in avoiding exposure to fraud.

Best practices include:

- Accepting online payment, even with established credit cards, exposes the seller to some risk. According to Cybersource's 2010 11th Annual Online Fraud Report (*cybersource.com*), U.S. merchants continue to reject three times as many international orders (7.7%) as domestic orders (2.4%). Merchants reject orders they have reason to believe may be fraudulent. But there is some good news: the same survey notes that actual international e-commerce fraud rates for U.S. merchants fell from a 2008 average of 4.0% of total online orders to 2.0% in 2009. The drop can be attributed in part to firms that use various methods to safeguard against unauthorized use of credit cards.
- Although the trends in online fraud are encouraging, U.S. firms need to continue to be vigilant. This is true especially in countries

that used to be considered *safe* for e-commerce retailers. The U.S. Commercial Service has a long history of reports from U.S. export-ers about online fraud coming from China and Nigeria, but now fraudulent activity is occurring in places where it was once rare; the U.S. Commercial Service is now receiving complaints about fraudu-lent activity in Singapore and the Scandinavian countries, among other previously low-risk countries.

• The key is to address fraud concerns proactively with due diligence and reasonable care standards.

This will reduce fraud opportunity and maximize the best outturns.

SUCCESS IN GLOBAL E-COMMERCE

A guide for success in global e-commerce—provided by Department of Commerce/Pitney Bowes

INTRODUCTION

We find ourselves in the midst of a global e-commerce boom, with eMarketers projecting that global e-commerce sales will eclipse $3.5 trillion by 2019.1 If your business has not already taken steps to take advantage of this juggernaut by implementing a global sales strat-egy, the time to get started is now or you risk being left in the retail dust.

While domestic sales in the United States have remained relatively flat, there is huge potential beyond America's shores. Any retailer, large or small, looking for growth should be focusing overseas. The good news is that much of this potential is still untapped. The global e-commerce market is projected to continue growing at a double-digit rate, with the Asia-Pacific region growing faster than any other at a rate of 35.2% year after year. Much of that growth is coming from consumers in rural areas making online purchases from mobile phones. In fact, the region was expected to gain about 80 million new online shoppers in 2015.

Even in more mature e-commerce markets, such as the United Kingdom (one of the strongest e-commerce markets globally), online sales are still expected to grow by 15% in 2016. What is more,

(Continued)

the demand for U.S. goods is high. For international shoppers, the most desirable e-destinations for consumers looking to purchase goods outside their own countries are the United States (71%) and the United Kingdom (44%). Your audience is ready and waiting!

WE LIVE IN A GLOBAL ECONOMY, IT IS TIME TO FULLY ENGAGE IT

Despite the phenomenal potential, many retailers have shied away from the global market due to the complexities involved in setting up shop internationally. They know that it is not as simple as just putting up a website. Many of those that are successful today are working with a partner that understands the challenges of global e-commerce and has experience navigating and mitigating the risks and regulations on a country-by-country basis.

WHAT YOU NEED TO KNOW TO GROW

Selling online to international consumers has historically offered a poor customer experience marked by expense and unpredictability: a clunky web interface, compliance issues that impact delivery times, unexpected additional fees and duties, and an impossible returns process.

As e-commerce has matured, domestic buyers have come to expect mobile-optimized sites, personalization, a broad choice in payment and delivery options, and a flexible returns policy. Today, these niceties—now mandates—must also be offered to international buyers. It is what they have come to expect from an online shopping experience.

Going global is not easy. It brings new challenges that most retailers have not yet encountered. Creating a top-notch international customer experience is just one of many. In the sections that follow, we take a look at some of the major challenges to going global and offer some real-life examples that illustrate how retailers are meeting them.

Regional and Cultural Differences

When extending your domestic brand experience to a global audience, there is much to consider. A *one size fits all* website will almost

(Continued)

always miss the mark. Global consumers have unique shopping preferences and behaviors that vary by country. Each region comes with its own set of characteristics, not to mention rules and regulations.

Start by defining your market focus by country, differentiating your product offerings based upon what your target audience is looking for. For example, consumer electronics and apparel are the biggest draws for Chinese buyers, while books, DVDs, and music are important to Australians. Household goods and auto parts are top categories for Russian e-commerce consumers.

It is also important to align your digital presence to international consumers in a way that meets your buyers' expectations. Consider cultural norms and shopping preferences. Provide localized and personalized content that is available on the device of choice in that region. Consumers must feel served and understood, and be able to find what they are looking for, so they will want to return.

Though language is important, the look and feel of your website must also appeal to local preferences and match customer expectations. And in some markets, setting up a standard website is not the best approach. For example, in China, consumers are more likely to find and make purchases through online marketplaces. International brand familiarity is low, so selling via a domestic online marketplace can be a better way to build trust among Chinese consumers. Popular domestic marketplaces such as Taobao and Tmall account for 76% of online sales.

Understanding these cultural differences and tailoring your website accordingly can be a mammoth undertaking. Working with a partner can help. An upscale U.S. department store chain working with Pitney Bowes is able to sell and ship to more than 220 countries via a website that reflects regional differences based on the currency the shopper chooses. In fact, the company recently began selling in China using Alipay's ePass solution and has seen great results. By offering free or low-cost shipping promotions to most countries—popular in any language—the company has been able to build its customer base. Today, the retailer is able to offer a seamless global customer experience that complements its brand image.

(Continued)

Shipping and Logistics

Global consumers say that the biggest barriers to online cross-border shopping are high shipping costs (64%), additional fees owed at delivery (48%), and slow delivery (39%). Clearly, if you wish to succeed, these issues must be addressed and resolved.

Shipping is an important area that requires a lot of attention. First, a different set of rules pertaining to what you can ship applies to each country you are doing business in. And while shipping overseas takes more time and money, international buyers increasingly expect delivery speeds and costs that match their domestic options. If you are managing your shipments independently, you may not be getting the best rates.

What is more, you must be able to navigate internal delivery infrastructures and local carriers, while meeting delivery dates and managing returns. Providing detailed tracking information to buyers from the time the order is placed until delivery is also a must. Having reliable shipping partners on the ground, in country, is critical because those delivering your packages become an extension of your brand.

Then you have to consider duties and taxes, which are based not only on where the item was shipped from, but where it was made. No customer wants to be asked to pay an unexpected additional sum when their merchandise is delivered. The ability to quote customers a fully landed cost at checkout, inclusive of delivery, taxes, and duties, is key to building a loyal customer base.

International import and export laws are another issue. Shipping certain items is prohibited in certain countries—for example, do not try shipping umbrellas to Brazil or playing cards to Italy. And customs clearance can be daunting, especially in some Asia-Pacific markets, causing delays, fines, penalties, and higher duties if not handled properly. Is the merchandise legally acceptable in the destination country? Are appropriate documentation requirements met?

Delivery challenges can interrupt the customer experience you are looking to provide. Having a partner that is expert in managing country-specific logistics issues can help reduce challenges that can make or break your customer's experience.

(Continued)

An iconic British retailer with a well-heeled international clientele and a large volume of overseas sales was unable to offer pricing in local currencies with duties and delivery costs included. Having to collect duties and taxes from customers at time of delivery was not consistent with the retailer's world-class image or the first-class service it wished to provide. Partnering with Pitney Bowes now allows the company to guarantee a fully landed cost to customers—with all taxes, duties, and delivery charges included and paid at time of sale—in approximately 70 currencies.

Payment and Pricing

Risk abounds where money is concerned. You must ensure that you protect your customers and business against currency fluctuations that affect your pricing and margins, as well as various types of consumer fraud. For example, your customers expect that if they return something, they will get the same amount back that they originally paid. But what if the currency used to purchase the item took a dive in the meantime?

You probably know that consumers want to see prices and final costs in their own currencies, but is your retail site equipped to accept the alternative payment methods they might prefer? Online payment preferences vary by geography. For example, shoppers from the United Kingdom, Canada, France, and the United States predominantly use credit cards, while other parts of Europe prefer to use money transfer or prepaid cards. Local payment systems are also prevalent. For example, mobile wallets specific to China such as WeChat and Alipay are becoming increasingly popular.

Consider working with a partner that understands payment preferences and will take pricing risks out of the equation. The right partner will guarantee the price quoted to the customer at checkout. If currency fluctuations cause that cost to change, your partner will honor the original exchange rate for the life of the transaction, even through a return, if necessary, absorbing any difference.

A U.S. fashion brand turned to Pitney Bowes for help building an international online strategy that would support the opening of

(Continued)

international brick-and-mortar stores. It was vital that the online and brick-and-mortar sites feed each other, with consistent pricing and brand experience. Pitney Bowes technology has given this retailer peace of mind in being able to align country-specific online pricing to match that in local stores, despite any currency fluctuations.

DEMAND GENERATION

For retailers that do not wish to establish brick-and-mortar stores internationally, the digital approach offers an entrée into new, untapped markets. But creating demand and visibility in those markets is another hurdle. Running promotions on shipping in local currency is one way to create demand. Observing local holidays and shopping events such as Chinese New Year and Diwali with flash sales is another.

Knowing where to reach consumers is important too. Globally, the majority of online shoppers (62%) prefer to use a search engine to find products to purchase online, but this varies by country. Seventy percent of shoppers in Japan and the United Kingdom use search engines, while 51% in Canada and India prefer to visit a retailer's site directly. Social media is also a popular source in India, at 38%. While many Chinese shoppers use a search engine to find products, that search engine is not Google, but rather Baidu. With mobile accounting for about half of retail e-commerce sales in China in 2015, you must have a viable mobile and social strategy if you want to meet these customers where they shop.

Develop and deliver the right message to the right audience by working with a partner who has this kind of expertise. Working with Pitney Bowes, a large U.S. discount retailer launched an international version of its website available to shoppers in more than 200 countries just in time for the 2015 holiday shopping season. It also allows U.S. shoppers to ship to family and friends around the world. Pricing is the same as that offered on the U.S. site and can be shown in nearly 60 different currencies. The checkout page appears in the customer's local language, with a price inclusive of shipping, duties, and taxes.

(Continued)

WEBSITE LOCALIZATION AND LANGUAGE

Your website should be localized so customers feel welcome when they visit. A welcome mat in their language is just the start. Prices and checkout in the customer's familiar currency, choice of payment type based on local preferences, and multiple shipping options and delivery times geared to what each region expects will result in a customer experience that feels like home.

Product descriptions and checkout in the customer's own language are also ideal, especially for countries where English is little understood, but care must be taken with translation to maintain brand voice and observe cultural differences.

A high-end retailer with international brick-and-mortar stores wanted to increase its digital presence domestically and internationally. As a luxury brand, the retailer sought to create a seamless global online experience that was a reflection of the brand's uniqueness. To capture the greatest audience, however, a single website would not work. The retailer chose to work with Pitney Bowes because of our proven expertise in connecting the dots between the retailer's stores and online presence and providing a consistent customer experience optimized for each country served.

CUSTOMER CARE AND RETURNS

Offering customers first-class service is what keeps them coming back, but this can be particularly challenging with international customers. As often as possible, customer care should be offered in the customer's own language and time zone and returns must be easy and not cost-prohibitive. Global consumers (33%) cite online return policies as a deterrent to cross-border shopping.

A popular U.S. fashion retail chain wanted to offer international customers the same rich purchasing experience and high level of customer support it offers to U.S. customers, including a no-questions-asked returns policy. International returns create challenges for U.S. retailers. Because it partners with Pitney Bowes, the company is able to provide customers with a refund of the original merchandise price plus the duties and taxes originally paid in the same currency and using the same exchange rate

(Continued)

as the original order. Pitney Bowes acts as the merchant of record and absorbs any currency fluctuations.

LIVE AND LET BUY: BILLY REID AND THE 007 CONNECTION

In the summer of 2012, stills from Skyfall featuring Daniel Craig as James Bond wearing a navy blue pea coat from U.S. luxury clothing designer Billy Reid were leaked in the United Kingdom. Within days, requests for the coat—which was from a prior season—were pouring in from Western European fans. Until just a few months earlier, this would have caused a significant problem for the retailer, which previously had a very limited ability to sell internationally.

Fortunately, Billy Reid had deployed the Pitney Bowes global e-commerce solution, which provides fully landed international delivery costs including country-specific duties and taxes, parcel tracking, parcel protection, and some of the lowest shipping costs around. The company immediately began manufacturing and shipping the pea coats, for which international demand went viral. To date, Pitney Bowes has helped Billy Reid deliver more than 1000 pea coats overseas, and helped to grow the Billy Reid brand globally—one of its primary business strategies.

FROM ANYWHERE TO EVERYWHERE™

There is clearly a lot to be gained by going global. Consider the numbers from China's Singles Day 2015: Total sales were $14.3 billion, and 80% of all Chinese online shoppers participated. Nearly 70% of sales were made on mobile devices, compared to around 40% in 2014. In 2015, Western brands got a piece of the action too, with more than 15,000 global companies participating by launching stores on China's T-mall or localized branded e-commerce websites.

Opening up new revenue channels is critical to business longevity. For retailers, developing and executing on an international e-commerce strategy is almost a mandate—but there are also many

(Continued)

challenges to address. Depending on the approach you decide to take, there can be very little to lose if you work with a partner that understands the complexities and can successfully manage them for you throughout the customer life cycle.

Choose the Right Partner

Pitney Bowes provides an end-to-end global e-commerce solution that covers everything from demand generation to customer care and can be integrated with your e-commerce platform for a seamless customer experience. Supporting global e-commerce in more than 220 countries and territories, we help you go global by providing:

- In language
- In currency
- Pay as you choose
- Ship as you like
- Duties loaded
- With tracking
- Dedicated customer service

Our experience working with over 200 name-brand clients becomes yours, helping you connect with international shoppers on their terms. We continually gather data that add to our understanding of global economies, shopping trends, and cultural nuances, which in turn can inform and differentiate your online storefront.

GETTING STARTED

International consumers are hungry for more options. Make it as easy for them to purchase from you as it is for your customers at home.

Whether you choose to simply test the waters or reap greater rewards by launching a full-fledged online global presence, the right partner can help ease the complexities, while taking on much of the risk.

To learn more about Pitney Bowes global e-commerce solutions, please visit pitneybowes.com/globalecommerce.

CREATING AN E-COMMERCE WEBSITE GLOBALLY

Step 1—Select a Domain Name

A key component to establishing a web presence is choosing a uniform resource locator (URL), also known as a web address. As with URLs aimed toward the domestic market, a URL for an online exporter's website should be short, simple, descriptive, and memorable to customers in the target market. Internet Corporation for Assigned Names and Numbers (ICANN)-Accredited Registrars will concurrently register your URL and domain name for each country in which you register.

Using Country-Level Domain Codes

Every country (and a few territories) in the world has a reserved, 2-letter country code domain (e.g., the United Kingdom has the domain .uk; for a complete list, visit *bit. ly/1NhhWkY*). An online exporter might want to choose domain names localized for their target markets. Locally branded domain names can increase brand awareness, web address recall, and even brand sales and loyalty. In addition, most local search engines display locally relevant content by filtering the search results to include local country code domains only—something to consider when deciding whether to localize or internationalize your site. Companies that want to have a local domain name should research the rules for the particular country, as registration requirements vary. For more information, please visit *iana.org.*

Internationalizing Your Domain Name

Companies seeking foreign customers may also consider an *internationalized* or *multilingual* domain name. Such domain names are web addresses written in characters other than the Roman alphabet. For example, a company called *Bright Light Bulbs* wishing to sell in China could have a domain name that would use the Chinese characters for *bright light bulbs* in its web address. Internationalized domain names allow customers to search and access sites in their native language. Again, most ICANN-Accredited Registrars can assist you in researching domain names in various countries.

Step 2—Register with Search Engines

Most people use search engines to find information on the Internet. Major U.S. search engines such as Google and Bing will find your website automatically, however, in some markets, you may need to register your site with multiple local search engines.

There are a number of international search engines. Some search engines, such as *baidu.com*, are in native languages and characters. Others are popular U.S. search engines with international links, such as *br.search. yahoo.com*. Online exporters should find out if they need to register with each target market's preferred search engines.

Step 3—Choose a Web Host

A *web host* is simply a company which *hosts* your website's files—basically, storing them on powerful Internet-connected computer systems, and allowing them to be accessed by users all over the world. A variety of free and subscription-based web host services are available. Hosting may be purchased from many different kinds of companies, many of whom offer a wide range of services.

Hosting services often go beyond website maintenance to include domain name registration, website design, and search engine registration. For some online exporters, it may be most feasible to use a web host in their target market to take advantage of all of these localized services. The location or nationality of the website host does not affect accessibility of the site. However, when choosing a host, companies should ensure that the host servers reside within a stable infrastructure and are maintained to ensure optimal reliability. Companies also should consider whether they will be storing the personal information of EU citizens, or citizens of other nations that restrict exporting personal data. The personal data of EU citizens can be sent only to countries deemed *adequate*, or to companies using approved model contracts and binding corporate rules, or to those participating in the U.S.–EU Safe Harbor program. Companies also should take into account potential negative perceptions if they store personal data in nations in which fraud or identity theft are rampant.

As with domestically located hosting services, agreements should be clear and enforceable regarding the ownership of intellectual property, performance specifications and warranties, security, privacy, the right to transfer the site to a different host, and contract termination. Your contract with a hosting service should provide the same level of security and privacy that your company promises clients whose information it collects, when applicable.

Step 4—Website Content: Localize and Internationalize

Companies seeking foreign audiences for their websites will want to localize or internationalize their site, or provide a mixture of both approaches. Forrester Research notes that "visitors linger twice as long [on international sites] as they do at English-only URLs; business buyers are three times more likely to buy if addressed in their own language; and customer service costs drop when instructions are displayed in the user's language."

Localization consists of adapting your website to meet the linguistic, cultural, and commercial requirements of a targeted market. Internationalizing a firm's website enables the company to be multilingual and to be sensitive to cultural conventions without the need for extensive redesign. Localization or internationalization must be part of the online exporter's corporate strategy for website and business development. Features that should be considered include:

- Language
- Cultural nuance, such as differences in color association and symbols
- Payment preferences
- Pricing in the appropriate currency
- Web metrics and visitor reports
- Regular maintenance and updating of content

More information on localization and internationalization can be found at *gala-global.org*.

Step 5—Execute Orders

Guidelines for order execution and after-sales service are similar for offline and online transactions. You can easily add a checkout app to your website from a growing number of vendors. You can specify the payment methods that you will accept. Keep in mind that overseas buyers will have different payment methods, and that the app or third-party checkout service you acquire needs to provide these options.

You can also create your own site and online store using vendors such as Shopify. These services provide templates, which can be customized up to a point. You can purchase a domain name and install a checkout function. Some vendors purport to enable their customers to have a store up, running, and taking orders within a couple of hours—and no computer programming skills are needed.

> *Creating a website responding to global orders is a critical step in establishing an international E-commerce presence*
> *IPR: Protecting International Property Rights/Department of Commerce*
> *The U.S. Commerce Department is proud to play a central role in protecting IP*

Among the nation's founders', many enduring legacies is their respect for and values of intellectual property rights by providing for patents and copyrights in Article I, Section 8 of the Constitution—"to promote the Progress of Science and useful Arts." Like other parts of the Constitution, the idea of promoting progress by rewarding the creation of intellectual property has become a nearly global aspiration. Over the decades, Congress, federal courts, and the executive branch have done a great deal to develop the nation's intellectual property system, and, in the process, we have established benchmarks for other nations seeking to emulate our success. Many of our national intellectual property rules are reflected in international treaties and agreements.

Today's world is infinitely more complex than eighteenth century society. Even where specific intellectual property rights are recognized, we face differing views on stakeholders' responsibilities in protecting and exercising these rights. The awareness of the importance of IP is not universal, and in today's interconnected electronic age, preventing IP theft faces many challenges. Products can move across the globe at the speed of light and factories can be quickly adapted to replicate commercially successful goods.

Working with Congress, the courts, and our sister agencies, the Commerce Department plays multiple roles in the national effort to address this complex set of issues. In broad strokes, we:

- Grant certain intellectual property rights on behalf of the U.S. Government.
- Provide administration leadership in developing policy that supports statutory and case law.
- Advocate for the establishment of global intellectual property norms.
- Support national and international IP enforcement efforts, advocating protection for product or category-specific U.S. interests.
- Work to build up capacity in other nations so that they can have more effective intellectual property regimes for their own benefit and the benefit of global commerce.

These activities are mutually reinforcing. Coordinating them across the U.S. Government and with our international partners can be a challenge, but the Commerce Department is committed to working tirelessly on this effort.

Policy-Advice

The U.S. Patent and Trademark Office's role in establishing patents and trademark rights is fundamental to our intellectual property system. By law, the office is "responsible for the granting and issuing of patents and the registration of trademarks" (see 35 USC § 2(a)(1)). The role complements the Copyright Office's registration creative works, and the courts' protection of trade dress and trade secrets under the common law.

Giving life to this law—applying it in specific instances and evolving it to keep up with advances in technology—requires sound policy making. Here, Congress has charged different parts of the Commerce Department with complementary missions:

- Congress has tasked the U.S. Patent and Trademark Office, through the Secretary of Commerce, with advising the President on intellectual property policy matters in the United States and internationally through the Office of the Under Secretary for Intellectual Property.

- Commerce provides policy guidance and advisory and technical assistance, consistent with administration policies, on domestic IP issues to members of Congress and staff, officials of government agencies, and other IP stakeholders.
- And as the Internet has become a leading global platform for economic growth and social progress, the role of Commerce's National Telecommunications and Information Administration (NTIA) also comes into play. By statute, NTIA is the President's "principal adviser on telecommunications policies pertaining to the nation's economic and technological advancement." Since the emergence of the Internet on the commercial scene, NTIA has played a leading role in shaping Internet policy in areas such as Internet domain names, technology innovation, privacy, and security. In these areas, NTIA and PTO have worked together to shape an intellectual property policy that balances strong intellectual property protection with flexibility to allow innovative new applications and services to flourish.

Of course, we perform these policy advice functions in collaboration with other U.S. Government stakeholders. They include entities within the Executive Office of the President, including the Office of Science and Technology Policy, trade negotiators at USTR, and others, as well as the Copyright Office, our diplomatic corps at the State Department, customs officials at the Department of Homeland Security, including law enforcement officers at U.S. Immigration and Customs National IPR Coordination Center (IPR Center), the Department of Justice and, increasingly, the Federal Communications Commission.

Visit doc.gov for specific guidelines on how government resources can assist with IPR concerns.

> Just really, really believe in what you are trying to do. Do not let people alter that. Let people advise you and lead you down paths to make smart business decisions. But trust your instinct and trust that overwhelming drive that made you put all your dreams and everything on the line.
>
> **Luke Bryan**

6

Decision Management

One of the major roles of management is to make decisions. Not all decisions will be the right ones.

The goal is to assure that the overwhelming majority of decisions are made correctly and that executives consider both qualitative and quantitative processes in how they approach making key strategic decisions.

Keep in mind that certain decisions will involve the acceptance of certain risks. Risk taking is an integral part of any business model.

It is the managing of that risk to acceptable levels where most executives will consider. A company that is completely risk adverse will grow more slowly as compared to one that is typically willing to accept certain levels of risk.

Appreciate that in the decision-making process, risk is a very important component of the thought process.

Additionally, that consistent and defined steps are managed to create a pathway to better decision making. That is the heart of this chapter ... how do we go about making better business decisions?

BETTER DECISION MAKING: QUALITATIVE VERSUS QUANTITATIVE

The decision-making effectiveness of a business executive, manager, and leader will be a defining character trait evidencing strong capabilities and wherewithal.

You will be faced with having to make business decisions every day of which many will impact the success of the organization.

Two key factors in decision-making effectiveness is the use of two measurement systems known generically as qualitative and quantitative analysis.

Understanding how to utilize these two methods of analysis in decision-making will lead to more consistent, well thought out, and better decisions.

Executives would be in a much better position in achievement when they know how to work both qualitative and quantitative analysis options.

DEFINITIONS

QUALITATIVE

Qualitative is associated with the subjective quality of a thing or phenomenon, such as feel, taste, expertise, image, leadership, and reputation.

Qualitative aspects are abstract: they either do not require measurement or cannot be measured because the reality they represent can only be approximated. Knowledge of these aspects is gained through observation combined with interpretative understanding of the underlying thing or phenomenon.

QUANTITATIVE

Quantitative is associated with an objective quality of a thing or phenomenon that is measurable and verifiable, such as lightness or heaviness, softness or hardness, and thickness or thinness.

The quantitative process can be easily measured, whereas … qualitative aspects are abstract: they either do not require measurement or cannot be measured because the reality they represent can only be approximated. Knowledge of these aspects is gained through observation combined with interpretative understanding of the underlying thing or phenomenon.

Having said that … qualitative analysis can be *weighed* and *compared* utilizing various mathematical formulas and algorithms.

The characteristics of qualitative analysis are:

- Based on experience
- Judgmental
- Subjective

- Highly based upon feelings and sensibilities
- Room for interpretation
- Easy to challenge

The characteristics of quantitative analysis are:

- Based on metrics and scientifically sound factors
- Derived from *hard data*
- More difficult to challenge
- Less room for interpretation

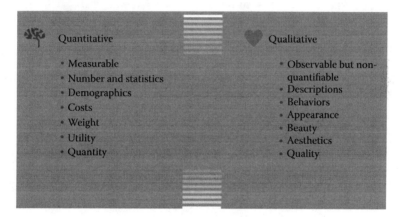

More senior executives with years of experience will rely on qualitative analysis as part of their decision-making process. It could be argued that they have earned that right.

The reason we even discuss this is that quantitative analysis takes time, resources, and money ... much more so then does qualitative analysis.

Executives with experience will tend to go down that road, as it is a *least path of resistance*.

Some, not many, will argue that experience *trumps* hard data. However, most scientists, analysts, and professional information gatherers will clearly dictate that *hard data* are always a much better analytical tool.

It has been my experience having utilized both processes that there is a *balanced* approach where both methods combined and collaborated with ... will always produce better results.

Over the course of 40 years+ I have come to the conclusion that both methods when synched are *golden* ..., but when they are in conflict ... it means back to the drawing boards and start the analysis over again until the results offer better synergy.

Sometimes redoing the analysis will produce different results. And sometimes you will have to do the analysis multiple times to obtain effective results.

A GREAT EXAMPLE

You are a purchasing manager for a 100 million dollar home delivery company, located in downtown NYC.

You have been charged with finding a new company for packaging material for which your annual spend is between 7 and 8 million.

You have four companies involved now and management wants you to consolidate the vendors and obtain savings of at least 12%–15% annually.

The four companies involved are Ajax, Bend, Cargo, and Evan. You have relationships with all four, but you believe that Cargo is the better vendor overall.

You set up a request for proposal involving all four companies. You create a fact sheet of critical data for each vendor, so they can provide a written and oral proposal to you within the next six weeks.

You have meetings with all four vendors and have answered all their questions and received back some initial ideas on what value add and differentiation each will bring ... along with some pricing discussions.

Along with your chief operating officer (COO), you create six points of analysis in making a *quantitative* decision.

You chose the following six areas of scrutiny:

1. Price
2. Customer service
3. Payment terms
4. Manufacturing flexibility
5. Off-hours accessibility
6. Experience in your industry

You then create an Excel-based grid where you will apply metrics to the decision-making process. The metrics will create a rating system of ranking each vendor in each area of review on a 1–5 basis … 1 being poor, and 5 being the best.

Area of Review/Vendor	Ajax	Bend	Cargo	Evan
Price	4	4	4	3
Customer service	3	4	5	3
Payment terms	4	4	4	4
Off-hours accessibility	3	3	5	3
Manufacturing flexibility	4	3	4	3
Experience in your industry	4	3	5	4
Total	22	23	27	20

Cargo clearly becomes the choice from a metrics standpoint. This aligned with your own sensibility and qualitative thoughts that you had on the subject.

This becomes the favored scenario where your *gut feeling* was supported by a detailed mathematical hard data and founded on a process of assessment.

Keep in mind how this would look if it turns out the decision was wrong, and the choice of Cargo presented issues six months later.

You could easily demonstrate how the decision was made and evidence the alignment of both qualitative and quantitative decision-making prowess.

In the same case study, but with a different outcome:

Area of Review/Vendor	Ajax	Bend	Cargo	Evan
Price	4	4	3	3
Customer service	3	5	5	3
Payment terms	5	4	4	4
Off-hours accessibility	3	3	4	3
Manufacturing flexibility	5	3	4	3
Experience in your industry	4	5	4	4
Total	24	24	24	20

In this analysis your gut sensibility in choosing Cargo … is not supported from the metrics and you have three of the four companies posting similar scores. One below par.

This creates a quandary, as your sensibility is not supported. This is where you might have to do any one of the following additional steps:

- Redo the analysis.
- Add additional areas of scrutiny.
- Bring more team members into the analysis to see if they post different scores.
- Go back to the vendors and see if they want to offer a revised proposal that would offer additional value add, services, or price reductions.

The best scenario of your qualitative and quantitative processes was not in synch. *Back to the drawing board* is your only option as outlined earlier.

As an executive becomes more seasoned and experienced, the alignment of qualitative and quantitative should fall in synch often. If it does not, you will need to question your thought process, subjective reasoning, and possibly even your ability to read circumstances well.

In the decision-making process, there are a number of steps you can take to assist you in making better decisions:

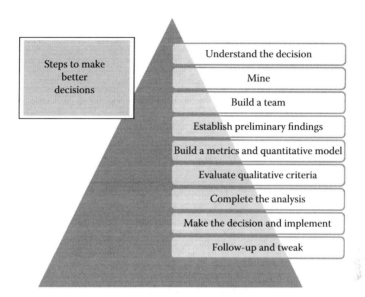

Understand the Decision

You are going to undertake making an important decision. It is always a good practice to make sure you are *framing* exactly what you are looking to decide on. Sometimes that may not be exactly clear.

Some executives will outline this area as clearly defining expectations, deliverables, and anticipated results.

You do not want to go through a complete analysis to find out later you were chasing the wrong question.

Mine

Information and intelligence is *gold*. The more informed you are … the better the opportunity to assess comprehensively and bring the thought process to a better decision.

Mining requires time, expense, and resources so you can collect data that can be figured into the decision-making process.

In my practice, I see a lot of issues raised within companies that result from decisions being made by personnel who were not completely informed of what their options are.

Mining is a commitment that must be practiced regularly. This means that executives have to have an information flow into their operations that is contemporary. This may include:

- Seeing vendors, channel partners, and business associates on a regular basis
- Attending trade shows and industry events
- Reading industry and trade magazines and periodicals
- Viewing key daily, weekly, and monthly subject matter e-mails
- Listening more intently when information is being offered by others

Build a Team

Important decisions sometimes have to be made by your lone self. But in business, the clear majority of decisions should be made by a number of individuals:

- Stakeholders
- Bosses
- Subordinates
- Colleagues
- Those with vested interests
- Those impacted by the decision
- Vendors, suppliers, and clients
- Channel partners, etc.

We have found over the years that building a *team* of people who can help you in the decision making process serves to mold a better decision-making model.

- First of all, you can delegate some of the responsibilities … mining, fact gathering, metric models, etc.
- You can obtain input and conflicting thoughts to help create varied perspectives.
- You can validate your thought process for *peace of mind.*
- You can have the burden when making important decisions.

All of the above as a *team* opens the pathway to a better decision-making model.

Establish Preliminary Findings

As you think through the decision to be made, it is okay to start to develop your *heading* and start to formulate conclusions. You will still go through the entire process, even though you may be sure of the eventual conclusion.

Preliminaries will help you in moving forward and molding an eventual decision and solution, as long as you do not allow that fact to interfere with the mining and evaluation process that might move forward into a different direction.

Build a Metrics and Quantitative Model

As we identified earlier in this chapter, utilizing metrics is your best path to better decisions.

Your utilizing substantive hard data produces quality results. Building analytical models with mathematics and algorithms allow for science to enter the equation.

Metrics are also a cover your ass (butt) (CYA) initiative that is an accountable and responsible management practice.

Evaluate Qualitative Criteria

It is okay to bring experience, sensibilities, and gut feeling into the equation and thought process. The more seasoned you are with lots of experience makes qualitative reasoning more qualified.

Keep in mind that it is a balanced approach of sensibility combined with metrics and where they come together … is the nirvana of decision making.

Complete the Analysis

Hopefully, done on time, you will finalize the analysis and draw down on your viable options, narrowing your choices to one or a few.

Make the Decision and Implement

Now it is time to make the decision, communicate the conclusion to all necessary parties, and begin whatever the next step is … maybe implementation or execution or information flow.

Follow-Up and Tweak

Decisions have to be followed up to determine their success and/or effectiveness. Often they have to be *tweaked or modified* adjusting to the revised analysis and what needs to be done to make the decision work.

Emotional Intelligence

Emotional intelligence (EQ/EI) is an important aspect regarding decision-making prowess. I contend that people with higher EQ's tend to make better decisions. They are more stable, thoughtful, and have a lot more street smarts, allowing qualitative thoughts to provide intuitive results.

EQ can be a huge distinguishing point, which separates good from great. Managers and leaders who have high levels of EQ can find solutions better and have an easier time at leading people in a direction to everyone's mutual interests.

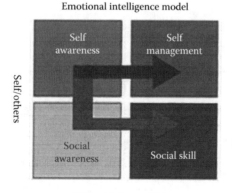

Emotional intelligence model

When one studies some of the great leaders of the world … past and present, after reading this section, you will be able to clearly define their EQ traits, which helps to define their greatness.

Emotional intelligence (emotional quotient, EQ) is a hot discussion point in corporate America coming from a group of progressive corporate cultural icons who have studied the subject in great depth. Some attribute the discussion to Adele Lynn, Robert Cooper, Ayman Sawaf, Bob Kelly, and Dan Coleman. They all identify EQ as the dimension of intelligence responsible for our ability to manage ourselves and our relationships with others.

EQ is the distinguishing factor that determines whether we make lemonade when life hands us lemons, or whether we spend our life in bitterness. EQ is the distinguishing factor that enables us to have wholesome, warm relationships or cold, distant ones. EQ is the distinguishing factor between finding and living our lives' passions or just existing.

In the business world, I believe that EQ is the major factor of differentiation between mediocre managers and leaders and great ones. In the business world, however, so much of our emphasis has been placed on intellect. It has all been on intelligent quotient (IQ) and the analytical, factual, and measured reasoning power that IQ represents. Make no mistake, intellect has proven invaluable to drive success in business and life. Financial decisions based on analytical details, sound strategies based on facts and data, and processes and procedures based on review and analysis are all critically important.

To get to the next level of business, we combine IQ and EQ to raise the bar of all our skill sets and merge them into a persona and action that exude confidence and prowess, causing our own inspiration, as well as providing a reason for others to follow.

In life, IQ would be akin to the athlete who practices all the time, is in the best shape and physical condition, continually studies all the plays, but is time and time again unable to deliver wins. It is also the actor who can sing, dance, and act, who works really hard and knows all the lines, but is never pursued by the directors, as he or she totally lacks *stage presence*. It is also the beautiful women who have the looks, the figure, the intelligence, all the perceived talent, and who are constantly being pursued, but who have difficulty in relationships and go through life alone. It is also the businessman whose father started the business, who has all the schooling, the training, and did all the right things, but who never rises to his father's place.

In all these examples, the formula for success was there, but it just did not happen. We all know numerous situations like this in our business and personal lives. They all seem to get to *third base*, but cannot get *home*. And even in our own circumstances, we have probably had times when we felt like these examples. Some use the phrase, "not seeing the forest through the trees"; or "the ship has sailed, but it does not know where it is going"; or "there are many animals to herd, but no pastures to show them."

In business, I found that these people lose out because they are unable to connect the dots. They have good intentions, all the fundamentals, but lack the ability to make it all bear fruit.

When we add *globalization* into the business equation ..., EQ becomes much more complicated and intense ..., therefore even that much more important.

Consider the case of a very intelligent CEO from an Ivy League school. He has 20 years of training, worked his way up the ladder, and has always been successful. He seems to go through life and business without a care-king of the golden child. He finally has his first major challenge, where all can be won or lost, and he loses. He is unable to muster the troops and lead the team through turbulent waters or navigate them to resolution. It seems he has all the talents, but is unable to bring it all together and make it happen.

Most highly regarded leaders have EQ. They are commanding, intelligent, intuitive, and most of all can get others to follow. Few people have the skill sets and a high degree of EQ.

As this concept of EQ develops into more of a science and its traits and characteristics are identified, sales managers will look to raise the bar of their capabilities and ultimately, their performance.

Some EQ considerations:

- Understanding that the job is not just thinking and doing, but to get others to think and do
- Seeing yourself realistically and getting others to be more honest with themselves and with the world
- Getting others to be their very best
- Learning the relationship between thinking and acting, imagining and creating, and believing and living
- Recognizing that everything is connected directly and indirectly

- Being able to connect the dots to conclusion, and remembering that everything eventually needs closure and that the timing of this is critical
- Understanding that articulation often separates the good from the best
- Recognizing that perception is very often reality, and knowing when it is not
- Learning how and why people behave the way they do, studying human nature
- Seeing the big picture and also paying attention to vital details
- Learning to focus
- Recognizing that health is everything—physical and emotional
- Learning to command, yet be respectful
- Listening well
- Understanding that business is business and that personal is personal, learning to know when they are the same, and when they are different
- Being street smart
- Recognizing when to be patient and when not to be
- Being more responsible, less fair
- Showing common sense, intuition, and realistic perspective, and a forthright demeanor, all of which are virtues
- Being honest, considerate, direct, and no nonsense
- Being traditional, contemporary, and futuristic
- Thinking globally, acting locally
- Always influencing in a positive way
- Realizing that stimuli influence mindset (beliefs), which causes thoughts, which influences behavior, which causes actions that influence results (we generally choose our stimuli, the beginning of how we perceive, and, ultimately, influence the world)
- Not sweating the small stuff
- Approaching every day with a positive can-do mindset
- Compromising everything, except your values
- Creating win–win scenarios
- Being sensitive to multicultural issues
- Reducing your emotional highs and lows to more of a steady demeanor
- Taking well thought out risks
- Knowing when to exercise passion and compassion

- Knowing when to delegate, mentor, and lead
- Always being grateful and living every moment and day as a gift

There has been both a seasoned and recent debate whether all these considerations are innate or whether they can be learned. For sure, they can be learned to some extent. For those who have the benefit of these innate gifts, they can certainly be enhanced and bettered.

To some, many of these EQ skills come naturally. For others, they have to be learned, practiced, and highlighted in everyday consciousness and action. For these EQ skills to work in building the character of a person, they must be practiced consistently and in all aspects of a person's business behavior and life persona.

The listed EQ considerations, when practiced with all the skill sets outlines in this book, will create a formula that will maximize your opportunities for ultimate success in sale, sales management, and in life.

And it is a necessary component of leadership and management where doing your very best is a behavioral trait.

> If people like you, they'll listen to you, but if they trust you, they'll do business with you.
>
> **Zig Ziglar**

7

Delivering Successful Negotiations

A critical skill set of all leaders and managers is the ability to bring the majority of all trade opportunities to a successful negotiation.

The author makes the point that a successful negotiation is defined where both or all parties compromise and benefit, which is the focus of this chapter.

Negotiating successfully means developing a strategy. This strategy is outlined in the following six steps:

1. Defining what we want to accomplish in negotiation and developing a strategic plan
2. Negotiating globally
3. The essence of compromise
4. Trust is the critical asset
5. Case studies
6. Negotiating for the millennium

DEFINING WHAT WE WANT TO ACCOMPLISH IN NEGOTIATION AND DEVELOPING A STRATEGIC PLAN

The strategic plan has seven considerations:

- Goal setting
- Assessment
- Mining
- Planning
- Action
- Tweaking
- Closure

Goal Setting

Negotiating is achieving something that you wanted to accomplish. Therefore, you need to first define what you are looking to accomplish. This becomes the goal, the deliverable or expectation of the negotiation. This means that we must make sure of the goal setting procedure referred to as specific, measurable, attainable, relevant, trackable, and *SMART.*

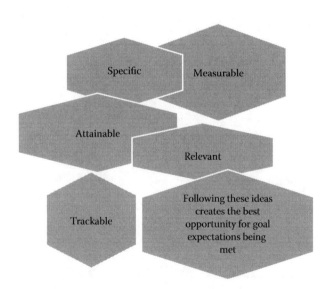

Making sure goals are *SMART* is a best practice and will very often help to assure successful negotiations.

Thinking through the five *SMART* concepts creates the best opportunity for strategically thinking out what you anticipate achieving and is the first step in the overall negotiation process.

Assessment

Following, the establishment of a goal ... the negotiator or negotiating team must create an assessment of the situation they are facing in the negotiation.

A *strengths, weaknesses, opportunities and threats* analysis has merit here. This standard practice creates for key points to measure, analyze and assess.

The assessment ties directly into information gathering in order to make better decisions.

Mining

Mining is a tool that *digs or mines* for information useful in assessing the circumstances surrounding the negotiation process. This will lead to making a decision about what strategy to utilize.

To make better decisions, one needs to get informed. This might include:

- Learning about competitor's programs and pricing
- Benchmarking alternative choices
- Evaluating your internal strengths and options
- Assessing anticipated risks versus rewards

Mining becomes an important tool to utilize as you are *stacking up* your opportunity to negotiate successfully when you are fully informed.

Information can be your most valuable resource.

Planning

From your assessment and mining processes, you will begin to draft a strategy and plan of action on how best to move forward with the negotiation.

This planning becomes your strategic blueprint and creates the outline of how to make your anticipated goals come to reality.

Action

The plan is strategic. Action is the tactical approach. It becomes the actual steps and actions that you make happen as you move forward on the negotiation. Setting up meetings, conference calls, site visits, and so on.

The plan moves your negotiation initiative forward.

Tweaking

The initial plan is your *best guess*. As the process moves forward, experience is gained. Information and your adversary's position become revealed.

This may cause you to reconsider your strategy and change direction, modify, alter plans, and so on.

This tweaking is an essential aspect of the negotiation process. It requires you to be nimble and quick, adaptive and intuitive. This then allows you to put a new foot forward with the hope of bettering your negotiation position and obtaining a favored outcome.

Sometimes you have to take two steps backward to move one step forward. And that is okay as long as you are moving forward and getting closer to a favored position.

Remember, negotiation is a *process* that adapts over time.

Remember negotiation is a *process* that adapts over time!

Closure

Negotiations that are successful close naturally. No one has to ask ..., it happens because everything was in order and everyone involved understands that it is over and moved forward.

When we have to *ask* ..., the negotiation has vulnerability.

But we need always to bring the negotiation to a close, win or lose ..., but over!

NEGOTIATING GLOBALLY

There is one very dominant issue we need to consider when negotiating globally.

Culture is a unique factor we must bring into every strategic action we consider.

Important aspects about culture:

- As Americans, we need to raise the bar about our knowledge and empathy for understanding the various cultures of the world we work and live in.
- Cultures can vary dramatically from one region and one country to another.
- Additionally, within countries, cultures can vary greatly.
- Negotiating internationally and not being tuned into diversity and culture is putting your being successful and your negotiation in jeopardy.
- Culture always is an impactful part of how people act, react, interpret, and make decisions with.
- Being rude culturally cannot only kill a negotiation, but could create irreparable harm.

One most learn the basics about culture in the various countries you are doing business with Some resources are:

- U.S. Government … doc.gov
- Various books on culture
- Your service providers accessing their overseas offices and networks for local information including cultural concerns

---

THE ESSENCE OF COMPROMISE

The important learning element of a good negotiation result is based upon compromise and consensus.

This includes creating a *win–win* scenario between all parties involved.

Heading into a negotiation with a mindset that you are going to obtain everything you want at the cost of the other party is not only selfish and self serving, but sets the stage for failure.

A mindset that both parties can walk away feeling successful, is one that those who understand the basis of compromise and consensus have.

You give up something to gain something and in the overall and in the big picture ... both parties have given something up, but they both gained, as there is now an agreement in place on how to move forward, having compromised, and finding common ground.

TRUST IS THE CRITICAL ASSET

The most important aspect of being able to negotiate well is to obtain the *trust* of the other party(s).

Trust makes you believable even when the information being passed is suspect. Trust allows the other party to feel comfortable.

Trust is made up of their sensibility that you have been honest, forthright, and straightforward. Trust binds you in a positive way with the other person(s) and dramatically increases the odds that you can be influential and lead someone into favored positions.

Trust may just be the most important tool you have to obtain compromise and consensus.

NEGOTIATION BEST PRACTICES

Key questions to ponder in *negotiation management*

- Perspective ... purchasing/supply chain versus sales.
- People negotiate ... not companies.
- Is negotiation an art or science?
- Can everyone negotiate and negotiate successfully?
- Is everything negotiable?
- What do we mean by *win–win*?
- Where does compromise come into the negotiation and when does it not?
- What are the typical problems that fall into play when we negotiate?
- Explain the importance of *timing* in negotiation.
- Explain *value add*.
- Explain the consequences of not paying attention to *value add*.

(*Continued*)

- Explain value versus spend and the importance of putting the concept into practice.
- What is a purchasing mantra and the importance?
- Explain the difference between strategy and tactics and action plan and the importance in negotiation success.
- Discuss the importance of people skills and psychology in negations management.
- Betterments in business and personal life, when we know how to negotiate better.
- Knowledge is very critical in negotiations.
- Importance of transparency, honest, straightforward, no non-sense approach to negotiating.

Core business needs:

- Personal
- Financial
- Internal requirements
- Risk mitigation or management
- Time or money
- Ease and convenience
- Opportunities … growth, profits, etc.
- Minimizing problems, headaches, aggravations
- Makes good business sense

Current times in 2018 and the new world economy:

- New world order … what does that mean?
- New president and administration bringing about major changes
- Globalization
- Timeliness of communications
- Information availability and technology (Internet)
- Running lean
- Corporate structure changes
- Motivation changes
- Competitive pressures

(Continued)

- Price versus value-added
- Short-term versus long-term benefits
- Risk and spend management

Problem areas and positive actions

- Talking versus listening
  Asking lots of questions
  Framing questions that draw to conclusions
  Framing questions that close the deal, without asking
- Patience
  Counting to ten
  Painful …, but relax
- Deal from strength
  Confidence
  Information
  Prenegotiation
  Sales focus
- Negotiate for the long run
  Short-term versus long-term goals
  How long will you be doing this and be in business?
- Putting all your cards on the table … upfront
  Example: "Best price, do not waste my time"
- Relationship building
  Importance … trust … confidence
  Over time
  1. Establish credibility
  2. Offer and do
  3. Identify common areas … personal and business
  4. Raise and discuss common goals
  5. *Breaking bread* … establishing a personal and intimate relationship
  6. Gauge how to handle the personality
  7. Handling areas of disagreement … timing and actions
  8. Test
  9. Maintain

(*Continued*)

- Personalities
  What type of person are you dealing with?
  - Open, honest, direct
  - Anal
  - Holier than though ... crap does not stink
  - Condescending
  - Respected
  - Empire building
  - Sheepish and subservient
  - Detailed
  - Big picture person
  - Cheap
  - Bodacious
  - Where are they in the packing order?
- Decision makers
  Deciding who and to what extent
  Who else?
  What motivates them as a *team* versus *individual*?
- Intimidation as a conscious decision
  Bullying
  Scare tactic
  Consequences negatively ... to a positive eventually
  Manipulating
  Politics and personalities

(*Continued*)

- Do not sell, buy, or negotiate over the phone ... on big matters
  Why?
  Eyeball to eyeball
- Team efforts in negotiation
  Good guy/bad guy
  Personalities
  Work at several levels
  Diversify tactics
- Control the negotiation
  Control is king
  Dealing with stalemates and deadlocks
  Losing in the short term and winning in the long run
- Closing questions
  Close should come without asking
  But if not ..., know when to ask and ask with a subtle approach
  Examples ...
  Be prepared and anticipate
  Dealing with objections ... best approach
- Physicality of negotiating

Case studies

1. Freight negotiation
   You are a sales manager for a large local trucking company.
   One of your largest clients for whom you have enjoyed a 7-year
   relationship with is now considering a bid from a larger, more
   nationally based competitor. Price and technology seems to be
   major factors.
   How do you handle the customer with the goal of eliminating the threat?
2. Bank deal
   You are a bank relationship officer. You have been working on a
   new opportunity for the last four months on selling a customer
   of a stiff competitor to move all of his banking services to your
   company. He has been basically satisfied with their 2-year relationship, but is open to hear what you have to say. He is one of
   (Continued)

several decision makers, he is a controller, and reports into a vice president (VP) of finance, who reports into the president.

Design the negotiating strategy.

3. Insurance close

   You are an insurance adjuster and are working with a client who just had an automobile accident. The claimant received a quote from an auto body shop (their family) for an estimate of $7800.00 for a new front end. The insurance company's shop is claiming that the repair cost will come in around $4400.00. You think the customer is inflating the repair cost and will make money through the claim. How do you go about bringing this to a favorable close? The customer is strong willed and not very accommodating.

4. New employee

   You have hired a new technical assistant. So, after a few weeks you notice that performance is less than satisfactory. You like the person and she gets along well with her colleagues. Her credentials are fine. You need to elevate her performance ... motivate her to do better, but also warn her about being terminated if the situation does not improve significantly.

   Negotiate a successful conclusion.

5. Car dealership

   A car salesman observes a man who just came into the showroom eyeing a sporty new convertible. His goal is to sell him that car. What does he do to accomplish that? What is he thinking about? What preparatory things could he have done? Is his goal correct?

6. Advertising executive

   A senior advertising executive is told by his client that he does not like one of his team members and is pretty upset with this person's handling of the account. He wants the person removed off the team immediately. The person has five years' experience and has been involved in handling larger accounts only for the past year and has only worked on this account for the past eight months. The person seems to get along with everyone else and you have no problems with her. You reached out to a few other clients about her and they express no cause for concern.

(Continued)

You have everyone on your team stretched a little thin and this account has some technical requirements that this woman has already gone through a learning curve on. You want to keep her on the team. You need to negotiate her staying servicing this account.

What steps do you take?

7. Bank line of credit

You as a senior bank relationship officer have been working with an existing customer to increase their line of credit with the bank. They have been in business for 19 years and have grown their business from 20 million to 80 million in the last five years. Their rapid growth has caused a need for working capital or an increase in their operating line of credit, which now is at 5 million ..., which they want to increase to 8 million. The client has never posed any concern over meeting their obligations until about two months ago, when their working line started to strain. Their financials are not strong from a profit standpoint, but the growth and potential has been amazing. The client has just added new management to help run the business more effectively as the founders tended to focus on creativity and growth. You are meeting with your credit committee tomorrow and are developing the strategy to convince them on why they should increase the credit line by 20%.

8. Bank promotion

You are a bank VP with over 20 years' experience in the industry including five years with this bank. You handle some of their key accounts and are responsible for developing business in the garment industry in NY. Up until a year ago you have always met the goals set for you and have been told that you have been doing a good job. You have five reports and for the most part the overall team performance has been good. The bank pulled back on credit availability, and this in the last two years has made your job a little more difficult. Some accounts were lost and new production has been subpar. The senior VP is retiring in 90 days, and they are looking for his replacement. The president of the bank has asked you to a meeting with he

(Continued)

and the executive committee to *interview* you for the position. It would mean a nice raise, more power and influence, and overall meet a career goal.

How do you prepare for the meeting and negotiate this promotion for yourself?

9. Union benefits

You are a city manager who is now faced with some major budget cuts. The board has directed that you negotiate with the three unions in town ... police, fire, and teachers ... a reduction in compensation. The goal is to cut health benefits by 7% and pension costs by 5%, effective October 1, 2015. The Unions, anticipating this initiative, have already and publicly stated they will go on strike before they give up on any compensation changes.

How do you go about entering this negotiation, which has a 90-day window to finalize?

10. Military conflict

You are head of a U.S. Military Special Forces team operating on the border of Afghanistan and Pakistan. You were just advised that a major terrorist leader has been seen about 30 miles from your position, but is in Pakistani territory, which is restricted. At your side is a Pakistani senior officer who could clear the way for your team to enter Pakistan. You believe that you only have 90 minutes to proceed or he will be too far along his way and out of reach.

You now only have moments to get permission from this Pakistani officer ... what do you say and do?

11. Date night

You have a real crush on this very nice-looking woman in your office. She seems really nice, and she would be considered a colleague in standing with you and has been employed there about the same amount of time. You would both be compatible by looks, personality, and standing.

Anytime you have flirted with her or reached out in any way ... she has really not paid any attention. There is a corporate outing that is going to take place for couples and you want to ask her to be your date. You overheard a few other guys

(Continued)

talking about asking her to this event, so you think you may only have a day or so before she will be taken up.

How do you proceed to make this date happen?

12. Cosmetic company: reluctant opportunity

You are a pretty successful sales woman in a cosmetics company. There are ten big retailers that all the cosmetic companies want to sell with. Your company has seven of them in their portfolio and you personally handle two of them ... and have been given charge to go after one of the three your company does not have. This retailer is about to put out a request for proposal/request for quote (RFP/RFQ) for another cosmetic line and your initial efforts have failed to get them to include you in this RFP/RFQ. They cite bad experience from five years ago with your company and seem to be pretty predisposed at not talking to you. Your goal is to get them to include you in this offering. You only have 30 days left before the bids go out.

Define your strategy.

13. Communications company

A TV company is attempting to increase the amount of money it receives from the cable network company that carries its channel. The current pricing falls in line with the rest of the marketplace, but your senior management team feels as though your channel is producing better shows, with better advertisers, and has a better opportunity for more revenue. You would be *buck heading* the already established market pricing set several years earlier. No one else is demanding a premium.

How do you negotiate a price increase in the face of market conditions against you?

14. Buying a new car

You were just given a nice raise and you intend to buy a new Maxima. The sticker price, fully loaded shows $31,500.00. You did a little market research before seeing the dealer and you believe you can get the price down to $26,500.00. Though you could pay cash, you were planning to lease the car and think you can at around $500.00/month.

Negotiate for the car without giving in on the price.

(Continued)

15. Coke/Pepsi

Coca-Cola has had the contract to sell Coke in Shea Stadium for 25 years. Shea's management group is looking to increase revenue on its beverage line, which now has allowed Pepsi an opportunity to bid. Coke has its claws dug deep here and is a stiff competitor. Pepsi has been invited in to give a *dog and pony* show on why Shea management should let them in and how this would benefit them.

Create the strategy and negotiation points.

Case studies in negotiation and purchasing/supply chain management

1. Managed printing services

You spend 10 million annually on managed printing service (MPS). You have nine divisions who all independently purchase their own MPS and were allowed to do so because of their unique requirements and the profit center structure within your company. A consulting company came in and advised your senior management that up to 20% could be saved by consolidating vendors.

How do you approach this negotiation?

2. Transportation spend

Your company spends 4.5 million with a specific trucking company who services ten locations nationally. They precede your engagement and have been the primary vendor for over 10 years.

Most managers like their service, and they have some strong roots with the owner of your company. The big problem with their operation is a lack of technology capability, which adds cost and a lot of internal manual manipulation of data and metrics. When they are approached about this ... they hide behind their tenure, their relationships, and the level of service.

If you were to take this vendor out ... a lot of internal screaming and strife would follow, but you need to get this technology.

How do you negotiate a resolve?

(Continued)

3. Technology services

   Your company manages third party technology services by each profit center, of which there are 12 divisions ... doing their own thing. Cumulatively, the spend exceeds 20 million and you have been directed as purchasing director to bring this under control and reduce risk and cost. Each division has its own independent needs and is a fierce control freak. You are not an IT sort of person and most of the technical side of all of this ... is very foreign to you.

   You want to make a favorable impact and negotiate a solution ... explain the strategy.

4. Redesign and upgrade corporate offices

   As purchasing manager, you are charged with the project of redesigning the old corporate offices and making them contemporary and more functional. You have about 300,000 square feet, over 1000 staff, and the existing facility has not been touched or over 20 years. You have a lot of input, opinions, and personnel thoughts on how this should be done and what the new look will be. As a matter of fact, it is overbearing. You have been given a tight budget and deadline. You want to make everybody happy.

   How to negotiate a realistic solution?

5. New CRM system

   Sales and marketing has come to you the PM to help them acquire a new CRM, Customer Relationship Management System. The one they have in place is not meeting their requirements and is ten years old. No RFP has ever been issued. Their new director of business development wants to manage the RFP process and not hand it into purchasing. The spend will just exceed 1.2 million. Your company has no specific guideline or dollar amount on required RFP's and purchasing.

   You know that this should be controlled by purchasing, so how do you navigate a favorable conclusion here?

6. Existing pricing

   You are putting out for bid in an informal process all your commercial insurances, spend approximately 8 million. You have no issues with the current broker or underwriter, but company

   (Continued)

policy requires that category spends in excess of 1 million must be rebidded every two years. A new broker has come in with some great business process improvements, better technology, and is discussing some price reductions, but is looking for you to advise on what your company is currently paying for these coverages. You are reluctant to release that information, as the incumbent will be annoyed and you are not sure what to allow for.

How do you negotiate through this issue?

Rank does not confer privilege or give power. It imposes responsibility.

Peter Drucker

8

Building the Sustainable Business Model

This chapter creates a refined outline in ten easy steps of what the business executive needs to accomplish to build a business, sustain, and profit greatly from.

- Overview of the sustainable business model
- The ten steps of sustainable business
- Summary

OVERVIEW OF THE SUSTAINABLE BUSINESS MODEL

The sustainable business model is best defined as an organizational structure, which assures tenure and longevity of the organization along with meeting, if not all, most of the company's objectives.

The sustainable business model might have the following traits:

- Profitability in successive years
- Little turnover of key personnel
- Meeting objectives on a regular and consistent basis
- Meeting growth, profitability, and margin targets
- Taking controlled risks
- Structure that allows independent thinking
- Collaborative internal business practices
- Technology driven

- Purchasing practices in place to reduce risk and spend
- Global trade in business model
- Ingrained training and education
- Key operations running well: manufacturing, distribution, finance, business development/sales, legal, risk management, supply chain, human resources, and trade compliance
- Internal auditing and assessing
- Resource gain and development
- Cyber security protections

Train to communicate better:
People relate to one another through various forms of communicating. Technology is impacting this concept dramatically every day and is advancing at a very rapid almost extraterrestrial rate.

There is also somewhat of a divide among younger (the millennials) and more seasoned executives.

This chapter delves into the various forms of communicating and more importantly how best to communicate globally to compete effectively.

- A brief overview of communication in business
- Young versus old ... *the millennials*
- Technology as a tool
- Keeping it simple, direct, and no nonsense
- Developing an image and communicating same

THE TEN STEPS OF SUSTAINABLE BUSINESS

The ten steps are tried and proven methods that company executives can take to assure their company prospers for years to come:

1. Develop leadership skill sets, starting at the top, filtering into the management team
2. Develop business skill sets for the management team in their respective disciplines
3. Encourage independent thinking and an open atmosphere with the exchange of ideas, even when potentially contentious

4. Integrative management: encourage an attitude of collaborative, transparency, and team behaviors
5. Maintain steady business development practices
6. Protect margins
7. Engage the international market
8. Diversify into collateral markets
9. Maintain a revolving, replacing, and redundant workforce
10. Team building

INTEGRATIVE MANAGEMENT

Integrative management is a concept that demands an executive making decisions within the area of their responsibility give serious consideration on the impact of that decision to the other profit and cost centers within and outside of the organization.

Internally, if the executive is managing distribution ... he or she would then consider the impact on warehousing, inventory management, sales, customer service, legal, finance, human resources (HR), and so on.

Externally, he or she would consider the impact on vendors, suppliers, subcontractors, third party manufacturers, channel partners, and on the other side ... customers, delivery providers, service providers, and so on.

The gain achieved in this approach has numerous channels of benefit:

- The collaborative approach allows additional insight from potentially impacted parties that might influence you to better decisions.
- The collaborative process demonstrates your leadership in a *team approach* and shows that you value their input.
- When decisions are made, and you have impacted parties participating in the decision-making process, then they will be more likely to *buy into* the resolutions and participate proactively and comprehensively in the implementation process.
- The broader reach into other business units internally and externally creates a much greater access to current and contemporary information that may prove valuable in making better decisions.

The integrative approach requires working with numerous skill sets:

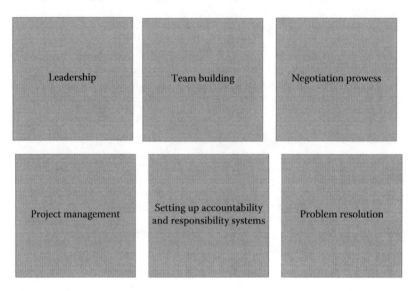

The integrative approach has these six areas: leadership, team building, negotiation prowess, project management, setting up accountability and responsibility systems, and problem resolution as critical areas of skill set development.

Leadership must be accomplished in order to lead and influence all impacted personnel into compromised decisions that benefit the organization.

Team building is a necessary aspect of managing any initiative successfully. Having greater participation and varied input will most likely produce more favorable results.

Negotiation prowess is a very important skill set, which enables a person to more successfully convince others of a particular direction, decision, or reasoning when you want to move others down a particular path to a specific decision.

Project management allows a structured format to pursue an internal initiative to come to some very specific goals. Projects will usually require leadership and team building.

Setting up accountability and responsibility systems is a thought process turned into actions, which makes sure that everyone does what is expected of them and creates both positive and negative consequences for success and/or failure. Setting up accountability and

responsibility systems creates the best opportunity to assure personnel participation and effort to work in the best interest of the company in completing a project successfully.

Problem resolution will be an important factor in the everyday activity
of senior professional executives who have to face an array of problems as they navigate through their cadre of overall responsibilities
tied into an interface ... in, out, down, and up!

Executives who develop a *mindset* of a collaborative and integrative
approach to their responsibilities have a much greater chance of succeeding, as this approach has proven within most organizations since the
industrialization of the Western world to accomplish better results.

There becomes a clear recognition that what one entity, division, silo, or
individual within an organization does ... impacts others and numerous
other parts of the organization.

And that to drive better management results is when collaboration is
accomplished working an integrated mindset into the thought process
and the actions of communication, camaraderie, and mutual best interest
are indeed accomplished.

Companies that create a team-based approach and master successful
camaraderie between management, staff, and personnel will then have the
best opportunity to achieve desired results.

The opportunity in an integrative approach maximizes the opportunity
to work through:

- Challenges
- Disputes
- Conflicts
- Differences
- Personnel behaviors

In corporations, we are always striving to create venues for making better
decisions and achieving mutual goals. In that process ... problems will
occur. The integrative approach therefore opens the likely path to resolution and conflict mediation.

Personnel, management, and staff that have camaraderie and a collaborative mindset are more likely to work through these challenges and create resolve ... rather than allowing them to disrupt access to favorable
resolves and conclusions.

DEVELOPING AND MANAGING TEAM INITIATIVES

Team Building

An effective tool in managing successfully is the ability to work within team structures.

This affords:

- Collaboration
- Camaraderie
- Effective delegation
- Mentoring effectiveness
- Crossing company silos
- Better results

Collaboration

When we take into consideration how others feel and value their input ... an appreciation is accomplished which allows for staff to feel more ingrained into the organization.

Additionally, their input may allow for wider and varied input, which can create a path to more workable and doable solutions.

Project management is often better accomplished through team initiatives. This becomes a collaborative process allowing for a better path to higher achievement.

Collaboration in the decision-making phase will also afford a better opportunity for successful implementation as you are obtaining everyone's *buy-in* during the assessment and analysis process that usually takes place in any team project.

Camaraderie

When a team successfully works together ... bonds are formed, friendships are established, and colleague ties are fostered.

This creates a work environment where the impossible can be accomplished.

The military has known and leveraged this concept for over 3000+ years ... develop camaraderie between the troops and you create a force to be reckoned with.

Camaraderie creates an environment where interpersonal relationships are matured into smooth running machines that make for the most effective and productive work forces.

Camaraderie creates the environment where team members watch each other's back and they care for one another. This atmosphere becomes conducive to working collaboratively at the highest levels, producing and meeting desired goals and expectations.

Effective Delegation

The team takes on tasks and responsibilities as delegated by the project manager and the collaborative process.

This creates a dispersion of responsibilities among the collective team. This delegating allows for the best opportunity for the project to both gain momentum and move forward successfully.

Effective delegation also allows for the best use of individual skill sets and capabilities among the team members.

It should also create a cooperative spirit where the team accepts the delegated responsibilities and tasks with a *can do* attitude and positive approach to getting the job done well.

Delegating also creates an opportunity for senior management to observe how team members accept responsibility and ultimately perform.

Additionally, you can also observe how well each team member *plays in the sand box.*

Effective delegation also makes the best use of limited resources among personnel who are already typically engaged at multiple levels within the organization.

Mentoring Effectiveness

Managers are given an opportunity to participate and demonstrate their prowess in mentoring staff members in:

- Collaborative ethics
- Building effective working relationships
- Participating effectively in *team-based activities*
- Taking responsibility in a project and bringing it to successful closure

Managers can show leadership skill in motivating a team initiative and taking charge of direction and forward movement.

Typically problems and disruptions will interfere with project scheduling so leadership can demonstrate problem resolution skill sets and how best to negotiate problems to favorable resolution.

Crossing Company Silos

Any team initiative and/or project will typically cross company silos. This will typically cause some issues, as silo managers are *protective of their turf.*

Silos also present different internal cultural concerns and many times have alternate agendas to other operational units.

This dynamic of *silo territory* is a challenge that often needs to be navigated carefully and even creatively.

It will challenge the team members to manage this challenge, which will be a good lesson for future benefit.

Better Results

The ultimate goal of any team or project effort is to make change, favorable impact, or bring an initiative to favorable closure.

The team concept for all the reasons outlined earlier creates the best structure and opportunity to make better collaborative decisions leading to *better results.*

A better process ... will usually produce better results.

Choosing Team Members

Choosing team members can be a challenge. The implications of making good or poor choices will have both favorable and not-so-favorable consequences.

Here are some guidelines:

- Introverts will kill a team. Look for extroverts.
- The *ability* to get a long and be a team player are important traits.
- Prior *team* experience is beneficial.
- Personnel with skill sets in communications, negotiations, obtaining compromise, and consensus and in working at collaborative alliances ... all prove beneficial.
- Personnel who know how to be organized and prioritize well will be beneficial.

- Bring teams together with personnel that have skill sets and behavior that bring diversity and an ability to meld.
- Make sure the team member has the time necessary to make a quality contribution and has complete authorization from their manager.
- Make sure team members understand and budget any serious time commitments.

Choosing team members following these basic guidelines will present the best opportunity to have success with the initiative or project.

Managing the Team

While a team may work independently, as a senior manager you must *watch-dog* the effort to make sure it is successful and stays on track.
Here are some suggestions:

1. Establish a clear and concise set of goals, expectations, and deliverables. Utilize the *SMART* process with goals.
2. Set reasonable timeframes.
3. Set up a system for weekly reports on progress.
4. Establish a *point person, leadership*, and *ownership*.
5. Allow independence, but make sure they are on *track, on schedule*, and moving forward at an acceptable pace.
6. Make sure they are communicating progress or set backs to impacted parties, stakeholders, and senior management.
7. Make sure you are made aware timely and comprehensively of any serious set backs or problems.
8. Create an atmosphere with the team of openness, straightforward dialog, and transparency.
9. And in closing, make sure the project closes out, whether successful or not. Do not let it *die on the vine* ... be proactive and open in bringing closure.

COMMERCIAL EXAMPLE

Google defines what makes a *team*.
The first step in answering this question of "what makes an effective team?" is to ask, "what is a team?" More than an existential thought exercise,

actually figuring out the memberships, relationships, and responsibilities of individuals all working together is tough, but critical to cracking team effectiveness.

The term team can take on a wide array of meanings. Many definitions and frameworks exist, depending on task interdependence, organizational status, and team tenure. At the most fundamental level, the researchers sought to distinguish a *work group* from a *team*:

- Work groups are characterized by the least amount of interdependence. They are based on organizational or managerial hierarchy. Work groups may meet periodically to hear and share information.
- Teams are highly interdependent—they plan work, solve problems, make decisions, and review progress in service of a specific project. Team members need one another to get work done.

Organizational charts only tell part of the story, so the Google research team focused on groups with truly interdependent working relationships, as determined by the teams themselves. The teams studied in Project Aristotle ranged from 3 to 50 individuals (with a median of 9 members).

Google defines *effectiveness.*
Once they understood what constituted a team at Google, the researchers had to determine how to quantitatively measure effectiveness. They looked at lines of code written, bugs fixed, customer satisfaction, and more. But Google's leaders, who had initially pushed for objective effectiveness measures, realized that every suggested measure could be inherently flawed—more lines of code are not necessarily a good thing and more bugs fixed means more bugs were initially created.

Instead, the team decided to use a combination of qualitative assessments and quantitative measures. For qualitative assessments, the researchers captured input from three different perspectives—executives, team leads, and team members. While they all were asked to rate teams on similar scales, when asked to explain their ratings, their answers showed that each was focused on different aspects when assessing team effectiveness.

Executives were most concerned with results (e.g., sales numbers or product launches), but team members said that team culture was the most important measure of team effectiveness. Fittingly, the team lead's concept of effectiveness spanned both the big picture and the individuals' concerns saying that ownership, vision, and goals were the most important measures.

So the researchers measured team effectiveness in four different ways:

1. Executive evaluation of the team
2. Team leader evaluation of the team
3. Team member evaluation of the team
4. Sales performance against quarterly quota

The qualitative evaluations helped capture a nuanced look at results and culture, but had inherent subjectivity. On the other hand, the quantitative metrics provided concrete team measures, but lacked situational considerations. These four measures in combination, however, allowed researchers to home in on the comprehensive definition of team effectiveness.

CYBER SECURITY ISSUES IN GLOBAL TRADE

Cyber security is a major concern for all business models. Internationally makes it even a greater risk. Sustainable business models are proactively involved in managing cyber security concerns. The following is a summary from a presentation I gave on the subject matter in late 2017.

Avoiding Costly Mistakes

- Global trade summary
- Specific areas of concern
- Case studies
- Best practices in mitigating potential security issues

Overview of Cyber Security

Cyber security is the body of technologies, processes, and practices designed to protect networks, computers, programs, and data from attack, damage, or unauthorized access. In a computing context, security includes both cyber security and physical security.

Cyber Security Impacts

- Application security
- Information security
- Network security
- Disaster recovery/business continuity planning
- Operational security
- Technology bullying
- Education and training

Application Security

Application security encompasses measures taken to improve the *security* of an *application* often by finding, fixing, and preventing *security* vulnerabilities.

Information Security

Information security, sometimes shortened to *InfoSec*, is the practice of preventing unauthorized access, use, disclosure, disruption, modification, inspection, recording, or destruction of information. It is a general term that can be used regardless of the form the data may take (e.g., electronic, physical). The chief area of concern for the field of information security is the balanced protection of the confidentiality, integrity, and availability of data, also known as the CIA triad, while maintaining a focus on efficient policy implementation and no major hampering of organization productivity. To standardize this discipline, academics and professionals collaborate and seek to set basic guidelines and policies on password, antivirus software, firewall, encryption software, legal liability, and user/administrator training standards.

Network Security

Network security consists of the policies and practices adopted to prevent and monitor unauthorized access, misuse, modification, or denial of a computer network and network-accessible resources. Network security involves the authorization of access to data in a network, which is controlled by the network administrator. Users choose or are assigned an ID and password or other authenticating information that allows them access to information and programs within their authority. Network security covers a variety of computer networks, both public and private, that are used in everyday jobs; conducting transactions and communications among businesses, government agencies, and individuals. Networks can be private, such as within a company, and others, which might be open to public access. Network security is involved in organizations, enterprises, and other types of institutions. It does as its title explains: It secures the network, as well as protecting and overseeing operations being done. The most common and simple way of protecting a network resource is by assigning it a unique name and a corresponding password.

Logical protection

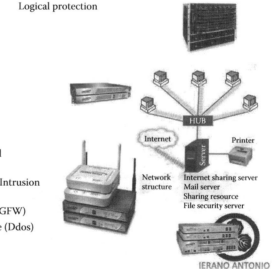

• Network security

  – Hardening

  – Patching

  – Remote access

  – Encryption

  – Secure sockets layer/Virtual private network (SSL/VPN)

  – Internet protocol standard/Intrusion detection system (IPS/IDS)

  – Next generation firewall (NGFW)

  – Distributed denial of service (Ddos)

  – ...

Internet

Printer

HUB

Network structure

Internet sharing server
Mail server
Sharing resource
File security server

Server

IERANO ANTONIO

Disaster Recovery and Continuity Planning

Disaster recovery and business *continuity planning* are processes that help organizations prepare for disruptive events—whether those events might include a hurricane or simply a power outage caused by a backhoe in the parking lot.

For cyber security, this would include internal *disruption or exposure* to technology interface, operations, and utilization.

Operational Security

Operations security is a process that identifies critical information to determine if friendly actions can be observed by enemy intelligence, determines if information obtained by adversaries could be interpreted to be useful to them, and then executes selected measures that eliminate or reduce adversary.

Technology Bullying

Utilization of technology through various means to hamper, disrupt, or harm business activity of another company or individual, that is, bad publicity, false and leading statements, fake news, e-mail bombing, and so on.

End-User Education and Training

In information technology, the term *end user* is used to distinguish the person for whom a hardware or software product is designed from the developers, installers, and servicers of the product.

The need to be informed, educated, and trained!

Global trade summary and its relationship to cyber security:

- Global trade: importing and exporting
- Foreign sourcing and overseas sales
- Foreign business development
- Direct, indirect, and third party
- Sharing on proprietary data and operational access

Specific areas of concern within most industry sectors:

- Proprietary information
- Client data
- Financial data
- Security breaches
- Impact to operations
- Third parties

Cyber Security Cases

There have been numerous examples of cyber security breaches that have occurred in recent years both within government jurisdictions and private companies:

- *Government*: National Security Administration (NSA), Ukrainian infrastructure, Central Intelligence Agency (CIA), German transportation, France electorate, and U.S. Electorate/Democratic National Committee (DNC)
- *Commercial*: Target, Equifax, Maersk, Amazon, Newsmax, and Twitter … and in all industry sectors and business models

Best Practices in "Mitigating" Potential Security Issues

- Assessment
- Professional support

- Mindset … cyber security is a very real threat!
- Establish cyber security initiative
- Train and educate staff

Assessment

- Benchmarking
- Internal or external support
- Sets the stage for proactive cyber security mitigation
- Exercising due diligence and reasonable care standards

Professional Support

1. Resources
2. Consultants
3. Insurance and brokerage companies
4. Hardware and software companies

Mindset … Cyber Security Is a Very Real Threat!

- Tens of thousands of incidents every month
- What the government believes, spends, and is committed to
- Has to become a *built-in* company silo, just like sales, customer service, accounting, and operations
- Must be integrated, collaborative, and synchronized into every nook and cranny
- Leadership from down, in, out, and up

Establish Cyber Security Initiative

- Who has ownership … point person
- Committee approach
- Learning issues, concerns, and resolutions
- Building technology-based protections
- Standard operating procedures (SOPs) and business protocols
- Setting stage for internal resource, training, and education
- Continued practice of being diligent

Train and Educate Staff

- Senior management awareness
- Specific skill set training
- Human resource engagement
- Training is a *work-in-process*
- New equipment and software ... updated training
- New operating systems ... updated training

Personnel Issues in Cyber Security

- Company size only dictates *extent*
- Written agreements in place over company information
- Background checks
- Restricted access
- Control over mobile and externally utilized equipment
- Continually changing access portals and entry codes
- Internal transparency and open-door policies
- Require continued and intense training

Additional International Cyber Concerns

- Operate globally ... participate in customs border and protection (CBPs)
- C-TPAT program, customs-trade partnership against terrorism
- Raises the bar of security in your global supply chain

> *Cyber Security* is a very real threat and must be taken seriously by everyone engaged in business and global trade
>
> There are significant resources available to help mitigate the exposures of *cyber risk*. A *best practice* strategy can be developed and implemented with high degrees of historical success to successful manage *cyber exposure.*

People are tremendous creatures, but only rise to the level you hold them accountable.

Thomas A. Cook

Appendix

- Terminology
- *White paper*: Time management
- *White paper*: Dispute resolution and conflict management
- *White paper*: Strategic planning and goal setting
- Export management program/bureau of industry and security
- *White paper*: International freight and trade compliance
- International Commercial (INCO) term overview
- Landed cost modeling Standard Operating Procedure (SOP)
- Trade compliance management article
- Trade compliance issues in mergers and acquisitions

TERMINOLOGY

Air Waybill

Bill of lading that covers both domestic and international flights transporting goods to a specified destination. It is a non-negotiable instrument of air transport that serves as a receipt for the shipper, indicating that the carrier has accepted the goods listed therein, and obligates the carrier to carry the consignment to the airport of destination according to specified conditions.

Antidiversion Clause

To help ensure that U.S. exports go only to legally authorized destinations, the U.S. government generally requires a Destination Control Statement (DCS) on shipping documents. The DCS must be entered for items subject to the Export Administration Regulations (EAR), except for items designated EAR99 or that are eligible for certain license exceptions.

Antidumping Duty

Special duty imposed to offset the price effect of dumping that has been determined to be materially harmful to domestic producers. (See also dumping.)

Arbitration

Process of resolving a dispute or a grievance outside of the court system by presenting it to an impartial third party or panel for a decision that may or may not be binding.

Bill of Lading

Contract between the owner of the goods and the carrier. For vessels, there are two types: a straight bill of lading, which is not negotiable, and a negotiable, or shipper's orders, bill of lading. The latter can be bought, sold, or traded while the goods are in transit.

Carnet

Standardized international customs document known as an admission temporaire or temporary admission (ATA) carnet that is used to obtain duty-free temporary admission of certain goods into the countries that are signatories to the ATA Convention. Under the ATA Convention, commercial and professional travelers may take commercial samples; tools of the trade; advertising material; or cinematographic, audiovisual, medical, scientific, or other professional equipment into member countries temporarily without paying customs duties and taxes or posting a bond at the border of each country to be visited.

Carriage and Insurance

Paid to Carriage and insurance paid for delivery to a named destination.

Carriage Paid to

Carriage paid to a named destination. This term is used in place of cost and freight and cost, insurance, and freight for all modes of transportation, including intermodal.

Cash in Advance

Payment from a foreign customer to a U.S. exporter prior to actually receiving the exporter's products (advance payment). It is the least risky form of payment from the exporter's perspective.

Central America and Dominican Republic Free Trade Agreement

One of a series of free trade agreements involving the U.S. and other countries. Benefits include duty-free or reduced-duty access, better overall market access, treatment equal to local companies, and intellectual property protection.

Certificate of Conformity

Signed statement from a manufacturer attesting that a product meets certain technical standards.

Certificate of Free Sale

Signed statement from the producer or exporter attesting that a product has been commercially sold within the country of origin.

Certificate of Origin

Signed statement required in certain nations attesting to the origin of the export item. Certificates of origin are usually validated by a semiofficial organization, such as a local chamber of commerce. A North American Free Trade Agreement (NAFTA) certificate of origin is required for products traded among the NAFTA countries (Canada, Mexico, and the United States) when duty preference is claimed for NAFTA qualified goods.

Commercial Invoice

Document prepared by the exporter or freight forwarder and required by the foreign buyer to prove ownership and to arrange for payment to the exporter. It should provide basic information about the transaction, including a description of goods, the address of the shipper and seller, and the delivery and payment terms. In most cases, the commercial invoice is used to assess customs duties.

Confirming House

Company based in a foreign country that acts as a foreign buyer's agent and places confirmed orders with U.S. exporters. The confirming house guarantees payment to the exporters.

Consignment

Delivery of merchandise to the buyer or distributor, whereby the latter agrees to sell it and only then pay the U.S. exporter. The seller retains ownership of the goods until they are sold, but also carries all of the financial burden and risk.

Consular Invoice

Document required in some countries that describes the shipment of goods and shows information such as the consignor, consignee, and value of the shipment. Certified by the consular official of the foreign country stationed in the United States, it is used by the country's customs officials to verify the value, quantity, and nature of the shipment.

Contract

Written or oral agreement that is legally enforceable.

Copyright protection granted to the authors and creators of literary, artistic, dramatic, and musical works, sound recordings, and certain other intellectual works. A computer program, for example, is considered a literary work in the United States and some other countries.

Cost and Freight

Cost and freight to a named overseas port.

Cost, Insurance, and Freight

Cost, insurance, and freight to a named overseas post. The seller quotes a price for the goods shipped by ocean (including insurance), all transportation costs, and miscellaneous charges to the point of debarkation from the vessel.

Countertrade

General expression meaning the sale or barter of goods on a reciprocal basis. There may also be multilateral transactions involved.

Countervailing duties are additional duties imposed by an importing country to offset government subsidies in an exporting country when the subsidized imports provide a measurable benefit to a specific enterprise or industry and cause material injury to domestic industry in the importing country.

Customs-Bonded Warehouse

Building or other secured area in which dutiable goods may be stored, may be manipulated, or may undergo manufacturing operations without payment of duty.

Customs Declaration

Document that traditionally accompanies exported goods bearing such information as the nature of the goods, their value, the consignee, and their ultimate destination. Required for statistical purposes, it accompanies all controlled goods being exported under the appropriate permit.

Customs Invoice

Document used to clear goods through customs in the importing country by providing evidence of the value of goods. In some cases, the commercial invoice may be used for this purpose.

Date Draft

Document used when the exporter extends credit to the buyer. It specifies a date on which payment is due, rather than a time period, as with the time draft.

Destination Control Statement

Required for all exports from the United States of items on the Commerce Control List that are not classified as EAR99. The statement is added to the commercial invoice.

Direct Exporting

Sale by an exporter directly to an importer located in another country.

Distributor

A merchant in the foreign country who purchases goods from the U.S. exporter (often at a discount) and resells them for a profit. The foreign distributor generally provides support and service for the product, relieving the U.S. exporter of these responsibilities.

Dock Receipt

Receipt issued by an ocean carrier to acknowledge receipt of a shipment at the carrier's dock or warehouse facilities.

Documentary Letter of Credit/Documentary Draft

Document used to protect the interests of both buyer and seller. A letter of credit requires that payment be made on the basis of the presentation of documents to a lender conveying the title and indicating that specific steps have been taken. Letters of credit and drafts may be paid immediately or at a later date. Drafts that are paid on presentation are called sight drafts. Drafts that are to be paid at a later date, often after the buyer receives the goods, are called time drafts or date drafts.

Dumping

Sale of an imported commodity at a lower price in one market than in another—that is, selling at less than *normal value* on the same level of trade, and in the ordinary course of trade. Dumping is considered an actionable trade practice when it disrupts markets and injures producers of competitive products in the importing country. Article VI of the General Agreement on Tariffs and Trade (World Trade Organization) permits the imposition of special antidumping duties on goods equal to the difference between their export price and their normal value.

E-Commerce

Buying and selling over the Internet.

Electronic Export Information, Formerly Known as Shipper's Export Declaration

Document used to control exports and act as a source document for official U.S. export statistics. Electronic export information (EEI) is required for shipments when the value of the commodities, classified under any single Schedule B number, is more than $2,500. EEI must be prepared and submitted, regardless of value, for all shipments requiring an export license or destined for countries restricted by the Export Administration Regulations.

Export-Import Bank of the United States

U.S. government organization that provides export finance products to U.S. exporters and foreign buyers of U.S. products.

Export License

Government document that authorizes the export of specific items (including technology), in specific quantities, to a specific destination. May be required for most or all exports to some countries, or for other countries only under special circumstances.

Export Management Company

Export management company (EMC) is one that performs the functions that would be typically performed by the export department or the international sales department of manufacturers and suppliers. EMCs develop personalized services promoting their clients' products to international buyers and distributors. They solicit and transact business in the names of the producers they represent or in their own name for a commission, salary, or retainer plus commission. EMCs usually specialize either by product or by foreign market. Because of their specialization, the best EMCs know their products and the markets they serve very well and usually have well-established networks of foreign distributors already in place. This immediate access to foreign markets is one of the principal reasons for using an EMC, because establishing a productive relationship with a foreign representative may be a costly and lengthy process.

Export Packing List

List that itemizes the exported material in each package and indicates the type of package, such as a box, crate, drum, or carton. An export packing list is considerably more detailed and informative than a standard domestic packing list. It also shows the individual net, tare, and gross weights and measurements for each package (in both U.S. and metric systems).

Export Processing Zone

Export processing zone (EPZ) is a site in a foreign country established to encourage and facilitate international trade. EPZs include free trade zones, special economic zones, bonded warehouses, free ports, and customs zones. EPZs have evolved from initial assembly and simple processing activities to include high-tech and science parks, finance zones, logistics centers, and even tourist resorts.

Export Quotas

Specific restrictions or ceilings imposed by an exporting country on the value or volume of certain exports designed, for example, to protect domestic producers and consumers from temporary shortages of the goods affected or to bolster their prices in world markets.

Export Subsidies

Government payments or other financially quantifiable benefits provided to domestic producers or exporters contingent on the export of their goods and services.

Export Trading Company

Export trading company (ETC) is a company that acts as an independent distributor, creating transactions by linking domestic producers and foreign buyers. As opposed to representing a given manufacturer in a foreign market, the ETC determines what U.S. products are desired in a given market and then works with U.S. producers to satisfy the demand. ETCs can perform a sourcing function, searching for U.S. suppliers to fill specific foreign requests for U.S. products.

Ex Works

The buyer is responsible for all export procedures, including vehicle loading, transportation, and costs arising after collection of the goods.

Foreign Agricultural Service

U.S. Department of Agriculture bureau with programs related to market development, international trade agreements and negotiations, and the collection of statistics and market information. It also administers the U.S. Department of Agriculture (USDA)'s export credit guarantee and food aid programs and helps increase income and food availability in developing nations.

Foreign Corrupt Practices Act

Foreign Corrupt Practices Act (FCPA) makes it unlawful for persons or companies subject to U.S. jurisdiction to offer, pay, or promise to pay money or anything of value to any foreign official for the purpose of obtaining or retaining business. It is also unlawful to make a payment to any person while knowing that all or a portion of the payment will be offered, given, or promised, directly or indirectly, to any foreign official for the purposes of assisting the company in obtaining or retaining business. *Knowing* includes the concepts of *conscious disregard* and *willful blindness*. The FCPA also covers foreign persons or companies that commit acts in furtherance of such bribery in the territory of the United States. U.S. persons or companies, or covered foreign persons or companies, should consult an attorney when confronted with FCPA issues.

Foreign-Trade Zones

Domestic U.S. sites that are considered outside U.S. customs territory and are available for activities that might otherwise be carried on overseas for customs reasons. For export operations, the zones provide accelerated export status for purposes of excise tax rebates. For reexport activities, no customs duties, federal excise taxes, or state or local ad valorem taxes are charged on foreign goods moved into zones unless and until the goods or products made from them are moved into customs territory. Thus, the use of zones can be profitable for operations involving foreign dutiable materials and components being assembled or produced in the United States for reexport.

Free Alongside Ship

A seller's price for the goods, including the charge for delivery of the goods alongside at the named port of export. The seller handles the cost of wharfage, while the buyer is accountable for the costs of loading, ocean transportation, and insurance. It is the seller's responsibility to clear the goods for export.

Free In

Pricing term that indicates that the charterer of a vessel is responsible for the cost of loading goods onto the vessel.

Free In and Out

Pricing term that indicates that the charterer of the vessel is responsible for the cost of loading and unloading goods from the vessel.

Free on Board

Free on board (FOB) is an international commercial term (Incoterm) and is used in international sales contracts. In an FOB contract, a buyer and a seller agree on a designated FOB point. The seller assumes the cost of having goods packaged and ready for shipment from the FOB point, whether it is the seller's own place of business or some intermediate point. The buyer assumes the costs and risks from the FOB point, including inland transportation costs and risks in the exporting country, as well as all subsequent transportation costs, including the costs of loading the merchandise on a vessel. If the contract stipulates *FOB vessel*, the seller bears all transportation costs to the vessel named by the buyer, as well as the costs of loading the goods on that vessel. The same principle applies to free on rail and free on truck.

Free Out

Pricing term that indicates that the charterer of the vessel is responsible for the cost of unloading goods from the vessel.

Freight Forwarder

Agent for moving cargo to an overseas destination. These agents are familiar with the import rules and regulations of foreign countries, the export regulations of the U.S. government, the methods of shipping, and the documents related to foreign trade.

Global Entrepreneurial Ecosystem

A local community support system for small- and medium-size exporters.

Gross Domestic Product

The total value of all goods and services produced by a country.

Incoterms

See: Terms of sale.

Indirect Exporting

Sale by the exporter to the buyer through a domestically located intermediary, such as an export management company or an export trading company.

Inspection Certificate

Document required by some purchasers and countries to attest to the specifications of the goods shipped. The inspection is usually performed by a third party.

Insurance Certificate

Document prepared by the exporter or freight forwarder to provide evidence that insurance against loss or damage has been obtained for the goods.

Intellectual Property

Collective term used to refer to new ideas, inventions, designs, writings, films, and so on that are protected by a copyright, patent, or trademark.

International Buyer Program

U.S. Department of Commerce program that matches U.S. exhibitors at select U.S. trade shows with foreign buyers.

International Trade Administration

A U.S. Department of Commerce bureau responsible for export promotion programs.

Joint Venture

Independent business formed cooperatively by two or more parent companies. This type of partnership is often used to avoid restrictions on foreign ownership and for longer-term arrangements that require joint product development, manufacturing, and marketing.

Letter of Credit

Instrument issued by a bank on behalf of an importer that guarantees an exporter payment for goods or services, provided that the terms of the credit are met. A letter of credit issued by a foreign bank is sometimes confirmed by a U.S. bank. This confirmation means that the U.S. bank (the confirming bank) adds its promise to pay to that of the foreign bank (the issuing bank). A letter of credit may be either irrevocable, in which case it cannot be changed unless both parties agree, or revocable, in which case either party may unilaterally make changes. A revocable letter of credit is inadvisable, as it carries many risks for the exporter.

Licensing

Arrangement in which a company sells the rights to use its products or services, but retains some control. Although not usually considered to be a form of partnership, licensing can lead to partnerships.

Market Survey

Report that provides a narrative description and assessment of a particular market along with relevant statistics. The reports are often based on original research conducted in the countries studied and may include specific information on both buyers and competitors.

Multilateral Development Bank

An institution created by a group of countries to provide development-related financing and professional advising.

North American Free Trade Agreement Certificate of Origin

Used by NAFTA signatories (that is, Canada, Mexico, and the United States) to determine if goods imported into their countries receive reduced or eliminated duty.

North American Free Trade Agreement

Trade agreement between the United States, Canada, and Mexico featuring duty-free entry and other benefits for goods that qualify.

Office of the U.S. Trade Representative

U.S. government agency responsible for negotiating trade agreements.

Packing List

See: Export packing list.

Patent

Right that entitles the patent holder, within the country that granted or recognizes the patent, to prevent all others, for a set period of time, from using, making, or selling the subject matter of the patent.

Piggyback Marketing

Arrangement in which one manufacturer or service company distributes a second company's product or service. The most common piggybacking situation is when a U.S. company has a contract with an overseas buyer to provide a wide range of products or services. Often, this first company does not produce all of the products it is under contract to provide, and it turns to other U.S. companies to provide the remaining products.

Primary Market Research

Collection of data directly from a foreign marketplace through interviews, surveys, and other direct contact with representatives and potential buyers. Primary market research has the advantage of being tailored to your company's needs and provides answers to specific questions, but the collection of such data is time consuming and expensive.

Pro Forma Invoice

Invoice prepared by the exporter before shipping the goods, informing the buyer of the goods to be sent, their value, and other key specifications.

Quotation

Offer by the exporter to sell the goods at a stated price and under certain conditions.

Regional Value Content

A technique used to determine whether a product meets a rule of origin.

Remarketer

Export agent or merchant who purchases products directly from the manufacturer, packing and marking the products according to his or her own specifications. Remarketers then sell these products overseas through their contacts in their own names and assume all risks.

Sales Representative

Representative who uses your company's product literature and samples to present the product to potential buyers. An overseas sales representative is the equivalent of a manufacturer's representative in the United States. The sales representative usually works on a commission basis, assumes no risk or responsibility, and is under contract for a definite period of time.

Secondary Market Research

Collection of data from various sources, such as trade statistics for a country or a product. Working with secondary sources is less expensive and helps your company focus its marketing efforts. Although secondary data sources are critical to market research, they do have limitations. The most recent statistics for some countries may be more than 2 years old, and the data may be too broad to be of much value to your company.

Sight Draft

Document used when the exporter wishes to retain title to the shipment until it reaches its destination and payment is made. Before the shipment can be released to the buyer, the original *order* ocean bill of lading (the document that evidences title) must be properly endorsed by the buyer and surrendered to the carrier. It is important to note that air waybills do not need to be presented in order for the buyer to claim the goods. Thus, risk increases when a sight draft is being used with an air shipment.

Small Business Development Center

National network of counselors for small enterprises. Offers services that can help first-time exporters.

Tariff

Tax imposed on a product when it is imported into a country. Some foreign countries apply tariffs to exports.

Technology Licensing

Contractual arrangement in which the licenser's patents, trademarks, service marks, copyrights, trade secrets, or other intellectual property may be sold or made available to a licensee for compensation that is negotiated in advance between the parties. U.S. companies frequently license their technology to foreign companies that then use it to manufacture and sell products in a country or group of countries defined in the licensing agreement. A technology licensing agreement usually enables a company to enter a foreign market quickly and poses fewer financial and legal risks than owning and operating a foreign manufacturing facility or participating in an overseas joint venture.

Terms of Sale

Terms that define the obligations, risks, and costs of the buyer and seller involving the delivery of goods that comprise the export transaction. These terms are commonly known as Incoterms.

Time Draft

Document used when the exporter extends credit to the buyer. The draft states that payment is due by a specific time after the buyer accepts the time draft and receives the goods. By signing and writing *accepted* on the draft, the buyer is formally obligated to pay within the stated time.

Trade Fair Certification Program

A U.S. Department of Commerce program that certifies international trade events so U.S. companies can know ahead of time if an event is high quality and offers opportunities.

Trademark

Word, symbol, name, slogan, or combination thereof that identifies and distinguishes the source of sponsorship of goods and may serve as an index of quality of a particular product.

Trade Statistics

Data that indicate total exports or imports by country and by product. They allow you to compare the size of the market for a product in various countries. By looking at statistics over several years, you can determine which markets are growing and which markets are shrinking.

Trading House

Company specializing in the exporting and importing of goods produced or provided by other companies.

U.S. Agency for International Development

U.S. government agency that procures goods and services from U.S. companies for use in developing countries.

U.S. Central Intelligence Agency

U.S. government agency tasked with gathering intelligence and statistics. Publishes the World Factbook, an important market research resource.

U.S. Commercial Service

The trade promotion arm of the U.S. Department of Commerce's International Trade Administration.

U.S. Department of Agriculture

U.S. government department responsible for developing and executing federal government policy on farming, agriculture, forestry, and food.

U.S. Department of Commerce

U.S. government department responsible for promoting domestic economic growth and handling other commerce-related responsibilities.

U.S. Small Business Administration

U.S. government agency that manages programs for U.S. exporters, including finance programs.

U.S. Trade and Development Agency

U.S. government agency that provides grants for feasibility studies in developing countries.

Warehouse Receipt

Receipt identifying the commodities deposited in a recognized warehouse. It is used to transfer accountability when the domestic carrier moves the export item to the port of embarkation and leaves it with the ship line for export.

WHITE PAPER: TIME MANAGEMENT

Executives who develop skill sets in managing their time will do a lot better in handling their overall responsibilities successfully.

In today's business environment, executives are busy with an array of responsibility and a huge demand to consistently perform.

Most executives have multiple responsibilities making them overbearingly busy. Their ability to manage time becomes critical in their managing their responsibilities well.

When time is not navigated successfully the consequences are numerous:

- Dissatisfied staff, customers, vendors, and bosses
- Failure to perform as required
- Inability to meet expectations
- Operational and financial losses
- Loss of business, margin, and staff

On the other side of the equation, when time is managed successfully, the rewards are grand:

- Satisfied customers, staff, suppliers, and bosses
- Opportunity to *move up the ladder*
- Keeping everyone *happy and moving forward* ... more smoothly
- More business and higher margins
- An easier managed business model

Reduction in Stress

When problems occur, and time is constrained, we become stressed. When stress becomes a common occurrence and grows in severity ... the potential consequences become critical:

- We tend to make hasty decisions which are not well thought out and could be mistakes.
- We emulate a nervousness, which could send out the wrong signal to those around us ... leading to their becoming nervous, upset, and dysfunctional.
- Stress can cause bad decisions, bad actions, and less than desirable results.
- The wrong signal is sent out leaving us potentially vulnerable in a relationship, a negotiation, or in a leadership posture.

This all leads us to the conclusion that excessive stress has mostly negative consequences, and we need to get it under control.

A leading cause of stress is not managing time correctly. The obvious conclusion is that if we manage time better, we then can operate in a less stressful environment, which will allow us to be more successful in whatever we are attempting to accomplish.

Stress has a positive consequence as well. It causes us to produce cortisol. In balance, this hormone allows various defensive mechanisms of the mind and body to heavily influence thoughts and actions.

As an example, stress may come from fear. We are on a walk in the woods and come across a bear. Fear allows us to pump adrenaline, to make us run faster. The stress of that moment and the production of key hormones allows the mind to think quickly and the body to move faster.

All that results in not being harmed by the bear.

Fortunately, in everyday life we do not often come across bears. But in business we do sometimes perceive *bears*, and the stress becomes overbearing and creates chaos and all sorts of negative consequences.

Too much stress too often can lead to more serious medical issues, as well as depression.

We must get stress under control.

So mastering time management is one of the tools we can utilize to manage stress concerns.

Additionally, stress comes from excessive fear, making a problem larger then it is and being over fearful of consequence taken way out of proportion to reality.

Stress can be better controlled by how we think through the everyday challenges of living and managing business responsibilities.

Some suggestions:

- We must work within ourselves and have reasonable expectations.
- We need to have people to talk to and be able to express our concerns and have them help us sort our perceptions from reality.
- Sometimes this will require specialized help from therapists, counselors, and psychiatrists.
- We must learn to recognize that problems and failures are part of the business model. They both must be minimized and brought under reasonable control, but they are both part of the deal, when we chose to live, and also when we chose to be in business.

- We must gain control and influence over what causes us to be fearful. This typically is better understanding *consequences* and putting that into the overall perspective and balance of our lives and our business responsibilities.
- We must learn our stress indicators and be proactive in managing them before the stress becomes consequential. Professional resources ... Internet, books, seminars, and therapy all are excellent options in understanding and managing stress indicators.

Stress is managed in two ways ... our mindset and actions and better managing time, which is further outlined in the following.

Managing Time Better

The big question then becomes how do we manage time better? In answering that question, we need to look at a number of variables that surround the topic of *time management*.

They are:

- Organizational skill sets
- Prioritization skill sets
- Delegation skill sets
- Establishing goals, boundaries, and sound time management practices

Organizational Skill Sets

If you are not organized well, you will never manage time well. Keeping yourself organized is a critical aspect of managing time well.

Organizing well means:

- Understanding what is expected of you
- A comprehensive list in some format of all you have on your plate
- Making sure you communicate to all vested interests what you have on your plate

Prioritization Skill Sets

Prioritizing ties directly into organizing, as it takes all that you have on your plate and structures an order of priority.

Then time frames for action and completion are accomplished.

This then engages a *strategy* that will make sure you accomplish all that you need to in a timely fashion.

Because we are busy, we never get everything done, so we need to make sure we are communicating what does not get done with readjusted time frames for completion.

Keep in mind that everyday problems will present themselves that will take us out of our preplanned day.

This means that priorities are a *work in process* that need to be tweaked consistently and communicated outbound timely and responsibly.

Delegation Skill Sets

Delegating is both an art and science following some of these guidelines:

- Understand what can be delegated and what cannot.
- Understand that who to and what is delegated must be well thought out.
- Delegation is also a *mentoring and coaching* task that allows you to mentor staff in how business should be handled.

It is very important to understand that when you delegate you are shifting a transactional responsibility to someone else. This does not mean you are giving up responsibility to make sure what you delegated is eventually completed satisfactorily.

This means you still have *ownership* of the delegated task from the person to whom you delegated to, who completes the task.

Delegation requires a system to *track and trace* individual delegated tasks, to make sure they are all done timely and responsibly. Microsoft office, various bolt-on technology options, and simplified Excel spreadsheets can all assist in this regard.

Irrespective of the system you utilize … having some *accountability and responsibility* practice in place is what is important.

Delegation has some of the following benefits:

- Allows you to move some minor tasks to subordinates to offer you more time and more important responsibilities.
- A source for mentoring and coaching, as well as evaluating performance of team members on how they approach this work and perform or not.

- A demonstration to your senior colleagues of how well you manage your responsibilities in delegating and in time management.
- It allows you to measure the performance of others and allow them to go through various learning curves that will eventually make them better employees and managers.

Effective delegators understand that there are certain responsibilities that cannot be delegated and that must be carried out by themselves. Knowing what can be delegated and what cannot is a very prized capability.

Delegating the wrong tasks can prove to be negatively consequential and bring on a resentment of all concerned with the choices and actions you have delegated rather than have assumed.

At the end of the day ... *delegating* is really a core competency of both good management and leadership.

Some leaders look at delegating as a burden, rather than an opportunity. This is being shortsighted. Delegation is a natural occurrence both in life and in business and sets the stage for other to follow and grow.

I have found over the years many executives who will not delegate or who do not delegate well have certain fears or paranoia's about being replaced by someone who is up and coming.

This is a fallacy and must be overcome.

Those who delegate must not delegate carelessly. Meaning they think though carefully as to what can get delegated and to who, based upon experience, capability, and their current workload.

It is well okay to push personnel to take on more, but one must be careful not to push so hard it becomes overbearing and leads to dismay. Personal and staff must be ready to be delegated to. The manager can best delegate by:

- Making sure the person is ready for the delegated task.
- Expectations and deliverables are concise and clear.
- There is an acknowledgement and acceptance of responsibility.
- Comprehensive and exact instructions are provided.
- Timelines are established and agreed to.
- All *stakeholders* are identified.
- Communication responsibilities are established.

Delegating can be an important asset to any busy executive to make him or her more successful in the execution of their overall responsibilities.

Establishing Goals, Boundaries, and Sound Time
Management Practices in "Delegating"

When thinking out delegation as a management tactic, you must first make sure you have established goals as to what you are attempting to accomplish.

Boundaries must also be established. What we mean by boundaries ... these are guidelines, protocols, and business practices that set both high and lower water marks for what can and cannot be delegated.

This can be established by business unit, division or vertical ... by individual, by scope of authority ... and along with company policies.

Boundaries help regulate delegating authorities and assure no one crosses the line into unauthorized delegating. Another example of this would be relative to financial and accounting controls within an organization, where *signing authority* has set limitations.

Or within the legal and contract requirements as to who has signing authority and to what limits?

Also establishing sound time management practices is tied into boundaries. What we mean here is to structure guidelines for staff and employees to follow regarding task and project completion.

Example of a sound time management practice policy:

XYZ Corporation, NYC 2018

- All tasks and projects will have clearly defined deliverables, expectations, and time frames for completion.
- No task or project can be delegated or received without establishing boundaries of authority.
- All stakeholders will be clearly recognized and the relevance to the task or project identified.
- Lines of timely and responsible communication will be established at the point of delegation and maintained throughout the life of the task or project delegated.
- A clear line of reporting problems and issues timely to management is required.

One of the important benchmarks within a company that makes *time management* an overall priority of a *best practice* in business management will also structure how delegating is best managed with an organization and have protocols and guidelines in place for their executive team to use as a reference guideline.

This prevents delegating from being over utilized and being a problem in the business model of the organization.

WHITE PAPER: DISPUTE RESOLUTION AND CONFLICT MANAGEMENT

While there are commonalities between dispute resolution and conflict management, we show clear delineation of them as two separate issues.

Dispute resolution is typically viewed as a *transactional* concern between two or more individuals or entities, usually germane to a particular aggravating factor.

Conflict management is typically viewed as a *longer-term* occurrence between at least two or more individuals or entities over the course of time, based on behavior, personalities, or wrong choices made in how situations were or are being handled.

Dispute Resolution

An example of a dispute might be as follows: In a company based in Jersey City, two managers (John and Sharon) share the responsibility of the receptionist (Lily), who has to report to the two of them.

From a management perspective, John and Sharon are very different individuals in how they approach their management responsibilities and how they interact with people.

John is a more stoic individual, not very personable and rigid in following company protocols. On the other hand, Sharon is very personable, very much a *people person*, and a very flexible and responsive manager to the needs of her staff.

A situation arises, where Lily needs additional time off due to a serious illness in her family. Sharon has no problem in accommodating the request, as she feels that Lily is a valued employee and her request is reasonable.

John is of the mindset that Lily has already taken her allowed time off and, as only being a *receptionist*, can easily be replaced, so there is no disruption in the office structure or flow of work. John also feels that if Lily is accommodated, others may also take advantage of the favored treatment.

As a result of the difference of opinions, Lily is frustrated as no favorable resolution has occurred and she needs action today.

John and Sharon report into Dick, VP of Operations. Lily decides to reach out to Dick directly to gain assistance in resolving her dilemma.

Dick listens intently to Lily and then a ½ hour later speaks with John and Sharon, attempting to hear their side and eventually bring a resolution to the dispute. Dick tells Lily that he will meet with John and Sharon and by the end of the day he will get back to her with a resolution ... one way or the other.

Dick is a tenured manager, part owner and has helped build the company over the last 15 years. His approach to management is balanced and responsible.

After hearing everyone out he advises the following:

- While receptionists are an easy hire, good receptionists are not. Lily is a great receptionist and therefore is a valued employee.
- The mantra of the company is to be supportive of the individual needs of valued staff.
- That John's position does not speak for the company's core values and Sharon's position does.
- He understands the potential disruption, but directs John and Sharon to spend the next hour together to find a solution to mitigate the company impact while Lily deals with her family issues.
- He then tells John to meet with Lily to advise her that the company would support her through this family need, and she is to keep him and Sharon advised on the *status* 2x weekly by phone calls and e-mails.

DISPUTE RESOLVED!

Conflict Management

An example of a conflict management situation:

Antares trading is a *tier one* supplier to Xenon Corp. for electronic components. In the last year, the Xenon manufacturing and purchasing teams have complained about various quality control issues on a number of parts.

Every attempt to fix the problem has not brought resolution. The CEO of Xenon is now paying attention to the problem, as it is beginning to impact the Profit and Loss (P&L) and is causing major delays in meeting customer demand.

The problem has been occurring for over a year without resolution and has caused major conflicts between the supplier's sales and customer service teams against the manufacturing and purchasing teams.

Personalities, fiefdoms, scope of responsibilities, and the quality control issues themselves ... have created an aura of major conflict. Threats are now being made by Xenon to cancel contracts that have spanned the last five years.

The Senior VP of Sales of Antares, under the threat of losing a long-time and large client and the property of continuing a 5-year future contract, ... reaches out to the CEO of Xenon to bring about a resolution to the conflict.

He starts off a dialog with the CEO of Xenon in creating a common interest in seeking a mutually beneficial solution.

Both senior executives designate a senior manager charged to work with one another to create resolve. The CEO and the Senior VP of Sales have a meeting with both key managers in delegating a transparent authority and confirming the mutual need and benefit to both parties to resolve the issues and quiet down the conflict within 30 days.

The two managers secure another meeting with their key players on both sides. At that meeting, the ideology of the senior executives is shared with both sides of this operating team.

The emphasis on a resolution within 30 days is emphasized. A process begins of each side outlining concerns and issues ... leading to where there are mutual opportunities ... then leading to create an action plan facilitating a short-term and long-term resolution to the conflict. Including steps to make sure the opportunity for future conflicts to be eliminated in advance.

The heart of the problem resulted in cost increases from the supplier so they can raise the performance of their QC processes and an oversight capacity from the buyer to make sure QC guidelines are being followed, as intended.

Additionally, the group agrees to meet by conference call weekly and on-site every other month to proactively review the resolution progress, tweak as necessary and continue creating actions for future business relationship developments between both parties.

Following this plan of action, six months later the QC issues has been seriously dissipated and both parties have renewed their *partnership* approach to a friendly and successful supplier/client relationship.

CONFLICT RESOLVED!

The Resolution Strategy Blueprint

In both dispute resolution and conflict management, there are a number of very specific steps that can be followed by managers:

Overview

The mantra of a person's resolving a conflict or a dispute must consider the following:

- Blame is not an immediate concern ... resolve is.
- Getting personnel to be honest and comprehensive must be quickly obtained.
- Some resolutions require a *confrontational* approach, while others may need a more *delicate* process.
- As you approach the resolution process as a senior manager, staff is observing your process, so this is a *coaching and mentoring* exercise, as well.
- Not all conflicts and disputes can be brought to a favorable resolution, but can often then be *mitigated* or *brought under control.*

The Process

Assessment

One needs to appreciate that a *serious fire* may be burning. A quick assessment needs to be accomplished ASAP!

This week in Las Vegas a gunmen killed over 60 persons and wounded another 400+ individuals attending an outdoor concert. It was a terrible tragedy and our hearts and prayers go out to all the families and those impacted by uniform collateral data (UCD) a horrendous crime against all of us.

But think about the first responders coming to the call of duty and seeing all the mayhem, chaos, wounded civilians, and so on, … how quickly they had to assess the situation, to know how best to respond.

In business, we typically do not have these sort of tragedies to deal with, but we know they can happen … BP Oil Spill in the Gulf of Mexico in 2014, Equifax Security Breach in 2017.

All these aforementioned events do portray *fires burning* in the corporate world, but the typical day-to-day events we face though they may have a serious element involved, are not so consequential as the examples outlined earlier.

The purpose of the examples was to show *fires and imminent* conflicts/ disputes do occur in business.

The commonality in all conflicts and disputes is that the first step in coming to a resolution is to accomplish an initial assessment of what you are dealing with.

Is this a problem that needs to be resolved right now, tomorrow, or next week? What are the potential risks and consequences of the conflict or dispute, if I do nothing? I say that because some conflicts and disputes are ok to leave alone as they may work themselves out over time.

We are not necessarily a *Mother* with situations all the time requiring our intervention. Some circumstances are best left to *inaction*, rather than *initiative*.

The primary goal of the assessment process is to then be in the best position to offer guidance on resolution.

Some considerations in the assessment process:

- Determine key players and those impacted.
- Interview quickly.
- Turn as many stones over as possible.
- Create a team or committee to assist.
- Review all pertinent documentation.
- Take good mental and written notes.
- Do not jump to a conclusion too quickly, complete the assessment before finalizing future actions.
- Utilize due diligence and reasonable care in your approach.
- Keep in mind about peoples sensibilities at what might be a very difficult time.

- Recognize that you may need to portray a high sense of urgency, while at the same time offering calm and patience to get to the right resolve.

Assessment leads to a strategy and action plan to bring about resolution, which is the next step.

Initial Action

Keep in mind that the initial action may be:

- Temporary
- Only dealing with certain aspects of the conflict or resolution

  The perfect example of this is in the *triage facility* in a theater of war. The wounded combat soldier is brought in for an immediate assessment ... "stop the bleeding," "keep him alive," "mitigate the pain," etc.

  Those steps do not necessarily deal with the injury, but deal with the symptoms so time can be gained ... to allow for the surgical process down the road when circumstances permit.

  In business ... your company has a distribution warehouse in South Florida, which when Hurricane Irma hit in the fall of 2017, caused major damage and a loss of availability to the organization for 60–75 days.

  Moving southeast distribution to come from sister warehouses in Ohio and Oklahoma on a temporary basis might be an action, done temporarily, but keeps the flow of materials and supplies to their clientele.

  In the longer term, the problem might be resolved by relocating the warehouse/distribution to higher ground where floodwaters may not be imposing a threat.

Initial actions should be as well thought out, as time and circumstance allows a best effort to move forward in order to bring resolution.

But often, initial actions need to be tweaked and adjusted based on new information and how circumstances develop and change.

Second Assessment

Time and circumstance will determine how effective your initial strategy and action plan is or is not ... effective in bringing resolution.

If the first actions are effective, that may bring the final step of closure into the cue. However, my experiences with most business problems have demonstrated that any initial action may work to some extent or maybe not at all ... but then will either need to be tweaked, modified, or maybe an action to go down a completely different path ... may be required.

If this is so, then another assessment will be required to understand what factors:

- May have changed
- Progressed
- Been altered

That now will cause a different strategy to have to be formed which will lead to different actions to happen.

Tweaking

A different strategy will lead to new actions or existing actions that just need to be altered or modified.

Tweaking allows analysis, debate, review, and scrutiny ... all leading to better decisions. Better decisions will allow the best opportunity for problem and dispute resolution.

Remember that success does not always come easy and may require several tries. Tweaking is just part of the process of determining what works and what does not.

It can sometimes be frustrating and add more aggravation and time, but in reality is just part of the overall process in obtaining the desired results.

Revised Action

The tweaking may alter the strategy and the specific actions required to achieve desired results and expectations.

Revisions need to be:

- Goal oriented
- Team accepted
- Communicated timely and responsibly
- Followed-up on comprehensively

Follow-Up

We too often take an action, for some reason believe it has worked, and we move on. Moving on can be a huge cause of continued grief.

The typical scenario is one in which because no one is *complaining* … we believe that everything is now okay.

It could not be further from the truth. Just because they are not complaining does not mean they are not happy, satisfied, or ready to find another supplier/vendor/partner or whatever.

Some people chose not to complain. Some people have complained once, maybe even twice …. but now they are so unhappy … they just leave and never complain about it. They just go and you find out about it after the fact.

Follow-up requires a high level of due diligence in making sure the problem, dispute, the conflict is actually resolved:

- You need to specifically and clearly communicate with all the impacted parties and question whether each or not they agree that the problem is resolved.
- If they agree … you move on.
- If they disagree or offer a *gray area* response … you must continue to dig and mine to determine what the remaining issues are … and then go back to step one and start the process all over to bring a resolution.
- You then follow-up again to see the results of that new or renewed process.
- Follow-up will create the basis for *closure* or *continued action and follow-up.*
- It demonstrates management prowess, caring, and ultimate levels of concern that personnel, vendors, clients friends, and associates all appreciate.
- Follow-up creates *mitigation.* It helps with how the impacted parties feel about you, your company, and ultimately the continuation of the business or personal relationship.

Closure

The final step after follow-up occurs, and it is determined that the problem, conflict, or dispute has been resolved, is to create an atmosphere that demonstrates legitimate remorse, concern, and resolve.

It is where reflection occurs. It may include an assignment of blame. It may include a reiteration of the problem, steps taken, and the resolution.

Sometimes we just need to talk about what happened, even after the fact. It tends to make people feel better about what happened. Often the reflection reduces harm, stress, and bad sentiment.

Closure allows you to move on.

In business, failure to gain closure successfully can seriously impact sustainability of long-term relationship opportunities.

Closing Remarks on Conflict and Dispute Resolution

In my 35 plus years in business, I have learned that at the end of the day bringing a problem to successful resolution is a *NEGOTIATION*.

You are negotiating with impacted parties to move them from distress to success. You are getting others to follow a protocol, a process, various steps that will provide the best opportunity to create a favorable resolve.

You are negotiating with people and their sensibilities and faults, challenges that any problem brings and even ... moats and dragons. All of which may be obstructing you to move forward on what needs to happen.

Navigating those potential obstructions is best accomplished by negotiating with each one as they pop up and occur. Successful people with intense levels of emotional intelligence and negotiation skill sets, both covered in separate sections of this book ... are some of the best attributes to have when dealing with obtaining the very best of favorable resolutions.

WHITE PAPER: STRATEGIC PLANNING AND GOAL SETTING

Successful organizations have clearly defined goals and expectations. These goals are best accomplished by developing successful strategies that create business plans, actions, and tactics that deliver results. This chapter dissects how goals are developed and transformed into business plans, through comprehensive strategies.

SMART Goals

Professional business executives typically utilize a model first created in the early 1980s as follows:

S ... Specific
M ... Measurable

A ... Attainable
R ... Relevant
T ... Trackable

Some professionals will vary slightly the meanings:

A ... Assignable
R ... Realistic
T ... Time specific

In either scenario, the concept is that those that practice these guidelines when first creating goals will increase the odds of more favorable outcomes and achieving desired results.

My experiences in dealing with hundreds of corporations are that goals fail because realistic assessments that they could even be achieved were never diligently accomplished. Because if they were, better and different goals would have been developed.

Our wishes and desires, particularly in business, need to have realistic and attainable goals following a granular assessment of identifying the *real opportunity* to accomplish same.

A basic overview of SMART:

S—Specific
Rhetorical statements such as a lot, more, or greater ... do not assign a more exact position of what we are attempting to achieve.
As an example. The chief operating officer (COO) tells a purchasing team to negotiate better deals to obtain savings on corporate spend.
The team after 6 months creates an average savings of 4.5% to the organization overall. Upon presentation to the COO, he is terribly disappointed, as he anticipated savings of 8%–10%.
Being that the COO never identified a more specific percentage of savings, nor was that pursued by the purchasing team ... the scenario for disappointment was *cast in stone* at the time the initiative was put into motion.
Both parties of the initiative to reduce spending needed to scrutinize the request and bring it to a more specific or range of specific numbers and figure out its' attainability.

M—Measurable

Goals and deliverables once set and agreed upon after careful analysis and scrutiny ... must have an ability to be measured so desired results can be found out and quantified and qualified.

An ability to *measure* allows a determination of the degree of success or failure of the setting of the goal and the strategic plan, which was developed and executed.

A—Attainable or assignable

Attainable refers to an analytical process to determine if the anticipated goal has a reasonable opportunity for success.

Many goals or deliverables are not obtainable because in analysis they are excessive and not likely to happen as intended.

One creating a goal must shoot high, but not so high it becomes out of reach. Only disappointment will follow.

Some reference this term as *assignable* ... meaning transferable to a third party.

R—Relevant

Relevant means closely connected or what is appropriate to what is being done or considered. In goal setting, this is critical as the *goal* must be relevant to reasonable expectation and the surrounding circumstances.

Sometimes the "R" refers to *realistic*, meaning having a sensible idea of what can be achieved, which directly supports *relevance*. Goals all need to be realistic and/or relevant.

T—Trackable

Once goals are established you must be in a position to determine the progression of your actions to either getting to the goal you established ... or not.

There needs to be a system or process to see how your action steps are progressing or *tracking*.

T can also mean time specific. In goal setting, this means the actions taken to get us to the goal should have some reference to *time* or another word for an anticipated completion date.

The structure for goal setting ... 12 steps:

1. Obtain input
2. Mine

3. Confer
4. Establish preliminary goals
5. Confer
6. Finalize goals
7. Confirm and identify true motivation
8. Establish strategy
9. Establish tactics
10. Review and tweak
11. Move forward
12. Bring closure

Goal Setting Finale

Crossing the finish line in *goal setting* is to get the desired results you had intended. Besides all the 12 steps outlined previously, once must also have the following traits:

- Persistence
- Creativity
- Bull persona
- Communication skills
- Negotiation skills
- Patience
- Selfishness
- Emotional intelligence
- Being grounded

(Grab your reader's attention with a great quote from the document or use this space to emphasize a key point. To place this text box anywhere on the page, just drag it.)

Having these traits will maximize the effectiveness of not only setting the goals, but more importantly in developing a strategy and then executing the tactics successful to obtain favorable outcomes.

Remember in *goal setting* ... it is not only the development of the goal, but in also making it happen.

The first known use of the term occurs in the November 1981 issue of *Management Review* by George T. Doran [1]. The principal advantage of SMART objectives is that they are easier to understand and to know when they have been done. SMART criteria are commonly associated with Peter Drucker's management by objectives concept [2].

EXPORT MANAGEMENT & COMPLIANCE PROGRAM

INTRODUCTION

This is a tool created for exporters to aid in the development of an export management and compliance program. It may be used to create a new program or to assess whether internal controls have been implemented within an existing program with the purpose of eliminating common vulnerabilities found in export compliance programs. Each company has unique export activities and export programs; therefore, this is an example to build upon and does not include all Export Administration Regulations restrictions and prohibitions.

This tool is a combination of best compliance practices implemented by U.S. companies, auditing practices, and Export Administration Regulations requirements.

METHODOLOGY

An effective export management and compliance program (EMCP) consists of many processes that connect and intersect. The connections and intersections must be planned, and then, clear directions must be given to those who are to follow the rules of the program. Without maps (instructions), chances are that personnel will all go in their own directions, leaving them vulnerable to getting lost on the way and chancing that key connections are missed, resulting in violations of the intended rules of the program. To use this self-assessment, first look to see if your program includes written instructions that create the connections and intersections needed to maintain compliance.

Within the self-assessment columns, "Y/N/U" stands for Yes/No/ Uncertain or Indeterminate.

PREAUDIT CHECKLIST

- Identify business units and personnel to be audited
- Send e-mail notification to affected parties
- Develop a tracking log for document requests
- Prepare audit templates such as interview questions, transactional review checklist, audit report format, etc.
- Each business unit should provide their written procedures related to export compliance before the audit
- Personnel at all levels of the organization, management, and staff should be interviewed to compare written procedures with actual business practices
- Identify gaps and inconsistencies

POSTAUDIT CHECKLIST

- Write draft audit report
  - Executive Summary (purpose, methodology, key findings)
  - Findings and Recommendations (organize in priority order)
  - Appendices (interview list, document list, process charts)
- Conduct postaudit briefing for affected business units to discuss audit findings and recommendations. Provide draft report. This is an opportunity for business units to address inaccuracies in report
- Obtain commitment from business units for corrective action. Include in audit report
- Brief executive management on audit findings and recommendations
- Track corrective actions. Within the year, audit corrective actions

Element 1: Management Commitment	Y	N	U	Initials Date Comments
Is management commitment communicated on an ongoing basis by:				
Company publications? Company awareness posters? Daily operating procedures?				
Other means, e.g., bulletin boards, in meetings, etc.?				
Does management issue a formal statement that communicates clear commitment to export controls?				
Is the formal statement distributed to all employees and contractors?				
Who is responsible for distribution of the statement?				
Is there a distribution list of those who should receive the statement?				
What method of communication is used (letter, e-mail, intranet, etc.)?				
Does the distribution of the statement include employee-signed receipt and personal commitment to comply?				
Is the formal statement from current senior management communicated in a manner consistent with management priority correspondence?				
Does the formal statement explain why corporate commitment is important from your company's perspective?				
Does the formal statement contain a policy statement that no sales will be made contrary to the Export Administration Regulations?				
Does the formal statement convey the dual-use risk of the items to be exported?				
Does the formal statement emphasize end-use/end-user prohibitions?				
Proliferation activities of concerns:				
• Nuclear?				
• Certain rocket systems and unmanned air vehicles?				
• Chemical and Biological Weapons?				
Does the formal statement contain a description of penalties applied in instances of compliance failure?				
• Imposed by the Department of Commerce?				
• Imposed by your company?				

(Continued)

Element 1: Management Commitment	Y	N	U	Initials Date Comments
Does the formal statement include the name, position, and contact information, such as: e-mail address and telephone number of the person(s) to contact with questions concerning the legitimacy of a transaction or possible violations?				
What management records will be maintained to verify compliance with procedures and processes (including the formal statement)?				
Who is responsible for keeping each of the management records?				
How long must the records be retained?				
Where will the records be maintained?				
In what format will the records be retained?				
Are adequate resources (time, money, people) dedicated to the implementation and maintenance of the EMCP?				
Is management directly involved through regularly scheduled meetings with various units responsible for roles within the EMCP?				
Is management involved in the auditing process?				
Has management implemented a team of EMCP managers who meet frequently to review challenges, procedures, and processes and who serve as the connection to the employees who perform the EMCP responsibilities?				
Does the statement describe where employees can locate the EMCP manual (on the company intranet or specific person and location of hard copies)?				
Are there written procedures to ensure consistent, operational implementation of this element?				
Is a person designated to update this element, including the management commitment statement, when management changes, or at least annually? (Note in comments the name of the person.)				
Who are other employees who are held accountable for specific responsibilities under this element? For example: • Company official charged with EMCP oversight and ongoing commitment to the program • Management team members who are responsible for connecting with all responsible employees in the EMCP • Persons charged with ensuring the EMCP is functioning as directed by management				

(Continued)

Element 1: Management Commitment	Y	N	U	Initials Date Comments
If the primary responsible person is unable to perform the responsibilities, is a secondary person designated to backup the primary designee?				
(If not, is a procedure in place to eliminate vulnerabilities of an untrained person proceeding with tasks that might lead to violations of the EAR?)				
Do responsible persons understand the interconnection of their roles with other EMCP processes and where they fit in the overall export compliance system?				
Is the message of management commitment conveyed in employee training through:				
Orientation programs? Refresher training?				
Electronic training modules? Employee procedures manuals?				
Other?				
Is management involved in EMCP training to emphasize management commitment to the program?				
Determination:				

Elements 2 and 5: Risk Assessment and Cradle-to-Grave Export Compliance Security and Screening	Y	N	U	Initials Date Comments
Are there written procedures for ensuring compliance with product and country export restrictions?				
Do procedures include reexport guidelines or any special instructions?				
Is there a written procedure that describes how items are classified under export control classification numbers (ECCNs) on the Commerce Control List (CCL)?				
A. Does a technical expert within the company classify the items?				
B. If your company does not manufacture the item, does the manufacturer of the item classify it?				
C. Is there a written procedure that describes when a classification will be submitted to the Bureau of Industry and Security (BIS) and who will be responsible?				
D. Is there a written procedure that describes the process for seeking commodity jurisdiction determinations?				
Is an individual designated to ensure that product/country license determination guidance is current and updated?				

(Continued)

Elements 2 and 5: Risk Assessment and Cradle-to-Grave Export Compliance Security and Screening	Y	N	U	Initials Date Comments
Is there a distribution procedure to ensure all appropriate users receive the guidance and instructions for use?				
Is there a list that indicates the name of the persons responsible for using the guidance?				
Is a matrix or decision table for product/country license determinations used?				
Are the instructions provided easily understood and applied?				
Do the instructions provided specify who, when, where, and how to check each shipment against the matrix?				
Does the matrix/table display ECCNs and product descriptions?				
Appropriate shipping authorizations, license required, license exception (specify which), or no license required (NLR)?				
Does the matrix communicate license exception parameters/restrictions?				
Are license conditions and restrictions included within the matrix/table?				
Does the matrix/table cross reference items to be exported with license exceptions normally available (based on item description and end destination)?				
Does the matrix/table clearly define which license exceptions are normally available for each item (also clearly state which license exceptions may not be used due to general prohibitions)?				
Are embargoed destinations displayed?				
Is country information in the table up-to-date?				
Are item restrictions displayed? (i.e., technical parameter limitations, end-user limitations)				
Is the matrix automated?				
Is a person designated for updating the tool?				
Are reporting prompts built into the matrix/table?				
Are Wassenaar reports required? Does the matrix/table denote when they are required?				
Is the matrix manually implemented?				
If so, is a person designated to update the tool?				
Is there a *hold* function to prevent shipments from being further processed, if needed?				
Is there a procedure to distribute and verify receipt of license conditions?				
Is there someone designated to distribute and follow-up with acknowledgment verification?				

(Continued)

Elements 2 and 5: Risk Assessment and Cradle-to-Grave Export Compliance Security and Screening	Y	N	U	Initials Date Comments
Are there written procedures to ensure that checks and safeguards are in place within the internal process flows, and are there assigned personnel responsible for all checks?				
Is the order process and all linking internal flows displayed visually in a series of flow charts?				
Is there a narrative that describes the total flow process?				
Are the following checks included in the internal process?				
• Preorder entry screen checks performed (i.e., know your customer red flags)				
• Denied persons				
• Entity list				
• Unverified list				
• Specially designated nationals list				
• Boycott language				
• Nuclear end-uses				
• Certain rocket systems and unmanned air vehicles end-uses				
• Chemical and biological weapons end-uses				
• Product/country licensing determination				
• Diversion risk check				
Do the order process and other linking processes include a description of administrative control over the following documents: Shipper's Export Declarations (SED)/Automated Export System (AES) Records, Shipper's Letter of Instruction? Airway bills and/or Bills of Lading, Invoices?				
Does the procedure explain the order process and other linking processes from receipt of order to actual shipment?				
Does the procedure include who is responsible for each screen/check throughout the flow?				
Does the procedure describe when, how often, and what screening is performed?				
Are hold/cancel functions implemented?				
Does the procedure clearly indicate who has the authority to make classification decisions?				
Are supervisory or EMCP administrator sign-off procedures implemented at high risk points?				
Does the company have an ongoing procedure for monitoring compliance of consignees, end-users, and other parties involved in export transactions?				
Determination:				

Elements 2 and 5: Risk Assessment and Cradle-to-Grave Export Compliance Security and Screening Review Orders/Transactions against the Denied Persons List (DPL)	Y	N	U	Initials Date Comments
Is there a written procedure to ensure screening of orders/ shipments to customers covering servicing, training, and sales of items against the DPL?				
Are personnel/positions identified who are responsible for DPL screening (consider domestic and international designee)?				
Is there a procedure to stop orders if a customer and/or other parties are found on the DPL?				
Is there a procedure to report all names of customers and/ or other parties found on the DPL?				
Do the procedures include a process for what is used to perform the screening, and if distribution of hard copies is required, who is responsible for their update and distribution?				
Is the DPL checked against your customer-base?				
A. Are both the customer name and principal checked?				
B. Is there a method for keeping the customer-base current?				
C. Is there a method for screening new customers?				
Is the DPL checked on a transaction-by-transaction basis?				
A. Is the name of the ordering party's firm and principal checked?				
B. Is the end-user's identity available? If so, is a DPL check done on the end-user?				
C. Is the check performed at the time an order is accepted and/or received?				
D. Is the check performed at the time of shipment?				
E. Is the check performed against backlog orders when a new or updated DPL is published?				
Does documentation of screen (whether hard copy or electronic signature) include:				
A. Name of individuals performing the checks?				
B. Dates screen checks performed?				
C. Date of current denied person's information used to perform the check?				
D. Is the date of the DPL used to check the transaction documented? Is it current?				

(Continued)

Elements 2 and 5: Risk Assessment and Cradle-to-Grave Export Compliance Security and Screening Review Orders/Transactions against the Denied Persons List (DPL)	Y	N	U	Initials Date Comments
Are other trade-related sanctions, embargoes, and debarments imposed by agencies other than the Department of Commerce checked?				
A. Department of Treasury (Office of Foreign Assets Control):				
1. Specially designated terrorists?				
2. Specially designated nationals and foreign terrorist organizations?				
B. Department of State:				
1. Trade-related sanctions (Bureau of Politico-Military Affairs)?				
2. Suspensions and debarments (Center for Defense Trade, Office of Defense Trade Controls)?				
Are domestic transactions screened against the DPL?				
Determination:				

Elements 2 and 5: Risk Assessment and Cradle-to-Grave Export Compliance Security and Screening Diversion Risk Profile See Export Administration Regulations Part 732, Supplements 1 and 3	Y	N	U	Initials Date Comments
Are there procedures to screen orders for diversion risk red flag indicators?				
Is a checklist used based upon the red flag indicators?				
Does the written screening procedure identify the responsible individuals who perform the screen checks?				
Is the division risk profile (DRP) considered at all phases of the order processing system?				
Is a transaction-based DRP performed?				
Is a customer-based DRP performed?				
Is a checklist documented and maintained on file for each and every order?				
Is a checklist documented and maintained on file in the customer profile?				
Is the customer base checked at least annually against the red flag indicators or when a customer's activities change?				

(Continued)

Elements 2 and 5: Risk Assessment and Cradle-to-Grave Export Compliance Security and Screening Diversion Risk Profile See Export Administration Regulations Part 732, Supplements 1 and 3	Y	N	U	Initials Date Comments
General Prohibition 6—Prohibits export/reexports of items to embargoed destinations without proper license authority. Are embargoed-destinations prohibitions communicated on the product/country matrix and part of the red flag indicators?				
General Prohibition 10—Prohibits an exporter from proceeding with transactions with knowledge that a violation has occurred or is about to occur. Is there anything that is suspect regarding the legitimacy of the transactions?				
Determination:				

Elements 2 and 5: Risk Assessment and Cradle-to-Grave Export Compliance Security and Screening Prohibited Nuclear End-Uses/Users, EAR, Section 744.2	Y	N	U	Initials Date Comments
Are there written procedures for reviewing exports and reexports of all items subject to the Export Administration Regulations (EAR) to determine, prior to exporting, whether they might be destined to be used directly or indirectly in any one or more of the prohibited nuclear activities?				
Are personnel/positions identified who are responsible for ensuring screening of customers and their activities against the prohibited end-uses?				
Does the procedure describe when the nuclear screen should be performed?				
A. Is your nuclear screen completed on a transaction-by-transaction basis?				
B. Is the screen conducted against an established customer base? If yes, is there a procedure for screening each new customer before the new customer is added to that customer base?				
C. Is the nuclear screen completed before a new customer is approved?				
Is there a list of all employees responsible for performing nuclear screening?				

(Continued)

Elements 2 and 5: Risk Assessment and Cradle-to-Grave Export Compliance Security and Screening Prohibited Nuclear End-Uses/Users, EAR, Section 744.2	Y	N	U	Initials Date Comments
Does the check include documentation with the signature/initials of the person performing the check, and the date performed, to verify consistent operational performance of the check?				
Is the customer base checked and the check documented at least annually in the Customer Profiles? (see EMCP Guidelines, Diversion Risk Screen.)				
Is it clear who is responsible for the annual check?				
Is there a procedure to verify that all responsible employees are performing the screening?				
Are nuclear checklists (and/or other tools) distributed to appropriate export-control personnel for easy, efficient performance of the review?				
Have export/sales personnel been instructed on how to recognize situations that may involve prohibited nuclear end-use activities?				
Does the procedure include what to do if it is known that an item is destined to a nuclear end-use/user?				
Determination:				

Elements 2 and 5: Risk Assessment and Cradle-to-Grave Export Compliance Security and Screening Rocket Systems and Unmanned Air Vehicles Prohibited Missile End-Uses/Users, EAR, Section 744.3	Y	N	U	Initials Date Comments
Are there written procedures for reviewing exports and reexports of all items subject to the EAR to determine, prior to exporting, whether the items are destined for a prohibited end-use?				
Are personnel/positions identified who are responsible for ensuring screening of customers and their activities against the prohibited end-users/users?				
Does the procedure describe when the missile systems and unmanned air vehicles screen should be performed?				
Does the procedure include a check against the entity list?				
If yes, is there a procedure to maintain documented entity list screen decisions on file to verify consistent operational review?				

(Continued)

Elements 2 and 5: Risk Assessment and Cradle-to-Grave Export Compliance Security and Screening Rocket Systems and Unmanned Air Vehicles Prohibited Missile End-Uses/Users, EAR, Section 744.3	Y	N	U	Initials Date Comments
A. Is your rocket/unmanned aerial vehicle (UAV) screen completed on a transaction-by-transaction basis?				
B. Is the screen conducted against an established customer base? If yes, is there a procedure for screening each new customer before the new customer is added to that customer base?				
C. Is the rocket/UAV screen completed before the new customer is approved?				
Does the check include documentation with the signature/ initials of the person performing the check, and the date performed, to verify consistent operational performance of the check?				
Is the customer base checked and the check documented at least annually in the Customer Profiles?				
Is it clear who is responsible for the annual check?				
Is there a list of all employees responsible for the annual check?				
Is there a procedure to verify that all responsible employees are performing the screening?				
Are missile systems and unmanned air vehicles checklists (and/or other tools) distributed to appropriate export-control personnel for easy, efficient performance of the review?				
Have export/sales personnel been instructed on how to recognize prohibited missile systems and unmanned air vehicles end-use activities?				
Does the procedure include what to do if it is known that an item is destined to a prohibited end-use/user?				
Determination:				

Elements 2 and 5: Risk Assessment and Cradle-to-Grave Export Compliance Security and Screening Prohibited Chemical and Biological Weapons (CBW) End-Uses/Users, EAR, Section 744.4	Y	N	U	**Initials Date Comments**
Are there written procedures for reviewing exports and reexports of all items subject to the EAR for license requirements, prior to exporting, if the item can be used in the design, development, production, stockpiling, or use of chemical or biological weapons?				
Are personnel/positions identified who are responsible for ensuring screening of customers and their activities against the prohibited end-use/users?				
Does the procedure describe when the chemical and biological weapons screen should be performed?				
A. Is your chemical and biological weapons screen completed on a transaction-by-transaction basis?				
B. Is the screen conducted against an established customer base? If yes, is there a procedure for screening each new customer before the new customer is added to that customer base?				
C. Is your chemical and biological weapons screen completed before the new customer is approved?				
Does the check include documentation with the signature/initials of the person performing the check, and the date performed, to verify consistent operational performance of the check?				
Is the customer base checked and the check documented at least annually in the Customer Profiles?				
Is it clear who is responsible for the annual check?				
Is there a list of all employees responsible for performing chemical and biological weapons screening?				
Is there a procedure to verify that all responsible employees are performing the screening?				
Are chemical and biological weapons checklists (and/or other tools) distributed to appropriate export-control personnel for easy, efficient performance of the review?				
Have export/sales personnel been instructed on how to recognize prohibited chemical and biological weapons end-use activities?				
Does the procedure include what to do if it is known that an item is destined to a prohibited end-use/user?				
Determination:				

Elements 2 and 5: Risk Assessment and Cradle-to-Grave Export Compliance Security and Screening Review Orders/Transactions against Antiboycott Compliance Red Flags	Y	N	U	Initials Date Comments
Is there a written procedure to screen transactions and orders/shipping documents for restrictive trade practice or boycott language included in Part 760 of the EAR?				
Are personnel/positions identified who are responsible for performing this screen?				
Is the antiboycott screening performed by using a profile checklist?				
Does the checklist include the following:				
A. The firm's name? (as *Consignee*)				
B. Name/initials of personnel performing the screen check?				
C. Date screen check is performed?				
Is there a procedure to *hold* orders if there is a red flag during the processing of orders?				
Is a person designated to resolve red flags or report them to the BIS Office of Antiboycott Compliance?				
Have all units that might possibly come into contact with the red flags been trained to identify the red flags?				
Are antiboycott red flags included in training materials?				
Determination:				

Elements 2 and 5: Risk Assessment and Cradle-to-Grave Export Compliance Security and Screening Review Customers and Other Parties against the Entity List	Y	N	U	Initials Date Comments
Is there a written procedure to screen transactions against the entity list to determine whether there are any license requirements in addition to normal license requirements for exports or reexports of specified items to specified end-users, based on BIS determination that there is an unacceptable risk of use in, or diversion to, prohibited proliferation activities?				
Is the screening documented, including the following?				
A. The firm's name?				
B. Names/initials of individuals performing the check?				
C. Date checks are performed?				
D. Is screening check combined and performed with another check (e.g., denied persons list check)?				
Is the Federal Register monitored daily for the addition of new entities to the entity list?				
If matches occur, is there a *hold* function implemented within the order processing system that stops the order until a decision is made as to license requirements?				
Determination:				

	Y	N	U	**Initials Date Comments**
Element 3: A Formal Written EMCP				

Are there written procedures that describe how information will flow among all the elements to help ensure EMCP effectiveness and accountability?

Is the written EMCP developed and maintained with input from all the corporate stakeholders in the export process?

Do the written procedures clearly describe detailed step-by-step processes that employees are expected to follow, and are contingencies addressed?

Are the written procedures reviewed for update at least annually and when major changes occur?

Are the written and operational procedures consistent?

Has an administrator been designated for oversight of the EMCP?

Is there a table that identifies individuals, their positions, addresses, telephone numbers, e-mail addresses, and their respective export transaction and compliance responsibilities?

Does it include all domestic sites? Does it include all international sites?

Is a person designated as responsible for management and maintenance of this element?

Is a person assigned responsibility for distribution of information related to this element?

Is a person assigned to retain the records?

Is the length of time the records are to be retained included?

Is the location of where the records are to be retained included?

Is the format of the records to be retained included?

If the primary responsible persons are unable to perform the assigned responsibilities, are secondary persons designated to backup the primary designees?

Where there are no backup designees, are there procedures in place to prevent untrained/unauthorized personnel from taking action?

Are all EMCP tasks clearly summarized in this element and consistent with detailed information in other corresponding elements?

(Continued)

Element 3: A Formal Written EMCP	Y	N	U	Initials Date Comments
Does each employee designated with tasks understand the importance of his/her role related to the overall export compliance system?				
Do the responsible persons understand how the processes they are responsible for connect to the *next* process? ("… and then what happens next?")				
Do all the appropriate personnel have the ability to hold a questionable transaction?				
Are the necessary systems to allow employees to perform their tasks readily available to them?				
Is training for understanding and use of the EMCP provided on a regular basis to the necessary employees, and are records of the training kept?				
Based on an organization chart and assignment of tasks, does it appear that there are conflicts of interest in the chain of command and the tasks to be performed?				
Determination:				

Element 4: Training	Y	N	U	Initials Date Comments
Are there written procedures that describe an ongoing program of export transaction/compliance training and education?				
Do the written procedures clearly describe detailed step-by-step processes that employees are expected to follow?				
Is a qualified individual designated to conduct training and to update the training materials? (Note in comments the name of the person.)				
If the primary responsible person is unable to perform the responsibilities, is a secondary person designated to backup the primary designee? (If not, is a procedure in place to eliminate vulnerabilities of an untrained person proceeding with tasks that might lead to violations of the EAR?)				
Is there a schedule to conduct training (including date, time, and place)?				

(Continued)

Element 4: Training	Y	N	U	Initials Date Comments
Does the training component of the EMCP include what training materials are used (module, videos, and manuals)?				
Are training materials accurate, consistent and current with operational company policy, procedures, and processes? (If not, note in the comments section what corrective actions are needed.)				
Are attendance logs used for documentation, which includes agenda, date, trainer, trainees, and subjects?				
Is frequency of training defined?				
Is a list of employees/positions defined who should receive export control/compliance training?				
Are responsible persons trained to understand the interconnection of their roles with other EMCP processes and where they fit in the overall export transaction/compliance program?				
Is the list of employees/positions to be trained consistent with other elements?				
Is a person identified and responsible for keeping the training records?				
Is the location of where these training records are to be maintained included?				
Is the format of how these training records will be maintained noted?				
Do training methods include:				
• Orientation for new employees?				
• Formal (structured setting, agenda, modules used)?				
• Informal (less structured basis, verbal, daily, on-the-job exchanges)?				
• Circulation of written memoranda and e-mails to a small number of personnel, (usually group specific instruction)?				
• Refresher courses and update sessions scheduled?				
• Employee desk procedure manuals?				
• Backup personnel training?				

(Continued)

	Y	N	U	Initials Date Comments
Element 4: Training				

Does content of training materials include:
- Organizational structure of export-related departments and functions?
- Message of management commitment—policy statement
- The role of the EMCP administrator and key contacts?
- U.S. export/reexport regulatory requirements?
- EMCP company operating procedures?
- The purpose and scope of export controls?
- Licenses and conditions/license exceptions and parameters?
- Regulatory changes and new requirements?
- Destination restrictions?
- Item restrictions?
- End-Use and End-User prohibitions?
- How to perform and *document* screens and checklists?
- Various process flows for each element?
- New customer review procedures?
- Identification and description of noncompliance?

Determination:

	Y	N	U	Initials Date Comments
Element 6: Recordkeeping (EAR, Part 762)				

Are there written procedures to comply with recordkeeping requirements?

Do the written procedures clearly describe detailed step-by-step processes that employees are expected to follow?

Are all records in each process included in the records maintained?

Are the written procedures reviewed for update at least annually and when significant changes occur?

Are the written and operational procedures consistent?

Is there a designated employee responsible for management and maintenance of this element? Is name and contact information provided?

(Continued)

Element 6: Recordkeeping (EAR, Part 762)	Y	N	U	Initials Date Comments
Identify all other employees who are held accountable for specific responsibilities under this recordkeeping element?				
Do the designated employees know who is responsible for the next action to be taken in the process?				
If the primary responsible person is unable to perform the responsibilities, is a secondary person designated to backup the primary designee?				
Where there are no backup designees, are there procedures in place to prevent untrained/unauthorized personnel from taking action?				
Do employees understand the importance of their roles related to the overall recordkeeping requirement?				
Do employees have the appropriate budgetary, staff, and supporting resources to perform their responsibilities?				
Do employees have access to all the appropriate systems, tools, databases, and records to perform their responsibilities and ensure compliance with recordkeeping procedures?				
Is appropriate and specific training provided regarding this element?				
Is the training included on an annual schedule of employee training?				
Have appropriate parties been identified who will retain records? Are names and contact information provided?				
Has the length of time for record-retention been identified?				
Have secure physical and electronic storage locations for records been identified for the retention of records?				
Have determinations been made regarding the formats that all of the different types of records will be retained in?				
Is there a list of records that are to be maintained (see Guidelines and the following for checklists)?				

(Continued)

Element 6: Recordkeeping (EAR, Part 762)	Y	N	U	Initials Date Comments
Does the procedure include a list of records to maintain, including the following: *Administrative Records*: Commodity Classification records? Commodity Jurisdiction letters?				
Advisory Opinion letters? Copy of the EMCP BIS 748P, Multipurpose Application Form BIS 748P-A, Item Appendix				
BIS 748P-B, End-User Appendix				
BIS 711 Statement by Ultimate Consignee and Purchaser? Electronic version BIS 748P, Simplified Network Application Process (SNAP) ACCN Number?				
Accompanying attachments, rider, or conditions? International Import Certificates?				
End-user Certificates?				
License Exception TSR Written Assurance? AES Electronic Filing Authorization?				
High Performance Computer Records?				
Transmittal and acknowledgement of license condition?				
Log administering control over use of Export/Reexport license?				
Is a log maintained to ensure return or commodities previously exported under License Exception transportation motor pool (TMP)?				
Is a log maintained to ensure License Exception LVS limits are not exceeded?				
Humanitarian Donations GFT Records?				
Are there instructions for the accurate completion and filing of the following *Transaction Records*:				
1. Commercial invoices?				
2. AES electronic filing authorization?				
a. Description of items(s)				
b. ECCN(s)				
c. License number				
d. License exception symbols or exemptions				
e. Schedule B number(s)				
3. Air Waybills and/or Bills of Lading Value of shipments				
Is there conformity regarding the aforementioned documents?				

Determination:

Element 7: Audits/Assessments	Y	N	U	Initials Date Comments
Are written procedures established to verify ongoing compliance?				
Is there a qualified individual (or auditing group) designated to conduct internal audits?				
Is there a potential conflict of interest between the auditor and the division being audited?				
Is there a schedule for audits?				
Are internal reviews performed annually, every six months, quarterly, etc.?				
Is there a step-by-step description of the audit process?				
Is a standard audit module or self-assessment tool used?				
If yes, does the audit module or self-assessment tool evaluate: Corporate management commitment in all aspects of the audit not just the Written policy statement element?				
If yes, does the audit module or self-assessment tool evaluate: Formalized, written EMCP procedures compared to operational procedures?				
If yes, does the audit module or self-assessment tool evaluate: Accuracy and conformity of export transaction documents by random sampling or 100% verification?				
If yes, does the audit module or self-assessment tool evaluate: Whether there is a current, accurate product/license determination matrix consistent with the current EAR and Federal Register notices?				
If yes, does the audit module or self-assessment tool evaluate: Whether correct export authorizations were used for each transaction?				
If yes, does the audit module or self-assessment tool evaluate: Maintenance of documents, as required in the written EMCP.				
If yes, does the audit module or self-assessment tool evaluate: Whether internal control screens were performed and documented as required in the EMCP?				
If yes, does the audit module or self-assessment tool evaluate: Whether there are flow charts of the various processes for each element?				
If yes, does the audit module or self-assessment tool evaluate: What is used to provide verification that the audits were conducted?				

(Continued)

Element 7: Audits/Assessments	Y	N	U	Initials Date Comments
If yes, does the audit module or self-assessment tool evaluate: Whether there is a procedure to stop/hold transactions if problems arise?				
If yes, does the audit module or self-assessment tool evaluate: Whether all key export-related personnel are interviewed?				
If yes, does the audit module or self-assessment tool evaluate: Whether there are clear, open communications between all export-related divisions?				
If yes, does the audit module or self-assessment tool evaluate: Whether there is daily oversight over the performance of export control checks?				
If yes, does the audit module or self-assessment tool evaluate: Does it include sampling of the completed screens performed during the order processing and/or new (or annual) customer screening?				
If yes, does the audit module or self-assessment tool evaluate: Whether export control procedures and the EMCP manual are consistent with EAR changes that have been published?				
If yes, does the audit module or self-assessment tool evaluate: Whether the company's training module and procedures are current with EAR and Federal Register notices?				
Is there a written report of each internal audit?				
Are there written results of the review?				
Is the appropriate manager notified, if action is needed?				
Are spot checks/informal self-assessments performed? Are they documented?				
Is there evidence of a conflict of interest between the reviewer and the division being reviewed?				
Are records of past audits maintained to monitor repeated deficiencies?				
Is there a *best practice* that should be shared with other divisions in the company to improve effectiveness and efficiency of export controls and promote consistency of procedures?				
Are other departments aware of their export-control-related responsibilities, e.g., legal dept., human resources, information management, etc.?				
Determination:				

Elements 8 and 9: Reporting, Escalation, and Corrective Action	Y	N	U	Initials Date Comments
Are there internal procedures in place to notify management within the company if a party is determined to be in noncompliance? Is contact information provided for each official in the chain?				
Does the company policy/guidelines address accountability and consequences for noncompliant activity? Are the appropriate incentives, rewards, requirements, and penalties in place, and is an appropriate business culture of compliance being fostered to facilitate notification of any possible noncompliance?				
Are there internal procedures in place to notify the appropriate				
U.S. Government officials (e.g., Export Administration's Office of Exporter Services Export Enforcement, etc.) when noncompliance is determined?				
Has a central corporate point-of-contact been defined for all communications with the U.S. Government?				
Is the management chain clearly defined for voluntary self-disclosures and are there clear guidelines for voluntary self-disclosures?				
Do all employees receive export control awareness training (including for potential deemed exports and hand-carry scenarios)? Does this training detail reporting, escalation, and corrective action requirements?				
Is there a 24-hour mechanism for notifying compliance management of possible export violations or problems?				
Does the company have an anonymous reporting mechanism for employees?				
Do compliance guidelines provide defined criteria for when a formal internal investigation is required? If yes, are the procedures to be followed defined? Are the reporting and documentation requirements defined?				
Do compliance guidelines include policy and procedures for follow-up reporting to management and the reporting employee? Is there a process for evaluating lessons learned?				
Determination:				

WHITE PAPER ON INTERNATIONAL FREIGHT AND TRADE COMPLIANCE

Overview

The key to successful logistics in international business is to move freight:

- Timely
- Safely
- Cost effectively
- Trade compliantly

Global businesses that are engaged in global trade, importing, exporting, and distributing products worldwide face numerous challenges.

The ability to move goods in the international arena will make or break a sale or even maintain a client relationship.

The ability to deliver parts and equipment on a timely and loss free basis is a critical component to business managers worldwide.

This *white paper* addresses *Eight Steps* to follow to help reduce risk and cost in the area of international shipping, freight, and logistics.

The Eight Steps

The following eight steps originate from the authors 35 year experience in moving freight all around the world and in assisting corporations with global logistics that are cost effective and reduce risk to themselves and their clients.

1. Recognize the importance of shipping and logistics in your business model
2. Chose the best International Commercial Term (INCO) term
3. Insure the shipment
4. Chose the right freight forwarder and carrier
5. Track all shipments proactively
6. Understand the total *landed costs*
7. Be trade compliant!
8. Leverage free trade agreements

Recognize the Importance of Shipping and Logistics in Your Business Model

Customer satisfaction is often dictated by how well you ship parts and equipment on a timely, safe, and cost-effective method.

A critical aspect of overall performing consistently for your clients is being able to ship your products and service your clients' needs responsibly.

This brings freight and logistics to the forefront of your client's relationships ... and not as a secondary area or relevance, but as a primary consideration.

Quality and reliable shipping can be as valuable in client relationships as any other aspect ... including overall responsiveness, price, and value-added services.

Responsible shipping can also differentiate you as a valued provider of parts, equipment, and related products.

Keep in mind that shipping, while sometimes an aggravation and a headache, is a necessary area as part of your business model in satisfying your clients' needs to obtain parts and equipment on a timely and inexpensive basis.

Our firm helps companies manage their shipping needs better, and we have now been working with global firms over the last 30 years with many successful initiatives.

Outlined here are another seven steps to consider in the world of international freight and logistics.

Choose the Best INCO Term

The INCO Term, established by the International Commerce Commission is followed by all countries belonging to the United Nations for goods that pass through international borders.

There are 11 options in the 2010 Edition.
Incoterms for any mode or modes of transport:

- *EXW*: Ex works
- *FCA*: Free carrier
- *CPT*: Carriage paid to
- *CIP*: Carriage and insurance paid
- *DAT*: Delivered at terminal (*new*)
- *DAP*: Delivered at place (*new*)
- *DDP*: Delivered duty paid

Incoterms

Incoterms for sea and inland waterway transport only:

- *FAS*: Free alongside ship
- *FOB*: Free on board
- *CFR*: Cost and freight
- *CIF*: Cost, insurance, and freight

The INCO term is a term of sale between a seller and a buyer that picks a point in time in the transaction where risk and cost is transferred from one party to the other.

It does not address other contractual concerns, such as payment method, title, and details of marine insurance.

What it really does is advise an exporter to what time and place in a transaction is it responsible for cost and risk to and, conversely, where the importer picks it up on.

Depending upon the INCO term utilized ... the risks and costs could be dramatically impactful for either the seller or the buyer.

We recommend that all operations, purchasing, and sales personnel in the International Distributors Association (IDA) membership learn at a very detailed level all they can about INCO terms and, more specifically, how to best leverage the term to reduce risk and cost in their transaction.

The author is available to the membership at bringing in-house classes on INCO terms to the IDA membership and always available to assist IDA members with any questions (tomcook@bletigerintl.com, kellyraia@bluetigerintl.com).

Insure the Shipment

The typical importer, exporter, and domestic shipper never worry about loss or damage until it occurs.

And at that point, everyone from the forwarder to the carrier is blamed for the occurrence.

Freight will always get lost or damaged at some point in time, when you ship frequently and all over the world.

It is very important to make sure that you first identify through the purchase or sales contract who has risk of loss or damage. What INCO term is being utilized? How is payment being made?

Once the risk is understood ... then marine cargo insurance should be acquired ... on an *All Risk, Warehouse to Warehouse* basis with a reputable international cargo insurance underwriting company.

Additionally, some loss control elements need to be considered to mirror the insurance policy that considers:

- That the freight is packed, marked, and labeled well
- A responsible forwarder and carrier is utilized
- Freight needs to pass through the system quickly ... delays at border points open the door for loss and damage
- Freight needs to clear customs ... thoroughly, legally, following all import regulations, and timely ... all that will mitigate the potential for loss and damage

Chose the Right Freight Forwarder and Carrier

As an extension of your shipping personnel the forwarder and carrier take responsibility to move your freight through the global system.

They need to do this:

- Timely
- Safely
- Cost effectively
- Trade compliantly

Choosing the right company that is qualified, experts in parts and equipment distribution becomes some very important criteria to make sure the shipment, the freight, and the logistics move your package to your customer's satisfaction.

Blue Tiger International with over 35 years of experience has developed some very key relationships with an array of freight forwarders and carriers and can assist you in making sure you have all the necessary information to make the best choices.

Other organizations like the National Customhouse Broker and Forwarder Association (NCBFAA), Air Forwarder Association (AFA), and Transportation Intermediaries Association (TIA) ... all freight trade associations can produce members who specialize in this IDA Industry Vertical.

Track All Shipments Proactively

Making sure the shipments arrive on time and in workable condition is the guarantee of customer satisfaction, long-term relationships, less headaches, and greater margins.

This can be a service your freight forwarder or carrier provides, but it needs to be clearly identified in that vein, and it must be done proactively ... through every step of an international shipment.

Depending upon distances involved, countries of export and import, and choices of mode and carrier ... some freight can travel 12,000 miles, through 4–5 carrier handoffs, via several customs authorities, and in several modes of transit.

All these convolutions can create exposure to loss, damage, or delay. All three concerns we want to avoid. They lead to loss of revenue, customer dissatisfaction, and lots of stress within your organization.

To mitigate this concern, you need to structure a proactive system to *track and trace* all your international shipments through all the convolutions, hand-offs, and modes of transit.

Many *track and trace* systems can be electronic and advise you through web portals, e-mails, and other electronic means on all your shipping activity.

The benefits of proactively in lieu of a *reactionary* mind set will pay off in spades over the course of time and client relationships.

Understand the Total "Landed Costs"

Landed costs are the total of all the accumulated expenses attached to a shipment moving internationally.

Many of these costs are outlined as follows:

- International freight
- Duties, taxes, and fees
- License charges
- Handling charges
- Domestic freight
- Clearance and handling charges
- ISF fees
- Carrier surcharges
- Demurrage
- Storage and warehousing

Landed cost:

"The total cost you will pay to have your item arrive at your international customer's door."

Sometimes the landed costs can exceed the value of the actual shipment.

In order to protect margins and profits ... it is critical to make sure *transactionally* that you completely understand what the *landed costs* are for your shipment ... then you can make sure these costs are covered in the eventual client invoicing that will follow.

Remember, no one likes surprises ... particularly those that have an additional price tag attached to them.

Be Trade Compliant!

It is imperative that both importers and exporters operate their global supply chains trade compliantly.

This is following procedures and operational practice that accomplishes:

- Due diligence
- Reasonable care
- Supervision and control
- Engagement

This includes:

- Understanding the regulations
- Building internal SOPs to comply with the regulations
- Training personnel on how to interpret and practice the SOPs and in a regulatory manner
- Engaging in government programs that provide evidence of managing secure and compliant global supply chains, such as C-TPAT, Customs-Trade Partnership Against Terrorism

C-TPAT is a voluntary program of security created for importers into the United States managed by CBP, Customs Border and Protection ... now open to include exporters from the USA.

Areas also included in trade compliance have to do with ... documentation, classification [Harmonized Tariff System of the United States (HTSUS)/Schedule B Number(s)], valuation, record keeping, export license requirements, and denied party listing ... to name a few of the operational concerns.

The penalties for noncompliance are fines, penalties, and potential loss of import or export privileges. More serious areas can include criminal prosecutions.

Leverage Free Trade Agreements

North American Free Trade Agreement (NAFTA), Central American Free Trade Agreement (CAFTA) the Caribbean Initiative, and the Israeli Free Trade Agreement are but a few of over 20 agreements in place that the United States engaged in to promote global trade.

These free trade agreements either lower or eliminate duties and taxes between participating countries, thereby lowering *landed costs* or, in other words, reduce logistics costs.

Many companies in an array of manufacturing and distributor verticals are benefiting from these free trade agreements.

Near sourcing in countries like Mexico with companies participating in NAFTA and/or the Maquiladora Program can reap huge financial benefits enhancing competitive advantages.

SUMMARY

Importing and exporting successfully means paying attention to detail. These six areas outlined earlier are a good foundation for creating a detailed and comprehensive approach to managing global supply chain responsibilities.

Our 35 years plus of global supply chain experience have demonstrated that those companies that are diligent about how they manage the freight, logistics, and distribution of parts and equipment will create the best opportunity to:

- Protect margins and grow profits
- Increase customer satisfaction
- Decrease stress and problem areas in global markets
- Better the reputation, which converts to client retention and expansion
- Leverage government programs to lower costs and increase profits and margins

THE AUTHORS

Cook

Tom is Managing Director of Blue Tiger International, (bluetigerintl. com) a premier international business consulting company on supply chain management, trade compliance, purchasing, global trade, and logistics.

Tom was former CEO of American River International in NY and Apex Global Logistics Supply Chain Operation in LA.

He has over 30 years of experience in assisting companies all over the world manage their import and export operations.

He is a member of the NY District Export Council, sits on the board of numerous corporations, and is considered a leader in the business verticals he works in.

He has now authored over 19 books on global trade and is in the middle of an eight book series, titled … *The Global Warrior … Advancing On the Necessary Skill Sets to Compete Effectively in Global Trade.*

Tom is also the Director of the National Institute of World Trade (niwt. org) a 30-year-old educational and training organization, based here on Long Island.

Tom can be reached at tomcook@bluetigerintl.com or 516-359-6232.

Kelly Raia

Kelly is a licensed customhouse broker and trade compliance specialist working for numerous companies assisting them in managing their import and export trade activities.

Kelly was formerly a Vice President at American River International and is now the Vice President of Trade Compliance for Blue Tiger International in NY. She is also involved with numerous companies as their *outsourced* Trade Compliance Manager.

Kelly is a specialist in import and export compliance, logistics, and supply chain management. Many companies depend upon her expertise in facilitating their export sales or import purchasing.

Kelly is a frequent lecturer on compliance and logistics and is a published author.

She can be reached at kelyraia@bluetigerintl.com or 516-236-5716.

INCO TERMS 2010 OVERVIEW

Incoterms 2010: Standard Trade Definitions
Used in International Freight Transactions

For those involved in international freight transactions, the following explanations of international standard trade definitions are useful in outlining risks and responsibilities between buyers and sellers.

This page highlights the Incoterms 2010 changes from Incoterms 2000.

Incoterms 2010

The International Chamber of Commerce has released the table of contents to the Incoterms 2010. Incoterms 2010 consists of only 11 Incoterms, a reduction from the 13 Incoterms 2000.
The Incoterms 2010 are organized into two categories:
Incoterms for any mode or modes of transport:

- *EXW*: Ex works
- *FCA*: Free carrier
- *CPT*: Carriage paid to
- *CIP*: Carriage and insurance paid
- *DAT*: Delivered at terminal (*new*)
- *DAP*: Delivered at place (*new*)
- *DDP*: Delivered duty paid

Incoterms for sea and inland waterway transport only:

- *FAS*: Free alongside ship
- *FOB*: Free on board
- *CFR*: Cost and freight
- *CIF*: Cost, insurance, and freight

The reduction in Incoterms from 13 to 11 different terms was accomplished by substituting *two new Incoterms, DAT (Delivered at terminal)* and *DAP (Delivered at place)*, for DAF (Delivered at frontier), DES (Delivered ex-ship), DEQ (Delivered ex-quay) and DDU (Delivered duty unpaid).
Incoterms 2010 also addresses duties to provide information regarding security-related clearances, such as importer security filings and other chain-of-custody information.
Contrary to some predictions, Incoterm *FAS remains* in Incoterms 2010, since that Incoterm is important in bulk and break-bulk trade.
This interpretation is provided as a guide only.
Please feel free to print this summary of Incoterms 2010.

Incoterms 2010: Expanded Summary

EXW (Ex works)	The buyer bears all costs and risks involved in taking the goods from the seller's premises to the desired destination. The seller's obligation is to make the goods available at his premises (works, factory, warehouse). This term represents minimum obligation for the seller. This term can be used across all modes of transport.
FCA (Free carrier)	The seller's obligation is to hand over the goods, cleared for export, into the charge of the carrier named by the buyer at the named place or point. If no precise point is indicated by the buyer, the seller may choose within the place or range stipulated, where the carrier shall take the goods into his charge. When the seller's assistance is required in making the contract with the carrier, the seller may act at the buyer's risk and expense. This term can be used across all modes of transport.
CPT (Carriage paid to)	The seller pays the freight for the carriage of goods to the named destination. The risk of loss or damage to the goods occurring after the delivery has been made to the carrier is transferred from the seller to the buyer. This term requires the seller to clear the goods for export and can be used across all modes of transport.
CIP (Carriage and insurance paid to)	The seller has the same obligations as under CPT, but has the responsibility of obtaining insurance against the buyer's risk of loss or damage of goods during the carriage. The seller is required to clear the goods for export, however, is only required to obtain insurance on minimum coverage. This term requires the seller to clear the goods for export and can be used across all modes of transport.
DAT (Delivered at terminal)	**New Term—May be used for all transport modes** Seller delivers when the goods, once unloaded from the arriving means of transport, are placed at the disposal of the buyer at a named terminal at the named port or place of destination. *Terminal* includes quay, warehouse, container yard or road, and rail or air terminal. Both parties should agree the terminal and, if possible, a point within the terminal at which point the risks will transfer from the seller to the buyer of the goods. If it is intended that the seller is to bear all the costs and responsibilities from the terminal to another point, DAP or DDP may apply. **Responsibilities** • Seller is responsible for the costs and risks to bring the goods to the point specified in the contract • Seller should ensure that their forwarding contract mirrors the contract of sale • Seller is responsible for the export clearance procedures • Importer is responsible to clear the goods for import, arrange import customs formalities, and pay import duty • If the parties intend the seller to bear the risks and costs of taking the goods from the terminal to another place then the DAP term may apply

(Continued)

DAP (Delivered at place)	**New Term—May be used for all transport modes** Seller delivers the goods when they are placed at the disposal of the buyer on the arriving means of transport ready for unloading at the named place of destination. Parties are advised to specify as clearly as possible the point within the agreed place of destination, because risks transfer at this point from seller to buyer. If the seller is responsible for clearing the goods, paying duties, etc., consideration should be given to using the DDP term. **Responsibilities** • Seller bears the responsibility and risks to deliver the goods to the named place • Seller is advised to obtain contracts of carriage that match the contract of sale • Seller is required to clear the goods for export • If the seller incurs unloading costs at place of destination, unless previously agreed, they are not entitled to recover any such costs • Importer is responsible for effecting customs clearance and paying any customs duties
DDP (Delivered duty paid)	The seller is responsible for delivering the goods to the named place in the country of importation, including all costs and risks in bringing the goods to import destination. This includes duties, taxes, and customs formalities. This term may be used irrespective of the mode of transport.
FAS (Free alongside ship—named port of shipment)	The seller must place the goods alongside the ship at the named port. The seller must clear the goods for export. Suitable only for maritime transport, but NOT for multimodal sea transport in containers [see Incoterms 2010, International Chamber of Commerce (ICC) publication 715]. This term is typically used for heavy-lift or bulk cargo.
FOB (Free on board—named port of shipment)	The seller must load themselves the goods on board the vessel nominated by the buyer. Cost and risk are divided when the goods are actually on board of the vessel (this rule is new!). The seller must clear the goods for export. The term is applicable for maritime and inland waterway transport only, but NOT for multimodal sea transport in containers (see Incoterms 2010, ICC publication 715). The buyer must instruct the seller the details of the vessel and the port where the goods are to be loaded, and there is no reference to, or provision for, the use of a carrier or forwarder. This term has been greatly misused over the last three decades ever since Incoterms 1980 explained that FCA should be used for container shipments.

(Continued)

CFR (Cost and freight)	The seller must pay the costs and freight required in bringing the goods to the named port of destination. The risk of loss or damage is transferred from seller to buyer when the goods pass over the ship's rail in the port of shipment. The seller is required to clear the goods for export. This term should only be used for sea or inland waterway transport.
CIF (Cost, insurance, and freight)	The seller has the same obligations, as under CFR, however, he is also required to provide insurance against the buyer's risk of loss or damage to the goods during transit. The seller is required to clear the goods for export. This term should only be used for sea or inland waterway transport.

Note: An Incoterm must be accompanied by a *named place* ex. FOB *Sydney, EXW Tahiti*

LANDED COST MODELING SOP

Effective January 1, 2018, all divisions of your company will utilize a landed cost calculator for import shipments in determining the *true and real* cost(s) to Systemax when comparing vendor options in the decision-making process.

It is critical that we comprehensively understand what our *total costs* are in making the decisions on where, what, and how much we buy from overseas or domestic suppliers.

- We also need to document this process in our product files, available for review upon request
- Following is an outline of what are landed costs as an overview in general, followed with some additional thoughts on specifically sourcing from China, where the majority of our imports derive from
- This SOP concludes with a draft calculator, which should be utilized as a guide for actually determining landed costs for your products

What is Landed Cost?

Establishing *landed costs* for the products that a company handles can be difficult and convoluted. All businesses that import or export need to understand what the total cost of goods is for what they are buying or selling. In order to accurately calculate the landed cost, all factors beyond the obvious primary price must be considered. Calculating *landed cost* is critical in understanding what a product actually costs and therefore what is can be sold for.

This impacts margin considerations, which are one of the most important aspects of managing a business in a public market.

Landed Cost Definition

Landed cost is the total cost of a product once it has arrived at the buyer's door. This list of components that are needed to determine landed costs include the original cost of the item, all brokerage and logistics fees, complete shipping costs, customs duties, tariffs, taxes, insurance, currency conversion, crating costs, and handling fees. Not all of these components are present in every shipment, but all that are must be considered part of the landed cost.

Clearly it is advantageous to reduce the cost of each or any component of landed cost. Each one will allow the seller to lower the final selling price or increase the margin associated with that sale.

When considering the *landed cost or true cost* of any item that is shipped internationally, there are components that need to be included. For instance, determining *Harmonized system codes* (HS codes) or Harmonized tariff codes (HTS codes) is essential for over 98% of global trade. Once the HS code or HTS code is obtained, the mandated duties and tariffs can be established. Accuracy of these harmonized codes is of significant importance, as misclassification will result in incorrect tariff codes, incorrect duties, and eventually customs delays and fines. When customs delays and fines are levied, they themselves need to be calculated into the landed cost model.

Global trade management, supply chain management, and international logistics all have many moving parts. In this economic climate, trade agreements are being forged and modified at a very high rate. HTS codes vary from place to place, cost of fuel can drastically affect shipping costs, currency valuations ebb and flow constantly, and the list of variables goes on and on. Limiting the variables to a manageable few will streamline operations and keep overall cost structures as stable as possible.

Additional variables, such as, but not limited to: quantity purchased, INCO term, insurance, inland freight, and storage/warehousing all impact landed costs, but are often not considered by purchasing and sourcing personnel at the time of product acquisition.

Controlling costs, ensuring timely deliveries, and customs compliance are serious issues that every international business is concerned with. Landed cost is a significant component of all of these concerns. Establishing a *landed cost model* is not just important, it is essential.

ADDITIONAL CONSIDERATIONS: HOW TO CALCULATE LANDED COST WHEN IMPORTING FROM CHINA

As an importer, made in China is a good choice for many products which can sell locally or online with a good profit. Though your company purchases goods from all over the world and the diversity will continue to grow ... China presents itself as our largest source of imported goods.

Making sure we are earning the correct margins on merchandise sales from China is a key responsibility of all purchasing and sourcing managers. Additionally, supply chain and logistics considerations must be contemplated, therefore those Systemax managers with these specific responsibilities, must be considered as part of the landed cost model.

Congruently, Systemax trade compliance consultants must be in the loop, as total costs will be impacted by various areas in import and export trade compliance issues, such as, but not limited to ... vendor choices, INCO terms, and HTS codes utilized.

But in fact, too many both *seasoned* and new-to-China buyers focus only on product purchase price and then get an ugly surprise when they have an accumulation of additional costs when the goods arrive in their destination country, which they did not plan for in the budget or when margins were considered.

Find a supplier and get a quote is just the first step. All buyers should calculate a landed cost of the product they are purchasing before actually importing it. *Do not go through the trouble of importing and then finding out you spent more than you can sell it for.*

This outline will help you study and understand the true cost of the product you are buying from China. Let's begin.

What is Landed Cost?

This kind of cost is the total cost of a product once it has arrived at the buyer's door.

This list of components that are needed to determine include *the original cost of the item, all brokerage and logistics fees, complete shipping costs, customs duties, tariffs, taxes, insurance, currency conversion, crating costs, and handling fees.*

Not all of these components are present in every shipment, but all that are must be considered part of the total cost.

You can check through a chart in the following:

Incoterms 2010

	A	B	C	D	E	F	G	H	I	J	K
1	Incoterm	Loading on truck	Export - Customs declaration	Carriage to port of export	Unloading of truck in port of export	Loading charges in port of export	Carriage to port of import	Unloading charges in port of import	Loading on truck in port of import	Carriage to place of destination	Insurance
2	EXW	Buyer	Buyer	Buyer	Buyer	Buyer	Buyer	Buyer	Buyer	Buyer	N/A
3	FCA	Seller	Seller	Seller	Buyer	Buyer	Buyer	Buyer	Buyer	Buyer	N/A
4	FAS	Seller	Seller	Seller	Seller	Buyer	Buyer	Buyer	Buyer	Buyer	N/A
5	FOB	Seller	Seller	Seller	Seller	Seller	Buyer	Buyer	Buyer	Buyer	N/A
6	CFR	Seller	Seller	Seller	Seller	Seller	Seller	Buyer	Buyer	Buyer	N/A
7	CIF	Seller	Seller	Seller	Seller	Seller	Seller	Buyer	Buyer	Buyer	Seller
8	DAT	Seller	Seller	Seller	Seller	Seller	Seller	Seller	Buyer	Buyer	N/A
9	DAP	Seller	Seller	Seller	Seller	Seller	Seller	Seller	Seller	Seller	N/A
10	CPT	Seller	Seller	Seller	Seller	Seller	Seller	Seller	Seller	Seller	N/A
11	CIP	Seller	Seller	Seller	Seller	Seller	Seller	Seller	Seller	Seller	Seller
12	DDP	Seller	Seller	Seller	Seller	Seller	Seller	Seller	Seller	Seller	N/A

The Incoterms rules are intended primarily to clearly communicate the tasks, costs, and risks associated with the transportation and delivery of goods. As you can see, the table shows several fees. Some advise that the INCO term advises a point in time where risk and cost passes between a seller and a buyer.

Of course, you can choose DDP. In this case, you do not need to do any calculation by yourself. But obviously, a considerable amount of money is potentially at risk.

That's why most importers will choose FOB, which means let the supplier deliver the cargo to the outbound gateway, border crossing, port, or airport and you'll take it from there. Imports from China are typically purchased on a FOB or FCA basis.

Then you can handle most of the rest by working together with your international transportation provider, customhouse broker, and/or your freight forwarder.

An example:

There are many variables involved, so use the following as a guide:

- *Cost of goods*: $ variable depending on unit price and quantity
- *Import assistance company*: $ variable depending on level of service
- *Freight*: $ variable, depending on volume, port it is coming from/ going to, time of year, freight company used, etc. Allow $2000–$5000
- *Duty*: $ variable percentage of the value customs put on your goods
- *Tax* (*goods and services tax or value added tax*): $ variable percentage of (the customs value of cost of goods + freight + insurance + customs duty)
- *Insurance*
- Inland freight
- Other, e.g., customs clearance, document fees, wharf charges, etc.— Allow another 3% on top of everything else

The most complex part:

Import Customs Duties and Taxes

One common mistake here is to ask the supplier in China to confirm the taxes and duties in the destination market. Suppliers may not be knowledgeable about how your government would classify the given product and what regulations apply.

U.S. Customs (CBP) regulations make Systemax totally responsible for HTS classification.

Before finding the tariff amount for a particular product, you need to identify the harmonized tariff schedule number for their product.

Find HS Code of Your Products

HS codes (Harmonized commodity description and coding system) are part of an international classification system, which is simple for customs locating the specific item among catalogs, and it associates an imported product category with a specific import duty.

Please note: HS code is also referred to as *tariff codes, customs codes, harmonized codes, export codes, import codes, and harmonized commodity description and coding system codes.* So never get confused. When there's a code representing the product, that's the HS code.

HS codes can be varied in different countries. The code that your supplier provided for you is just a basis. You can find the most accurate classification according to the first four or six numbers here.

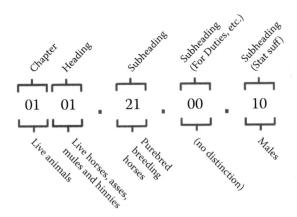

It should be listed on the commercial invoice correctly. Customs duties and taxes will be calculated by HS code of different products and the declared value (see Section Declared Value) on the commercial invoice.

Knowing the right code of your product is of central importance to your importing process. Without it or error using it may not only delay customs clearance, but could also incur unexpected costs. You can find more details here.

Declared Value

Customs duties and taxes are percentages calculated based on the customs value. The customs value is based on the declared value, which in turn shall be stated on the commercial invoice—a document issued by the supplier for clearance.

In the United States, the FOB purchase value is what is typically the declared value to U.S. Customs (CBP).

Duty/Tax Free Amount (De Minimis Value)

The de minimis value of the destination country is the declared value of your shipment below which duty and tax will not apply. Meaning, if you are importing a shipment with a total declared value LESS than this amount, duty and tax do not apply (certain products may be subject to other types of fees or taxes, that is, alcohol and tobacco).

Certain countries have a separate threshold. In what follows we show you some data from publicly available sources or our practical experiences. We accept that it may not be perfectly accurate or up to date.

- *Australia*: 1000 AUD
- *Canada*: 20 CAD
- *Europe*: 22 EUR
- *Japan*: 130 USD
- *New Zealand*: 308 USD (incl. freight)
- *Russia*: 10,000 RUB
- *Singapore*: 307 USD
- *South America*: 50 USD
- *United Kingdom*: 15 GBP
- *United States*: 200 USD

Please note: It's always the importer's responsibility to ensure that the correct declared value is stated on the commercial invoice. This responsibility cannot be shifted to the Chinese supplier.

Import Customs Duties

Duty

A duty is a kind of tax, often associated with customs, levied by a state on the import or export of goods in international trade. A duty levied on goods being imported is referred to as an import duty. What we mentioned as duty here are all import customs duties.

A free tool online http://www.importcalculator.com/.

3.1.1

Almost all countries have three levels of duties for origin countries. Following is a screenshot from the *Harmonized tariff schedule of the United States*.

General	Rates of Duty 1		2
		Special	
6.7%	Free (A, AU, B, BH, CA, CL, CO, E, IL, JO, KR, MA, MX, OM, P, PA, PE, SG)		90%
4.4%	Free (A, AU, B, BH, CA, CL, CO, E, IL, JO, KR, MA, MX, OM, P, PA, PE,		35%

- Imports from most countries are dutiable at the normal trade relation's rates under the general header in column 1.
- Goods from countries that do not have normal trade relations with the United States are dutiable at the full rates in column 2.
- Goods from some countries enjoy duty-free status. They are shown under the special header in column 1 of the tariff schedule.

You can take the three different rates as most loved (1), most hated (2), and others (general).

The first column (general) is referred to as the *most favored nation*, and China is considered a *most favored nation* by most countries. You can find a list of all countries under U.S. sanctions.

3.1.2

Between China and some countries, there're duty preferences. It's called certificate of origin.

- Certificate of origin form f for China-Chile FTA (Form F)
- Form for the Free Trade Agreement between the Government of the People's Republic of China and the Government of New Zealand (Form N)
- Certificate of origin China-Pakistan FTA (Form P)
- Certificate of origin Asia-Pacific Trade Agreement (Form B)
- Asean-China Free Trade Area Preferential Tariff Certificate of Origin (Form E)

Duty Calculation

It's easy to imagine: Products that are not manufactured in your country tend to have lower customs duty rates, sometimes as low as 0%. On the other hand, the opposite is often true for products that are considered part of an important industry in your country, sometimes-punitive duties unlimited.

For example, you are an importer in the European Union (EU). And you want to import T-shirts for women or girls locally. You are told that the HS code is 6106900020.

As you know, all EU member states have the same customs duty rates on products imported from non-EU countries. An importer only pays customs once, for products imported from China. Custom duties are not added to products sold within the European Union. Thus, your Spanish and German customers will not need to pay customs on products that have already entered EU territory.

3.2.1
Go to http://www.hscode.org/ and type in *T-shirt* and search, or just type in "610690." You can try both reverse searches to make sure the HS code is correct.

3.2.2
Go to http://ec.europa.eu/taxation_customs/dds2/taric/taric_consultation.jsp and fill in the *goods code* and *country of origin*, which is 610690 and China-CN. Then dig to the final 12%.

In what follows is a list of common products and their respective duty rate to the EU:

- *Wristwatches*: 4.5%
- *Tablet PC*: 0%

- *Solar panels*: 0%
- *Electric bikes*: 6%
- *LED bulb lights*: 4.7%
- *Peanuts*: 12.8%

Please note: There are other types of duties except for the regular one.

For example, if you are an importer in the United States, you are responsible for knowing your goods from China are subject to an anti-dumping duty (ADD) or counter-veiling duty (CVD) case. If so, then your customs declaration must be of the type corresponding to the type of import duties imposed.

Some ADD or CVD rates are as much as 100% of the value of the goods.

Import Taxes

Value-Added Tax

A value-added tax (VAT) is a form of consumption tax. From the perspective of the buyer, it is a tax on the purchase price. From that of the seller, it is a tax only on the value added to a product, material, or service, from an accounting point of view, by this stage of its manufacture or distribution.

In the EU, for example, different member states have different VAT rates. However, the standard VAT rate applies to most consumer and industrial products imported from China. Here, shows a list of VAT rates in different EU countries.

Please note: The VAT added on the imports can be offset against VAT added on sales.

Goods and Services Tax

Goods and services tax (GST) applies to most products imported to Australia, 10% on most goods and services transactions. GST is levied on most transactions in the production process, but is refunded to all parties in the chain of production other than the final consumer.

Insurance

All goods imported from China and worldwide are insured by our master cargo insurance policy. This protects our merchandise on an *All Risk Warehouse to Warehouse* basis. Specific insuring terms and conditions can be found with our Corporate Risk Management Department in Port Washington, NY.

For landed cost calculation purposes, utilize $0.10/$100 of insured value. If a purchase is valued at $50,000 USD, then the insurance cost is calculated at 50,000 divided by 100 × 0.10 = $50 USD.

Inland Freight

Our merchandise will typically arrive at an ocean port, airport, or at the border. It will then move from the point to our final destination distribution location.

That inland freight cost must be obtained from our international transportation provider and included in the landed cost model.

LANDED COST CALCULATOR

Category	Cost(s)
FOB/FCA Cost of merchandise	
Pickup at supplier	
Inland transportation to a port or airport	
Origin terminal and port fees	
Export licensing, documentation, and duties	
Ocean, air, or truck international freight	
Import clearance, documentation, and handling	
Duties, taxes, VAT/GST	
Terminal and port fees at destination	
Customs review	
Harbor maintenance fees	
Cargo insurance	
Inland transportation to importer's location	
Storage/warehousing/distribution	

CONCLUSION

Protecting our profits and growing our business are key responsibilities of everyone involved in sourcing, purchasing, merchandising, logistics, or supply chain.

Making sure we are aware of all our costs, then applying sound practice to lower or costs and risks are all primary responsibilities.

Understanding landed cost modeling is necessary to control margins and accomplish our Systemax corporate goals.

TRADE COMPLIANCE MANAGEMENT

The *Link* Between Service Providers and Shippers

Trade compliance management is an integral part of every operation engaged in global trade. All carriers, service providers, freight forwarders, customhouse brokers, 3PL's, and all related companies that are *part and parcel* to the supply chain.

Too often those management teams engaged in moving the freight as carriers and service providers have determined that the principal responsibility for *Trade compliance management* rests with the principal shipper, importer, or exporter.

This is a misnomer and often misunderstood principal of global trade. Government authorities understand well ... the connection between service providers and their principal shippers ... and hold them equally responsible for the various aspects of trade compliance management.

While each entity is responsible to a certain extent and also in different ways ... the only true compliant supply chain is one in which all parties are collaborative and equally trade compliant.

An importer who is completely trade compliant and holds its internal controls to the highest standards, yet utilizes a customhouse broker who is not as trade compliant as they need to be ... *does not have a trade compliant supply chain!* As a mistake made by the customhouse broker could have ramifications to that importer even though the action was indirect and unforeseen.

Quality and experienced trade compliance officers working for shippers understand they need to have reach, influence, and in some cases an *override* in the decision-making process when it comes to choosing and managing service providers.

Well-managed trade compliance managers recognize the importance of four elements of a successful trade program:

- Due diligence
- Reasonable care
- Supervision and control
- Proactive engagement

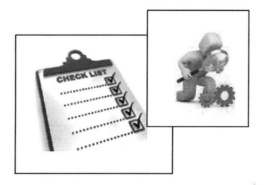

In the category of *supervision and control* …, it is understood by government authorities that principal shippers of cargo (importers and exporters) are likely to utilize third party service providers to assist them in the logistics of the supply chain.

Though this responsibility is *outsourced* …, the importer or exporter still has a responsibility to make sure the freight forwarder or customhouse broker is managing their responsibilities compliantly.

Many shippers I have come across look to the service provider as the experienced party in trade compliance and defer to their expertise for not only guidance, but also for *managing and handling* their trade compliance responsibilities.

In my experience, there are only a handful of service providers with a serious and comprehensive trade compliance capability; and these are few and far between.

It is a better practice to handle your own trade compliance aligned with industry professionals who specialize in trade compliance … consultants, attorneys, and trade compliance specialists.

Additionally, in managing service providers and carriers in respect to trade compliance management, *we make the following 10 recommendations*:

1. Deeply investigate and scrutinize the service providers in their trade compliance responsibilities and determine if they have dedicated personnel who have a matured expertise in this regard.
2. Do they work with and support their clients in mutual trade compliance areas of responsibility? Do they offer training programs?
3. Do they have a robust technology that helps manage import and export regulatory concerns?
4. Do they have a self-auditing capability to assure that they and their clients are trade compliant?
5. How are their relationships with the various government agencies that work with, such agencies as, but not limited to: Customs Border and Protection, Bureau of Industry and Security, Food and Drug Administration, Federal Maritime Commission, etc.? This would include both at a local level and in Washington, DC.
6. Do they have a record of any concerning violations?
7. If they have a multiple office and agency structure... do they enforce and train those local personnel in trade compliance management?
8. Are you aware how they manage their recordkeeping responsibilities? Do they have written SOP's and business protocols in place?
9. Are they C-TPAT certified?
10. Are they making sure … you as their customer … is trade compliant? A trade compliant service provider only has trade compliant customers!

Trade compliance is a very important element of managing global supply chains. There is a very strong connection between principal importers and exporters and those that service their logistics needs.

Managing this extension of your supply chain and developing a *partnership* approach will work in everyone's best interest in reducing risk and maximizing opportunity for successful global trade!

Thomas Cook is Managing Director of Blue Tiger International, a premier supply chain consulting company. Tom can be reached at tomcok@bluetigerintl.com or 516-359-6232.

TRADE COMPLIANCE ISSUES IN MERGERS AND ACQUISITIONS

As part of the due diligence process in mergers and acquisitions, companies must not overlook the trade compliance profile of the new business partner. In recent years, the Export Administration Regulations, Office of Foreign Asset Control Regulations, International Traffic in Arms Regulations, Customs Regulations, and Foreign Corrupt Practices Act have all played a role in enforcing successor liability.

Trade Compliance

Global supply chains require companies to be familiar with the rules and regulations of the various government agencies throughout all countries in which that supply chain operates. Trade compliance requirements are country specific and may also be commodity driven. For example, an export shipment of salted butter may not require an export license to be shipped, but will require an import license and approval from a Food and Drug/Health Dept. prior to importation. An import shipment of remote control cars may not require a license to import, but will require Federal Communications Commission approval at the time of import.

Frequently, trade compliance is looked at after the acquisition has been completed by the business development acquisition team. In these instances, a company may be in for a rude awakening as they discover there are duties owed to CBP and/or export violations to be disclosed to the BIS.

In many instances, the financial team working with the company prior to acquisition may be able to ascertain a considerable amount of information regarding compliance if they are trained to ask the right questions and have an understanding of trade compliance.

Managing trade compliance within a company is a detailed process that requires the cooperation of overlapping departments including shipping, logistics, finance, purchasing, sales, and legal. This process may be onerous on its own without the added disadvantage of not being familiar with the processes, commodities, sales destinations, and vendor agreements of a new acquisition. That said, the most basic trade requirements are the same for all companies whether they are importing screws and food products or exporting coal and aircraft parts.

When compliance violations are found in a company, massive amounts of time by internal personnel or the expense of hiring outside assistance to determine if the compliance issue is endemic or a onetime incident may be necessary.

Export Trade Compliance Basics

In the United States, there are several government agencies involved in the export process. Within the Department of Commerce there is the BIS and the Bureau of Census. The Office of Foreign Asset Controls is part of the Department of the Treasury. Companies that deal with items on the United States Munitions List will also fall under the jurisdiction of the Department of State Office of Defense Trade Controls (DTC). The Homeland Security's Bureau of CBP is also involved in the enforcement of export regulations.

The EARs are the rules by which the BIS regulates and controls the export of goods from the United States. The EAR also controls certain activities, such as the transfer of information to foreign nationals or engaging in restrictive trade boycotts not sanctioned by the United States. Companies that export from the United States are required to comply with these regulations and must have a process for managing their exports and international activities such as an export management compliance program. The export management compliance program becomes the game plan for staying compliant and avoiding export violations.

Export Management Compliance Program

As previously mentioned, the core elements of an effective EMCP are the same for all companies regardless of the commodities and services they are shipping and providing. However, there are additional steps that must be taken for those companies who are engaged in commodities that are controlled for export due to the type of commodity and/or for transactions with those companies and countries that are listed on a various denial list or companies that are domiciled in an embargoed country or restricted country.

The basic elements of an EMCP will minimally include:

1. Senior management commitment
2. Identification of risks in the current export program
3. Formal written manual
4. Training and awareness
5. Screening of business partners, customers, financial institutions, supply chain partners
6. Recordkeeping requirements
7. Periodic auditing and monitoring
8. System for reporting violations and handling compliance issues
9. System for implementing corrective actions where a compliance issue is indicated
10. Partnering with knowledgeable and compliant service providers

Senior Management Commitment

Managing compliance requires senior management support. Compliance touches many silos within a company, which in turn requires managing delicate relationships, such as between sales and shipping. Managing compliance may delay a shipment for a day or so while stones are turned to ensure the customer is not the *Jones Company* that is indicated on the Denied Parties List. Senior management's support of compliance efforts allows compliance measures to be successfully implemented within the supply chain. The lack of senior management support will be taken by anyone looking to skirt the compliance program as if management does not care, then why should I care.

In the due diligence process of mergers and acquisitions, it is simple enough to get a feel if a company has any compliance on its radar by a few key indicators such as: a mission statement that touches on compliance and/or regulatory matters; company website includes links to government regulatory sites; or company website lists harmonized tariff numbers and/or ECCNs. Any of these listed on a website does not ensure compliance exists within the organization, but it does indicate the company has minimally dabbled in compliance.

Identification of Risks in the Current Export Program

There are a few quick and dirty questions whose responses can identify potential risks in the company's export profile. Are there products subject to the CCL or U.S. Munitions List? What industries are our customers involved with? Where are our customers located? Do we have routed export transactions? Do we utilize any software programs for screening our customers and service providers? Blank stares or hemming and hawing will indicate these basic compliance measures are not in place.

If a company is exporting, they are subject to export controls. Identifying the potential risks in the export supply chain is key to determining what level of compliance should be in place and where the potential for fires exist within the supply chain.

For those companies that state they only have domestic sales, there are additional questions that need to be asked such as are any of the ship to/bill to details indicating a location in a foreign country? Are we using Federal Express, UPS, or a trucker to move the goods to a border location? Are we shipping the goods to a freight forwarder's warehouse? Each of these situations would indicate the goods will be moving internationally and subject to the export regulations. A written manual maps out the scope of the company's compliance program: responsible parties within the organization, identification of documentary requirements specific to the company's transactions, sample documents, and so on. The manual becomes the *go to* resource whether in hard copy or posted on the company intranet. The ability to obtain a copy of this document is priceless, as it may indicate the program to be robust and dynamic or a carbon copy lifted from an Internet site. Either outcome will give provide a good feel for the company's level of compliance.

Training and Awareness

In recent years, many companies under budget restraints have reduced training within the organization. A good compliance program provides personnel with the training to understand the importance of compliance, as well as to provide a forum for vibrant discussions on new business opportunities and existing customer issues.

Training can be in the form of webinars, attending outside forums, or a monthly *lunch and learn* update. Training may also be piggybacked with other meetings that are being held within a department, such as a quarterly sales meeting. All training should be documented as to who attended, as well as the content of the training and materials provided.

Asking general questions about company training in regards to Occupational Health and Safety Administration (OSHA) or any human resources training can easily include compliance training.

Screening of Business Partners, Customers, Financial Institutions, and Supply Chain Partners

As previously mentioned, identification of risks in the supply chain must include how the company screens its business partners. The U.S. Government maintains lists of companies, individuals, and countries that U.S. companies may not do business with or require the prior authorization of the U.S. Government in order to do business.

The key lists include:

Department of Commerce: Denied Party List, Unverified List, Entity List

Department of State: Debarred List and Nonproliferation Sanctions

Department of Treasury: Office of Foreign Asset Control, Specially Designated Nationals

List and Sanction Evaders List

This area of due diligence could be tested during the financial soundness testing portion of the acquisition by the accounting team responsible.

Recordkeeping Requirements

Recordkeeping requirements under the Export Administration Regulations and Foreign Trade Regulations are for five years from the date of export. Under the International Traffic in Arms Regulations, the DTC requires records to be kept for five years from the date of expiration of the export license.

All companies engaged in export activity must keep records including, but not limited to: memoranda, notes, correspondence, contracts, financial records, restrictive trade practice or boycott documents, electronic export information records, and corresponding documentation.

Recordkeeping should also include correspondence with the BIS or any other government agency in regards to requested information, warning letters, and/or issued penalty notices.

Periodic Auditing and Monitoring

Many companies have implemented compliance programs that limp along and have lost momentum once the initial training and awareness have taken place. Compliance programs are repetitive and personnel get into a groove of working within the program without much enthusiasm. This can set up the environment for a compliance program becoming lax and ineffective.

Periodic monitoring of shipments and a regularly scheduled audit keeps everyone on their toes. The ability to monitor AES Direct Monthly Compliance Report issued by Census, for examples, ensures the trade compliance manager as the AES account administrator is seeing the monthly picture if not the daily filings. Managing by exception and pulling those files that have a *verify* message for example, is a great tool for monitoring. Regularly scheduled audits of records should include pulling a few *test files* to see if the records are in place for everything from the customer's purchase order to the electronic export information copy and actual payment.

Once again this area of concern could be included as part of the diligence by the financial team as part of their questions.

System for Reporting Violations and Handling Compliance Issues

As part of the periodic auditing process, it is likely a problem will be uncovered. Depending on the nature and extent of the problem, it may be necessary to report the problem to the responsible government agency. Within the company, there may be reporting up to senior management or legal. Regardless of how the company is structured, make certain to involve management prior to any government reporting.

Each government agency has a different mechanism and even different requirement for disclosure. Census requires a company to make a correction to the electronic export information filing once that error is discovered. BIS encourages voluntary disclosure, but as of this writing, voluntary disclosure is not a requirement. While the majority of voluntary disclosures made to the BIS result in a warning letter and no monetary penalty, that is not always the case, as we will see further along in this chapter.

In many instances, it is possible to perform an Internet search to determine if a company has had BIS or the Office of Foreign Asset Controls violations, as these agencies make a point of publicizing violations.

System for Implementing Corrective Actions

As part of the reporting of the violation, the company will provide a plan of corrective action as part of the disclosure. Once the dust settles, the plan must be implemented. Many corrective action plans will include retraining, review of actions and section of compliance manual covering the area where the violation took place, interview of personnel, and rehashing the gory details to avoid future violations.

In the due diligence process, asking for the "well what happened after the violation took place" is important. If a reprimand was issued and everyone feels relieved, is there another chapter covering the next steps that were followed? Additionally, revisiting the issue by reviewing documentation and the actual parties involved in the violation will provide transparency and allow the trade compliance manager to get to the heart of the current view of compliance in the new company.

Partnering with Knowledgeable and Compliant Service Providers

Most companies work with a freight forwarder to handle their export transactions. The freight forwarder will prepare export documentation and arrange bookings with the air/ocean/rail carriers and truckers. By default, these companies consider their freight forwarder to be experts and heavily rely on the forwarder's expertise at moving the freight, as well as compliance with regulations.

In most penalty cases, the actual shipper is held responsible even if the actions of the freight forwarder caused the violation. Therefore, all shippers must confirm their freight forwarder is knowledgeable, has their own internal compliance program in place, and trains their personnel to follow the rules and regulations.

In making an acquisition, the company should obtain a list of the service providers being used and those companies should be interviewed to determine the level of compliance within that business partner's organizational structure. A compliant exporter aligns himself with a compliant forwarder.

Additional Note for those Companies Engaged in Exports under the International Traffic in Arms

Companies that are acquired and merging with a new parent that have licenses under the prior company's name must ensure they amend licenses and agreement with the Directorate of Defense Trade Controls. If the company is a new U.S. registrant, a list of open licenses and agreements should be provided to the Directorate of Defense Trade Controls to make the necessary name changes.

Failure to properly transfer over licenses and/or make necessary name changes by becoming a new registrant may result in freight delays, seizures, and monetary penalties.

Successor Liability and Export Violations

Sigma-Aldrich: Unlicensed exports made by the acquired company that took place prior to acquisition. Penalty: $1.7 million: Bureau of Industry and Security.

Qioptiq: Unlicensed exports made by the acquired company that took place prior to acquisition. Penalty: $25 million, Defense Trade Controls.

Sirchie fingerprint: Violation of denial order made by company acquired that took place prior to acquisition. Penalty: $12.6 million: Bureau of Industry and Security.

Case Study #1

Gator Enterprises is a computer software service that has decided to grow its business by moving into products complementary to the services they offer to their clients. The software designed by Gator Enterprises monitors gauges, actuators, and valves. Gator Enterprises has many customers in the construction industry and has determined a niche market for reselling these types of valves. Gator Enterprises closes a deal with Red Chair Valves, a valve manufacturer.

Red Chairs product line is diverse and includes items such as check valves for basement pumps and valves that are used in construction drilling. Gator Enterprises is excited about this expansion into new territory and following the due diligence on the acquisition side move ahead into selling their software services to Red Chair's customer base, as well as selling valves to the Gator Enterprise customer base.

Gator Enterprise has a sales manager who has fielded questions regarding export compliance in the past. The company is knowledgeable about screening potential customers through the various government Denied Party Lists, and the company has a list of countries that are embargoed and to which Gator Enterprises refuses to sell.

The challenge is that Red Chair has items they are now beginning to sell internationally. Some of the valve types are controlled for export. The sales manager has stumbled upon this while reading an export compliance blog post and recognizes their new acquisition has this issue.

The sales manager proceeds to perform a review of the Commerce Control List along with technical support from the Red Chair design staff. While the Department of Commerce permits a company to self-classify their products, the sales manager is not familiar enough with Red Chair and its product team and decides to reach out to the BIS for assistance. The sales manager registers for the SNAP on the BIS website. Through SNAP, the sales manager verifies the determinations made by the Red Chair design staff were correct. The sales manager now implements a compliance plan to manage these new products. The compliance plan includes:

- Training staff on export controls and restrictions on the specific controlled products
- Creating a freight forwarder letter of instruction for use by shipping as a compliance tool to supervise the actions of the freight forwarder
- Reviewing and updating the Gator Enterprise compliance manual to include the new product line

- Senior management rollout to bring management up-to-date on changes that have been made and to obtain budget approval for training for the following year

Import Trade Compliance Basics

The Bureau of CBP is part of the Department of Homeland Security. CBP has responsibilities for border control, immigration, border security, agricultural protection, and enforcement of the customs regulations. Any shipment being imported into the United States is subject to the customs clearance process and the payment of duties and taxes. Additional government agency requirements may be required depending on the nature of the commodity being imported.

Import Compliance Management Program

Importers are required to exercise reasonable care and supervision and control over the import process. Many importers hire a customs broker to handle the customs clearance and entry submission to CBP on their behalf. Unfortunately, many importers judge the performance of their customs broker by the success and expeditious delivery of the import shipment. This faith in the broker's expertise usually results in an ignorance of the rules and regulations by which the importer is held accountable.

CBP makes available many valuable resources to the import trade community. Among these resources are the Informed Compliance Publications. In reviewing the listing of the Informed Compliance Publications, importers will have a good idea of what the basic elements of their import compliance management program should include. In addition to the Informed Compliance Publications, an importer can access the Focused Assessment Preassessment Survey to better understand the expectations of CBP in the event the company is challenged on its import process.

Similar to the diligence in ascertaining export compliance levels, companies looking to acquire a company with imports as part of its profile need to establish the levels of compliance with CBP regulations and other government agency requirements.

Corporate Structure

CBP is very interested in how risk is assessed on import shipments including the frequency of assessments, changes made due to assessments, and who has the overall responsibility for these matters. Where compliance sits internally in an organization can determine how seriously compliance is taken, such as being a corporate function versus being a fall back responsibility on the receiving manager.

The setting for the compliance culture within a company is dictated by how management views compliance with the customs regulations. Is there a dedicated group that manages the import process together, for example the purchasing department works with business development or are import decisions made independently without following any guidelines? Is there a working compliance manual for personnel to follow? These factors add up to the corporate view of compliance and the overall level of import compliance within the company

Invoices

In addition to its many other responsibilities and functions, CBP is a revenue agency that protects the financial well-being of the United States. The manner in which import shipments are valued is one of the key elements to the entry process, as we will see in the next section. CBP does not examine each and every shipment that is imported into the United States.

CBP relies on the commercial invoice that is the heart of the transaction detailing many facts about the import transaction. The invoice is so key to the import process that the failure of an importer to present a proper invoice is a violation of the basic bond requirement, and the failure of a broker to correct the importer is a lack of reasonable care on the part of the broker.

Invoices must be in English and must include the following:

1. Probable port of entry
2. Name and address of importer of record
3. Name and address of ultimate consignee if known at the time of import and if different from the importer of record
4. Name and address of the manufacturer and shipper
5. Description of merchandise, including the name each item is known
6. Unit price of the merchandise
7. Currency of sale
8. Country of origin for each item
9. Statement of use in the United States (if applicable)
10. Discounts from price and rebates offered between buyer and seller
11. Values of assists including tools, molds, dies, and engineering work (performed outside the United States) and provided to the manufacturer to assist in product the imported items

12. Packing list
13. Endorsed by the person who prepared the invoice

The acquiring company should request a sample entry package, purchase order, as well as copies of the correspondence on a typical import shipment to review whether invoices appear to be in line with the transaction prior to performing a full import review.

Valuation

Importers tend to rely on the invoice value as the correct value for CBP without understanding the actual valuation methods, which CBP requires importers to use. Further to this, many import brokers are also not clear on how valuation has been determined by the importer. A customs broker reviewing an import invoice may not be aware of other factors that have been negotiated between the importing company's purchasing team and the foreign shipper such as assists.

Customs requires importers to declare the FOB/FCA value on the entry summary. This means customs is looking for the cost of goods and the inland freight costs to bring the goods to the port of departure. Should an importer purchase on a CPT or CIP basis, the importer can deduct the prepaid freight and insurance from the value on the invoice and declare the FOB/FCA value to CBP. Packing charges, if not included as part of the invoice value are also dutiable. As CBP is concerned with the value of the goods at the FOB/FCA point, the importer must make certain they are declaring a proper value and using a proper method of valuation.

The understanding of valuation concepts by the company being acquired may not be where it should be or may have been incorrectly interpreted by the broker working with the importer. In either case, the financial group handling the preacquisition work can ask about assists and valuation methods.

Harmonized Tariff Classification

Customs around the world utilize the HTS as the method for describing imports. Additionally, trade statistics are collected through the information submitted via entry declarations. The ten-digit number describes the product and is one of the factors in determining the correct amount of duty and taxes payable to customs in addition to the country of origin.

HTS numbers are not identical throughout the world. A vendor in Japan must follow the applicable rules of interpretation for Japan. The importer in the United States must follow the applicable U.S. rules of interpretation when making their entry declaration.

Many importers rely on their brokers to determine their tariff classifications without input from the importer. This is a lack of reasonable care on the part of the importer, as they need to be a part of the process. The importer should make drawings, full-blown product descriptions, and have someone available to answer questions from the broker regarding tariff classification. The broker should exercise reasonable care and work with the importer to come to a mutual decision that the correct number is being used and have the importer sign off on the classification. This classification process should also be documented.

HTS numbers should be maintained as part of the importer's product database and updated as the importer is advised of any changes to the HTS by the broker. Once a year, the HTS numbers should be reviewed against the new HTS numbers posted by CBP in January.

As previously mentioned, HTS numbers and the county of origin dictate the tariff rate. In some instances, there may be additional duties owed as a result of trade protection legislation. These duties are called ADD. ADD cases may take several years to be sorted out until a final duty rate is decided by the Court of International Trade. There have been several well-publicized cases of successor liability in which the company acquiring the importer was required to pay the additional duties owed for imports, which took place prior to the acquisition.

Country of Origin

There are many misunderstood ideas regarding the declaration of country of origin. In addition to the country of origin requirement on an import invoice, most imported products are required to be marked with the country of origin permanently marked indicating the country of origin to the ultimate purchaser.

Importers should include marking requirements as part of their purchase agreement. Customs states the marking must be legible, in English, and visible to the person in the United States who will receive the item in the form in which it was imported.

Containers of articles excepted from marking must be marked with the name of the country of origin of the article unless the container is also excepted from marking. CBP regulations contain a listing of items exempted from marking. While the item itself is exempted from marking, the outermost container in which the article reaches the ultimate purchaser is required to be marked. The items include screws, bolts, nuts, and washers among other items on the "J" list.

Determination as to the country of item is generally accepted as substantial transformation, but there are exceptions to this rule for certain commodities. Other exceptions to this rule include the various free trade agreements in which the United States participates. Products being imported under preferential duty treatment must meet an applicable Rule of Origin in order to avoid penalties.

The due diligence process should include questions as to country of origin determinations and participation in any free trade agreements.

Recordkeeping

Records are required to be kept for five years from the date of import. Recordkeeping requirements are extensive and can be found in detail on the Reference for Customs Regulations (A1A) list. Some of the records that must be included are the purchase order, invoices, bills of lading, customs entry documentation, communications, broker letter of instructions, and supplier payments.

Hard copy records must be retrievable for 30 days. Electronic records may be kept provided CBP has approved the importer's method of storage. Many importers make the mistake of assuming their broker has the documents required under the recordkeeping requirements. However, brokers are not privy to the internal documents an importer must retain, and in the event the importer severs ties with their broker, the importer will no longer have access to the broker's records. Brokers are required to keep their records in accordance with the requirements for brokers not for importers. Importers should retain their own records.

In requesting import documentation from the company being required, it will become evident pretty quickly if the company is correctly managing their recordkeeping.

Internal Controls and Supervision

An importer is not required to use a broker to handle their customs clearance. An importer is permitted to handle their own clearance and transmit entries to CBP if they choose to do so. Many companies choose to work with a customs broker as they have the electronic systems for dialoging with CBP, are considered experts, and it is a core skill set the broker has which the importer may not.

In choosing a broker, the importer must be diligent in choosing their partner. The importer should visit the broker's office and meet the personnel handling import shipments. These personnel will be handling import transactions, are they seasoned entry personnel with knowledge of customs regulations or data entry clerks, as this makes a difference in using the broker as a resource.

The importer should provide the broker with copies of their purchase orders for recommendations from the broker to streamline the clearance process and for the broker to understand if there are any other values that should be added to the declared entry value, such as assists.

Power of attorney documents provided to a broker should be dated in order to require the broker to follow-up on a yearly basis with the importer to understand if there have been changes in the inbound supply chain. Importers should require their brokers to provide their Importer Security Filing report cards, obtain Automated Commercial Environment (ACE) reports, and use their broker as a resource.

The importer is ultimately responsible for the declarations made by their broker. Due diligence by the acquisition team should request the number of brokers being used, and conversations with those brokerage offices should take place to ensure the brokers are operating in an environment conducive to compliance, which funnels down into a compliant resource for the importer.

Case Study #2

Flying High Imports purchases Sky Pie. Sky Pie is a small kite manufacturer that imports the materials used to manufacture its products. As part of the integration process, Flying High Imports has its trade compliance manager meet with the responsible parties for imports at the Sky Pie's offices. Sky Pie is a small company and the purchasing manager has worn the additional hat of issuing tariff classifications and managing the import process in addition to many other day-to-day responsibilities.

The trade compliance manager has a brief conversation with the purchasing manager to schedule time to review what has been done by Sky Pie prior to Flying High's acquisition of Sky Pie. Included in this conversation is the request for purchasing agreements, import entries, vendor payments, and so on.

Upon arrival at Sky Pie, the trade compliance manager meets with the purchasing manager and is walked through the import process including the assignment of Harmonized tariff system classification numbers. The purchasing manager advises they have always used the HTS numbers provided by the foreign shipper in China. The purchasing manager has not used their broker, a customs consultant, or a customs attorney for assistance nor have they requested any binding rulings from CBP.

The trade compliance manager accesses the International Trade Commission database and the Customs Ruling Online Search System and determines incorrect HTS numbers have been used and have been submitted to CBP on over 50 import entries in the past two years. The incorrect HTS numbers are at a lower duty rate resulting in roughly $20,000 in duties owed. In addition, the trade compliance manager is uncomfortable that there may be additional valuation and country of origin issues on the component materials, as well as supplemental items imported and sold by Sky Pie.

Successor Liability and Import Violations

Ataka America: Antidumping duties underpaid for wire rope: $189,000

Adaptive Engineering: Unpaid duties $6.8 million

Core Elements of an Effective Export Management and Compliance Program

1. *Management commitment*: Senior management must establish written export compliance standards for the organization, commit sufficient resources for the export compliance program, and ensure appropriate senior organizational official(s) are designated with the overall responsibility for the export compliance program to ensure adherence to export control laws and regulations
2. Continuous risk assessment of the export program
3. Formal written EMCP: Effective implementation and adherence to written policies and operational procedures
4. Ongoing compliance training and awareness
5. Pre/post export compliance security and screening: Screening of employees, contractors, customers, products, and transactions and implementation of compliance safeguards throughout the export

life cycle including product development, jurisdiction, classification, sales, license decisions, supply chain, servicing channels, and postshipment activity

6. Adherence to recordkeeping regulatory requirements
7. Internal and external compliance monitoring and periodic audits
8. Maintaining a program for handling compliance problems, including reporting export violations
9. Completing appropriate corrective actions in response to export violations

---

FOCUSED ASSESSMENT

Preassessment Survey Questionnaire

The purpose of this document is to obtain information from the importer about its import operations over compliance with CBP laws and regulations. The contents of the preassessment survey questionnaire (PASQ) will be tailored based on the auditors' analysis of the importer's import activity and the audit team's initial assessment of the potential risks for each of the audit areas that were identified in the PAR (face value). Auditors may adapt or modify this document as needed or may develop alternate formats. Auditors may also request copies of documentation in conjunction with the PASQ.

PREASSESSMENT SURVEY QUESTIONNAIRE
INSTRUCTIONS TO THE IMPORTER FOR COMPLETING THE PASQ

Please respond to all questions. The information you provide will assist us in focusing on the specific risks relative to your imported merchandise and the processes/procedures used to mitigate the risk of being noncompliant with CBP laws and regulations. In addition, your responses will help us to identify the individuals that are responsible for performing the procedures and the types of documentation that will be available for us to review.

The audit team will review your responses and prepare supplemental questions that will be discussed with your personnel to further our understanding of your processes and procedures. This PASQ file is a word document that may be filled in with your responses and returned to the auditors either as a word or portable document format (PDF) file. We request that your complete response be provided to us by insert date so we may prepare our questions prior to the Entrance Conference.

(Continued)

POINT OF CONTACT INFORMATION

Name(s) of the person(s) preparing the form:

If there are multiple preparers, you may identify a single person that can be contacted to obtain clarification of the responses.

Title(s):

Phone number(s):

E-mail address(es):

Section 1—Information about (name of importers)'s organization and policy and procedures pertaining to CBP activities

1.1   Describe the company's mission statement, code of ethics/conduct, and company's objectives?

1.1.1   How is the mission statement, code of ethics/conduct, and company's objectives disseminated within the organization?

1.2   Who is responsible for assessing the risks to achieving the company's objectives? *Indicate if there is a subgroup or individual responsible for assessing the risk for being noncompliant with CBP laws and regulations.*

1.2.1   Describe how the risk assessment is accomplished. *Indicate, for example, when/ how often the risk assessment is performed, what information is used, what thresholds/tolerances the company considers to be acceptable.*

1.2.2   When was the last risk assessment performed? *Describe any significant changes that were made as a result of the risk assessment.*

1.3   Who, within your company, has overall responsibility for ensuring compliance with CBP laws and regulations?
- *Indicate if there is an import function or department and describe the chain of command (e.g., identify who they report to).*
- *Alternately, your company may entrust compliance to a customs broker, customs consultant, or other outside agent. Identify them and indicate who within your company (i.e., individuals or groups) is/are responsible for interacting with the broker, consultant, or other outside agent (i.e., providing information to them and monitoring their work).*

1.3.1   If there is an import function or department, provide the following information:
- How is it staffed? *Indicate if an individual is assigned as the manager and identify the number of employees that report to them.*
- How long has the manager been assigned to his or her position?
- What are the responsibilities of the manager, and how are they accountable? *Indicate if they are responsible for providing weekly activity reports and describe any performance measures.*

1.3.2   If compliance has been entrusted to a customs broker, customs consultant, or other outside agent (i.e., no import department per se), provide the following information:
- How long has the company engaged the current broker, consultant, or other outside agent?
- Describe the processes used to communicate information and to monitor their work? *Indicate if there is a written contract or agreement.*

(Continued)

1.4   Who is responsible for developing and maintaining the written policies and procedures used to ensure compliance with CBP laws and regulations?
- How often are the written policies and procedures updated?

Section 2—Information about the valuation of imported merchandise

2.1   What basis of appraisement is used for the value of imported merchandise?

2.2   Who is responsible for transacting with the foreign vendors? *Identify all individuals or groups/departments that are responsible.*

2.2.1   Describe how transactions are negotiated with foreign vendors? *Describe all processes used and the conditions that apply.*

2.2.2   Describe the terms of sale used? *If there are different terms of sale, explain the conditions when each is used.*

2.2.3   If applicable, describe the terms/conditions when discounts or rebates are made?

2.2.4   If applicable, describe any additional expenses such as management fees or engineering services that are separately billed by the foreign vendors?

2.2.5   What documentation shows the terms of sale and prices (e.g., contracts, distribution and other similar agreements, invoices, purchase orders, bills of lading, proof of payment, correspondence between the parties, and company reports or catalogs/brochures)?

2.3   Describe the accounting procedures for recording purchases and payments.
- What accounts are used to record purchases of foreign merchandise? *Identify or provide a list of vendor codes.*
- What accounts are used to record payments made to foreign vendors? *Explain the methods of payments used (e.g., wire transfer, letters of credit).*

2.4   If applicable, what accounting data/reports are provided to the import function or department? *Indicate how often data/reports are provided (e.g., quarterly reports of price adjustments for purchases from foreign vendors).*

For risk pertaining to related party transactions

2.5   Describe the nature of the relationship between your company and the related foreign vendor/seller? *Indicate if your company is the exclusive U.S. importer.*

2.5.1   Describe any financial arrangements (e.g., loans, financial assistance, and expense reimbursement) between your company and the foreign vendor/seller?

2.5.2   If applicable, explain the terms and conditions of goods sold to your company on consignment.

2.5.3   Describe how prices between your company and the foreign vendor/seller/manufacturer are determined? *Identify all sources of data used and explain the accounting methodology or computational formulas where appropriate. If transaction value is used, indicate if your company supports circumstances of sale or test values.* If applicable, provide the following information:
- Describe when price adjustments are made.
- Identify any additional expenses such as management fees or engineering services that are separately billed to your company.

(Continued)

2.5.2   Explain how transactions are accounted for? Indicate if your company maintains its own accounting books and records.

2.5.2.1   What intercompany accounts are used?

For risk pertaining to statutory additions

2.6   **Assists**

2.6.1   If applicable, describe the type of assists that are provided to the foreign vendors for free or at a reduced cost (e.g., tooling, hangtags, art or design work).

2.6.2   Who decides (or determines) that the assists will be provided? *Identify all individuals or groups/departments that are involved in the decision.*
- When is it decided that the assists will be provided?
- What accounts are used to record the costs of the assists?

2.6.3   Describe the procedures used to ensure that the costs of the assists are included in the values declared to CBP. *Indicate who decides how the actual cost of the assist will be apportioned to the imported items and explain how the apportioned cost is tracked.*

2.7   **Packing**

2.7.1   If applicable, describe the type of packing (i.e., labor or materials), containers (exclusive of instruments of international traffic), and coverings of whatever nature that is separately paid to the vendor to put the imported merchandise in condition ready for shipment to the United States.

2.7.2   Who decides (or determines) that the cost of packing will be separately charged? *Identify all individuals or groups/departments that are involved in the decision.*
- When is it decided that the cost of packing will be separately charged?
- What accounts are used to record the costs of packing, containers, and coverings?

2.7.3   Describe the procedures used to ensure that the cost of the packing is included in the values declared to CBP.

2.8   **Commissions**

2.8.1   If applicable, describe the terms of sale with foreign vendors that require your company to separately pay for *selling agent* commissions. *Identify the vendors.*

2.8.2   Who decides (or determines) that *selling agent* commissions will be paid directly to the intermediary?
- When is it decided that the *selling agent* commissions will be paid directly to the intermediary?
- What accounts are used to record the payment of these commissions?

2.8.3   Describe the procedures used to ensure that these commissions are included in the values declared to CBP.

2.9   **Royalty and License Fees**

2.9.1   If applicable, describe the terms of sale with foreign vendors that require your company to pay, directly or indirectly, any royalty or license fee related to the imported merchandise as a condition of the sale of the imported merchandise for exportation to the United States. *Identify the vendors.*

(Continued)

2.9.2   Who decides (or determines) that royalty or license fees will be paid as a condition of the sale?

- When is it decided that royalty or license fees will be paid as a condition of the sale?
- What accounts are used to record the payment of the royalty or license fees related to imported merchandise?

2.9.3   What procedures ensure that royalty or license fees are included in the values declared to CBP?

2.10   **Proceeds of Any Subsequent Resale, Disposal, or Use**

2.10.1   If applicable, describe any agreements with the foreign vendors where the proceeds of any subsequent resale, disposal, or use of the imported merchandise accrue directly or indirectly to the foreign vendor. *Identify the vendors.*

2.10.2   Who decides (or determines) that the proceeds of any subsequent resale, disposal, or use of the imported merchandise will accrue directly or indirectly to the foreign vendor?

- When is it decided that the proceeds of any subsequent resale, disposal, or use of the imported merchandise will accrue directly or indirectly to the foreign vendor?
- What accounts are used to record the payment of these proceeds?

2.10.3   Describe the procedures used to ensure that proceeds of any subsequent resale, disposal, or use of the imported merchandise accruing directly or indirectly to the foreign vendor are included in the values declared to CBP.

Section 3—Information about the classification of imported merchandise

3.1   Who is responsible for determining how imported merchandise is classified? *Identify all individuals or groups that are responsible.*

3.1.1   What records and other information (e.g., product specifications, engineering drawings, physical items, laboratory analyses, etc.) are used to determine the classification of merchandise?

3.2   Does your company have a classification database?

3.2.1   If there is a classification database, do you archive previous versions of it? *Indicate how long previous versions are retained.*

3.2.2   If there is a classification database, is a copy provided to the broker? *Indicate how it is provided to the broker.*

3.2.3   If there is a classification database, what procedures ensure that the information in the database is accurate?

Section 4—Information about special classification provisions HTSUS 9801

4.1   Describe the type of merchandise that is imported under HTSUS 9801.

4.2   Who decides (or determines) that products of the United States will be returned after having been exported? *Identify all individuals or groups/departments that are involved in the process.*

- When is it determined that products will be returned after having been exported?
- What documentation/records are maintained for the exported items?

(Continued)

4.3   Describe the procedures that ensure the exported items have not been advanced in value or improved in condition by any manufacturing process or other means while abroad.

4.4   Describe the procedures that ensure that drawback has not been claimed for the exported items.

Section 5—Information about special classification provisions HTSUS 9802

5.1   Describe the type of merchandise that is imported under HTSUS 9802.

5.2   What documentation/records are maintained for the exported items?

5.3   *For items imported under HTSUS 9802.00.40/9802.00.50:* What documentation/records support the cost or value of the repair?

5.4   Describe the procedures or means (e.g., unique identifiers) used to ensure that the articles exported for repair or alterations are the same articles being reimported.

5.5   *For items imported under HTSUS 9802.00.40/9802.00.50:* Describe the procedures that ensure the foreign operation (e.g., repair or alteration process) does not result in the exported item becoming a commercially different article with new properties and characteristics.

5.6   Describe the procedures that ensure that drawback has not been claimed for the exported items.

Section 6—Information about GSP/FTA

6.1   If applicable, identify the name and Meat Inspection Divisions (MIDs) for all of the foreign vendors from whom items are imported under Generalized System for Preference (GSP)/Free Trade Agreement (FTA).

6.2   Describe any agreements with unrelated foreign vendors. *Indicate if the unrelated vendors are required to provide cost and production records to CBP or are legally prevented from releasing the records.*

6.3   Describe the procedures used to ensure the origin of articles imported under GSP (or FTA) is wholly the growth, product, or manufacture of the Beneficial Development Corporation (BDC) (or FTA country)? *Identify who performs the procedures and when/how often the procedures are performed.*

6.3.2   What documentation/records are verified? *Indicate if copies of the documentation/records are retained on file or may be obtained upon request.*

6.4   Describe the procedures used to ensure the cost or value of the material produced in the BDC (or FTA country), plus the direct processing cost, is not less than 35% of the appraised value of the articles at the time of entry into the United States? *Identify all individuals/groups that perform the procedures and when/how often the procedures are performed.*

6.4.1   What documentation/records are verified? *Indicate if copies of the documentation/records are retained on file or may be obtained upon request.*

6.5   What documentation is maintained on file showing that the articles are shipped directly from the BDC (or FTA country) to the United States without passing through the territory of any other country, or if passing through the territory of any other country, that the articles did not enter the retail commerce of the other country?

(Continued)

Section 7—Information about NAFTA

7.1 Who is responsible for maintaining the certificates of origin from NAFTA vendors?

7.2 Describe the procedures used to ensure that imported items are eligible for NAFTA?

Section 8—Information about AD/CVD

8.1 Who decides (or determines) that items may be subject to AD/CVD? *Indicate when and how often items are reviewed.*

8.1.1 What information is used to determine whether items may be subject to AD/CVD? *Identify all individuals or groups/departments that provide information as well as the documentation/records used.*

8.2 Describe the procedures used to ensure that the correct (true) country of origin is identified for items subject to AD/CVD.

8.3 Describe the procedures used to ensure that the correct AD/CVD case numbers are identified on the entry.

Section 9—Information about IPR

9.1 Identify all imported items for which your company has authorizations from the holders of IPR such as trade names, trademarks, or copyrights. *Describe the item and indicate the type of Intellectual Property Right (IPR).*

9.2 Who decides (or determines) that an imported item may have IPR belonging to other entities? *Indicate when and how often items are reviewed.*

- When is it decided that an imported item may have IPR belonging to other entities?
- What information is used to determine that the items have IPR belonging to other entities? *Identify all individuals or groups/departments that provide information as well as the documentation/records used.*

9.3 Describe the procedures used to ensure there is a valid authorization/agreement between your company and the owner of the trade name, trademark, copyright, or patent prior to the importation of the items?

9.4 What accounts are used to record royalties, proceeds, and indirect payments related to the use of the IPR?

REQUEST FOR DOCUMENTATION

DATE OF REQUEST:

RESPONSE DUE:

SUBJECT: *When submitted in conjunction with the PASQ, the subject matter may be "Information about the organization and policies and procedures relative to compliance with CBP laws and regulations."*

Item no.	Description of Documentation
1	A copy of the organizational chart, if there is one.
2	A copy of written policies and procedures used to ensure compliance with CBP laws and regulations (e.g., an Import Compliance Manual).

(Continued)

3	A copy of the General Ledger (GL) working trial balance for the period ending [xxxx] and description of accounts used.
4	A copy of written accounting procedures for recording purchases and payments.

FROM CBP INFORMED COMPLIANCE PUBLICATION: REASONABLE CARE

General Questions for All Transactions

1. If you have not retained an expert to assist you in complying with customs requirements, do you have access to the Customs Regulations (Title 19 of the Code of Federal Regulations), the Harmonized Tariff Schedule of the United States, and the government publishing office (GPO) publication Customs Bulletin and Decisions? Do you have access to the Customs Internet Website, Customs Bulletin Board, or other research service to permit you to establish reliable procedures and facilitate compliance with customs laws and regulations?

2. Has a responsible and knowledgeable individual within your organization reviewed the customs documentation prepared by you or your expert to ensure that it is full, complete, and accurate? If that documentation was prepared outside your own organization, do you have a reliable system in place to insure that you receive copies of the information as submitted to U.S. Customs and Border Protection; that it is reviewed for accuracy; and that U.S. Customs and Border Protection is timely apprised of any needed corrections?

3. If you use an expert to assist you in complying with customs requirements, have you discussed your importations in advance with that person and have you provided that person with full, complete, and accurate information about the import transactions?

4. Are identical transactions or merchandise handled differently at different ports or U.S. Customs and Border Protection offices within the same port? If so, have you brought this to the attention of the appropriate U.S. Customs and Border Protection officials?

QUESTIONS ARRANGED BY TOPIC

Merchandise Description and Tariff Classification

Basic question: Do you know or have you established a reliable procedure or program to ensure that you know what you ordered, where it was made, and what it is made of?

1. Have you provided or established reliable procedures to ensure you provide a complete and accurate description of your merchandise to U.S. Customs and Border Protection in accordance with 19 U.S.C. 1481? (Also, see 19 CFR 141.87 and 19 CFR 141.89 for special merchandise description requirements.)

2. Have you provided or established reliable procedures to ensure you provide a correct tariff classification of your merchandise to U.S. Customs and Border Protection in accordance with 19 U.S.C. 1484?

3. Have you obtained a customs *ruling* regarding the description of the merchandise or its tariff classification (see 19 CFR Part 177), and, if so, have you established reliable procedures to ensure that you have followed the ruling and brought it to U.S. Customs and Border Protection's attention?

4. Where merchandise description or tariff classification information is not immediately available, have you established a reliable procedure for providing that information, and is the procedure being followed?

5. Have you participated in a customs preclassification of your merchandise relating to proper merchandise description and classification?

6. Have you consulted the tariff schedules, customs informed compliance publications, court cases, and/or customs rulings to assist you in describing and classifying the merchandise?

7. Have you consulted with a customs *expert* (e.g., lawyer, customs broker, accountant, or customs consultant) to assist in the description and/or classification of the merchandise?

8. If you are claiming a conditionally free or special tariff classification/ provision for your merchandise (e.g., GSP, HTS Item 9802, NAFTA, etc.), how have you verified that the merchandise qualifies for such

status? Have you obtained or developed reliable procedures to obtain any required or necessary documentation to support the claim? If making a NAFTA preference claim, do you already have a NAFTA certificate of origin in your possession?

9. Is the nature of your merchandise such that a laboratory analysis or other specialized procedure is suggested to assist in proper description and classification?

10. Have you developed a reliable program or procedure to maintain and produce any required customs entry documentation and supporting information?

Valuation

Basic questions: Do you know or have you established reliable procedures to know the price actually paid or payable for your merchandise? Do you know the terms of sale; whether there will be rebates, tie-ins, indirect costs, additional payments; and whether assists were provided, commissions or royalties paid? Are amounts actual or estimated? Are you and the supplier related parties?

1. Have you provided or established reliable procedures to provide U.S. Customs and Border Protection with a proper declared value for your merchandise in accordance with 19 U.S.C. 1484 and 19 U.S.C. 1401a?

2. Have you obtained a customs *ruling* regarding the valuation of the merchandise (see 19 CFR Part 177), and, if so, have you established reliable procedures to ensure that you have followed the ruling and brought it to U.S. Customs and Border Protection attention?

3. Have you consulted the customs valuation laws and regulations, Customs Valuation Encyclopedia, customs informed compliance publications, court cases, and customs rulings to assist you in valuing merchandise?

4. Have you consulted with a customs *expert* (e.g., lawyer, accountant, customs broker, customs consultant) to assist in the valuation of the merchandise?

5. If you purchased the merchandise from a *related* seller, have you established procedures to ensure that you have reported that fact upon entry and taken measures or established reliable procedures

to ensure that value reported to U.S. Customs and Border Protection meets one of the *related party* tests?

6. Have you taken measures or established reliable procedures to ensure that all of the legally required costs or payments associated with the imported merchandise have been reported to U.S. Customs and Border Protection (e.g., assists, all commissions, indirect payments or rebates, royalties, etc.)?

7. If you are declaring a value based on a transaction in which you were/are not the buyer, have you substantiated that the transaction is a bona fide sale at arm's length and that the merchandise was clearly destined to the United States at the time of sale?

8. If you are claiming a conditionally free or special tariff classification/ provision for your merchandise (e.g., GSP, HTS Item 9802, NAFTA, etc.), have you established a reliable system or program to ensure that you reported the required value information and obtained any required or necessary documentation to support the claim?

9. Have you established a reliable program or procedure to produce any required entry documentation and supporting information?

Country of Origin/Marking/Quota

Basic question: Have you taken reliable measures to ascertain the correct country of origin for the imported merchandise?

1. Have you established reliable procedures to ensure that you report the correct country of origin on customs entry documents?

2. Have you established reliable procedures to verify or ensure that the merchandise is properly marked upon entry with the correct country of origin (if required) in accordance with 19 U.S.C. 1304 and any other applicable special marking requirement (watches, gold, textile labeling, etc.)?

3. Have you obtained a customs *ruling* regarding the proper marking and country of origin of the merchandise (see 19 CFR Part 177), and, if so, have you established reliable procedures to ensure that you followed the ruling and brought it to U.S. Customs and Border Protection's attention?

4. Have you consulted with a customs *expert* (e.g., lawyer, accountant, customs broker, customs consultant) regarding the correct country of origin/proper marking of your merchandise?

5. Have you taken reliable and adequate measures to communicate customs country of origin marking requirements to your foreign supplier prior to importation of your merchandise?

6. If you are claiming a change in the origin of the merchandise or claiming that the goods are of U.S. origin, have you taken required measures to substantiate your claim (e.g., Do you have U.S. milling certificates or manufacturer's affidavits attesting to the production in the United States)?

7. If you are importing textiles or apparel, have you developed reliable procedures to ensure that you have ascertained the correct country of origin in accordance with 19 U.S.C. 3592 (Section 334, Pub. Law 103-465) and assured yourself that no illegal transshipment or false or fraudulent practices were involved?

8. Do you know how your goods are made from raw materials to finished goods, by whom, and where?

9. Have you checked with U.S. Customs and Border Protection and developed a reliable procedure or system to ensure that the quota category is correct?

10. Have you checked or developed reliable procedures to check the Status Report on Current Import Quotas (Restraint Levels) issued by U.S. Customs and Border Protection to determine if your goods are subject to a quota category, which has part categories?

11. Have you taken reliable measures to ensure that you have obtained the correct visas for your goods if they are subject to visa categories?

12. In the case of textile articles, have you prepared or developed a reliable program to prepare the proper country declaration for each entry, that is, a single country declaration (if wholly obtained/produced) or a multicountry declaration (if raw materials from one country were produced into goods in a second)?

13. Have you established a reliable maintenance program or procedure to ensure you can produce any required entry documentation and supporting information, including any required certificates of origin?

Intellectual Property Rights

Basic question: Have you determined or established a reliable procedure to permit you to determine whether your merchandise or its packaging bear or use any trademarks or copyrighted matter or are patented and, if so, that you have a legal right to import those items into, and/or use those items in, the United States?

1. If you are importing goods or packaging bearing a trademark registered in the United States, have you checked or established a reliable procedure to ensure that it is genuine and not restricted from importation under the gray-market or parallel import requirements of U.S. law (see 19 CFR 133.21), or that you have permission from the trademark holder to import such merchandise?
2. If you are importing goods or packaging, which consist of, or contain registered copyrighted material, have you checked or established a reliable procedure to ensure that it is authorized and genuine? If you are importing sound recordings of live performances, were the recordings authorized?
3. Have you checked or developed a reliable procedure to see if your merchandise is subject to an International Trade Commission or court ordered exclusion order?
4. Have you established a reliable procedure to ensure that you maintain and can produce any required entry documentation and supporting information?

Miscellaneous Questions

1. Have you taken measures or developed reliable procedures to ensure that your merchandise complies with other agency requirements (e.g., Food and Drug Administration (FDA), Environmental Protection Administration (EPA)/Department of Transportation (DOT), Consumer Product Safety Commission (CPSC), Federal Trade Commission (FTC), Agriculture, etc.) prior to or upon entry, including the procurement of any necessary licenses or permits?
2. Have you taken measures or developed reliable procedures to check to see if your goods are subject to a Commerce Department dumping or counter-vailing duty investigation or determination, and, if so, have you complied or developed reliable procedures to ensure compliance with customs reporting requirements upon entry (e.g., 19 CFR 141.61)?
3. Is your merchandise subject to quota/visa requirements, and, if so, have you provided or developed a reliable procedure to provide a correct visa for the goods upon entry?

4. Have you taken reliable measures to ensure and verify that you are filing the correct type of customs entry (e.g., Temporary Import Bond (TIB), travel and entertainment (T&E), consumption entry, mail entry, etc.), as well as ensure that you have the right to make entry under the Customs Regulations?

I love the man that can smile in trouble, that can gather strength from distress, and grow brave by reflection. 'Tis the business of little minds to shrink, but he whose heart is firm, and whose conscience approves his conduct, will pursue his principles unto death.

Thomas Paine

Index

A

Accountability/responsibility systems, setting up, 192–193
Action process
  in dispute resolution, 26–27
  in strategic plan, 174
ADD (antidumping duty), 207, 305
Admission temporaire/temporary admission (ATA), 208
Air waybill, 207
Antidiversion clause, 207
Antidumping duty (ADD), 207, 305
Application security, 200
Arbitration process, 208
Assessment process, 25, 173, 204, 233–236
Assets/liabilities, 59
ATA (admission temporaire/temporary admission), 208
Attainable process, 53
Auditors, 309

B

Balance sheet, 59
Banking/creditor relationships, 59
Bill of lading, 207–208
Binding ruling process, 99
Blue Tiger International, 273, 293
BTI monthly management report, 50–51
Budgeting process, 60
Bullying technology, 202
Business culture, 127
Business development, 37–38, 221
Businesses goal, 72
Business management skill sets, 13
  communication, 14–19
  components, 3
  development, 37–38
  finance, 14
  growth strategies, 38–49
  negotiation, 30–31
  operations, 49–52
  people skills, 36–37
  problem resolution, 24–29
  project management, 21–23
  time management, 31–35

C

Camaraderie in team building, 194–195
Carnet, 208
Carriage and insurance paid to (CIP), 208, 276
Carriage paid to (CPT), 208, 276
Cash flow, 59
Cash in advance, 208
CBP. *See* Customs and Border Protection (CBP)
CCL (Commerce Control List), 111
Central Intelligence Agency (CIA) triad, 200
Certificate of origin, 209
CFR (Cost and freight), 210, 278
China, landed cost importing from, 280–283
  declared value, 285
  HS code, 284
  import customs duties, 285–288
  import taxes, 288
  inland freight, 289
  insurance, 288–289
CIA (Central Intelligence Agency) triad, 200
CIF (Cost, insurance, and freight), 210, 278
CIP (Carriage and insurance paid to), 208, 276
Closure process, 174
Coke/Pepsi company, 185
Collaboration process, 54–55, 191, 194
Commerce Control List (CCL), 111
Commerce Country Chart, 111
Commercial invoice, 209

Communication, 14–15
  articulation, 16
  capability, 15–16
  company, 184
  direct, 17
  feedback on, 19
  interesting, 16–17
  PowerPoint utilization, 20
  storytelling, 18
  style, 21
  timely, 19
  and time management, 35–36
  trust, 17
Competitive pressures, 77
Confirming house, 209
Conformity certificate, 209
Consignment, 210
Consolidated Screening List,
    109, 114
Consular invoice, 210
Consularization process, 115
Continuity planning, 202
Contract, 210
Cook, T. A., 273, 293
Cosmetic company, 184
Cost and freight (CFR), 210, 278
Cost, insurance, and freight (CIF),
    210, 278
Countertrade, 210–211
Country of origin/marking/quota,
    319–320
CPT (Carriage paid to), 208, 276
Credit and drafts, letters, 212, 218
C-TPAT. *See* Customs-Trade Partnership
    against Terrorism (C-TPAT)
Culture, aspects, 175
Customer Relationship Management
    (CRM) system, 186
Customer service
  in business development, 37
  program, 47
Customhouse brokers, 100–103
Customs and Border Protection (CBP),
    119–120, 302–303
  C-TPAT, 104, 122
  informed compliance publication, 316
Customs-bonded warehouse, 211
Customs declaration, 211
Customs invoice, 211

Customs taxes
  duty, 285–288
  GST, 288
  VAT, 288
Customs-Trade Partnership against
    Terrorism (C-TPAT),
    104–105, 271
  approach/guiding principles, 120–121
  benefits, 117–118
  exporters, 122
  external factors, 122
  overview, 118–120
Cyber security, 199–200, 205
  application security, 200
  assessment, 204
  bullying technology, 202
  cases, 203
  continuity planning, 202
  disaster recovery, 202
  end-user education and training, 202–203
  impacts, 200
  InfoSec, 200
  initiative, 204
  mistakes, 199
  network security, 201
  operations security, 202
  personnel issues in, 205
  professional support, 204
  train and educate, 205

D

DAP (Delivered at place), 277
DAT (Delivered at terminal), 276
Date drafts, 211–212
DCS (Destination Control Statement),
    207, 211
DDP (Delivered duty paid), 75, 277
Decision-making process, 155
  building team, 163
  complete analysis, 164
  decision understanding, 161
  follow-up and tweak, 165
  and implement, 165
  metrics/quantitative model, 164
  mining, 161–162
  preliminary finding, 163–164
  qualitative criteria evaluation, 164
  qualitative *versus* quantitative, 156–160

Delegating process, 34–35
  boundaries, 229
  skill sets, 227–228
  sound time management practice,
    229–230
Delivered at place (DAP), 277
Delivered at terminal (DAT), 276
Delivered duty paid (DDP), 75, 277
Denied party screening process, 114
Destination Control Statement (DCS),
    207, 211
Direct exporting, 212
Disaster recovery, 202
Dispute resolution and conflict
    management, 230–233
  action, 235–236
  assessment, 233–236
  closure, 237–238
  follow-up, 236–237
  remarks on, 238
  strategy, 233
  tweaking strategy, 236
Due diligence process, 293, 296, 299,
    306–307
Dumping, 212
Duty/tax free amount, 285

E

EAR (Export Administration
    Regulations), 110–111, 207, 295
EAR99, 111
E-commerce in global trade, 134–139
  domain name selection, 148
  localization/internationalization, 150
  order execution, 151–152
  overview, 212
  payment and pricing, 143–144
  policy-advice, 152–153
  regional/cultural differences, 140–141
  register with search engines, 149
  shipping and logistics, 142–143
  success in, 139–147
  web host, 149–150
  website localization and language, 145
Effective delegation, 195
Electronic Export Information (EEI),
    112, 213
EMC (export management company), 213

EMCP. *See* Export Management and
    Compliance Program (EMCP)
Emotional intelligence (EI), 165–169
Emotional quotient (EQ), 166–169
Employee costs/payroll, 60
End-user education/training, 202–203
EPZ (export processing zone), 214
EQ (emotional quotient), 166–169
ETC (export trading company), 214
Export Administration Regulations
    (EAR), 110–111, 207, 295
Export license, 213
Export Management and Compliance
    Program (EMCP), 242, 295
  audits/assessments, 262–263
  awareness, training and, 297
  business partners, screening, 297–298
  corrective actions, 299
  formal written, 256–257
  knowledgeable/compliant service
    provider, 299–300
  management commitment,
    244–246
  methodology, 242–243
  periodic auditing and monitoring, 298
  preaudit/postaudit checklist, 243
  recordkeeping, 259–261, 298
  reporting, escalation, and corrective
    action, 264
  risk assessment, 246–255
  risks identification in, 296–297
  senior management commitment, 296
  training, 257–259
  violations and compliance issues, 299
Export management company
    (EMC), 213
Export packing list, 214
Export processing zone (EPZ), 214
Export quotas, 214
Export sales concept, 73–75
  competitive pressures, 77
  distributors/agents uses, 78
  freight forwarders utilization, 76–77
  global expansion, 78–79
  INCO terms, 75
  landed costs, 77
  sound reasons, 73
  trade compliance issues, 77
Export subsidies, 214

Export supply chain, 109
   CCL, 111
   consularization/legalization, 115
   denied party screening, 114
   EAR, 110–111
   EEI, 112
   embargoed country screening,
      114–115
   FTAs, 116
   government agencies responsible,
      109–110
   Harmonized Tariff numbers, 113
   IPPC, 115
   ITAR, 110
   letter of credit, 116–117
   preshipment inspections, 116
   recordkeeping requirements, 114
   Schedule B numbers, 113
   USPPI, 112–113
   valuation, 113–114
Export trading company (ETC), 214
Ex works (EXW), 75, 215, 276

F

FAS (Free alongside ship), 216, 277
FCA (Free carrier), 276
FCPA (Foreign Corrupt Practices
     Act), 215
Financial considerations, 14, 57
   assets/liabilities, 59
   balance sheet, 59
   banking/creditor relationships, 59
   budgeting, 60
   cash flow, 59
   controls, 57–61
   employee costs/payroll, 60
   exposures/risks, 59
   insurance considerations, 59–60
   inventory, 60
   payables, 58
   P&L statement, 58
   receivables, 58
   reporting, 59
   revenue/expenses, 58
   taxes, 60
   technology in accounting, 60–61
Financial exposures/risks, 59

Financial reporting, 59
FOB (Free on board), 216, 277
Focused assessment, 309–316
Foreign agricultural service, 215
Foreign asset expansion, 79
Foreign Corrupt Practices Act
     (FCPA), 215
Foreign distributor, 212
Foreign purchasing, 88–92
Foreign-trade zones, 215–216
Forrester Research company, 150
Free alongside ship (FAS), 216, 277
Free carrier (FCA), 276
Free in and out, 216
Free on board (FOB), 216, 277
Free sale certificate, 209
Free trade agreements (FTAs),
     116, 209
Freight forwarders, 76–77, 90, 217
Freight negotiation, 180
FTAs (free trade agreements), 116, 209

G

Gator Enterprises, 300–302
Global entrepreneurial ecosystem, 217
Global sourcing, 79, 86–87
Global supply chain, 81–82
Goods and services tax (GST), 288
Google
   effectiveness, 198–199
   executives, 198
   qualitative assessments, 198
   team lead and member, 198
   team making, 197–198
Gross domestic product, 217
Growth strategies in business
     management
   closing deals, 46
   customer service, 47
   opportunity, 43–44
   in organic growth model, 38–39
   price, 46–47
   prospects, 44–46
   quality development/sales personnel,
     41–43
   sales strategy, 39–40, 48
GST (goods and services tax), 288

H

Harmonized system codes (HS codes), 279–280, 284
Harmonized Tariff numbers, 113
Harmonized Tariff Schedule of the United States (HTSUS), 94–95
HS codes (harmonized system codes), 279–280, 284
HTS codes, 279–280, 304–305
HTSUS (Harmonized Tariff Schedule of the United States), 94–95

I

IDA (International Distributors Association), 267–268
Import compliance management program, 302
   corporate structure, 302–303
   country of origin, 305–306
   HTS, 304–305
   internal controls and supervision, 306–307
   invoices, 303–304
   recordkeeping, 306
   valuation, 304
Import supply chain, 93–94
   bonds, 107–108
   country of origin marking, 95
   customhouse brokers, 100–103
   duties/fees, 94
   HTSUS, 94–95
   internal supervision/control, 103–104
   invoice requirements, 106–107
   reasonable care standard, 96–100
   record retention, 108–109
   supply chain security, 104–106
   textile declaration, 99
Income statement, 58
Incoterms. *See* International Commercial Terms (Incoterms)
Indirect exporting, 217
Information security (InfoSec), 200
Inspection certificate, 217
Insurance
   certificate, 217
   considerations, 59–60

Integrative management, 191
   accountability/responsibility systems, 192–193
   leadership, 192
   negotiation prowess, 192
   opportunity in, 193
   problem resolution, 193
   project management, 192
   team building, 192
Intellectual property rights (IPRs), 84–85, 90, 320–321
International business, 71
   Americans/world benefits, 88
   culture, 127–132
   export sales, 73–79
   foreign asset expansion, 79
   foreign cultures, 80
   global sourcing, 79
   global supply chain, 81–82
   goals, 72–79
   import/export operations/regulations/ procedures, 80–81
   legal/accounting/finance issues, 82
   marketing/sales/customer service, 82–85
   purchasing, 86–87
   skill sets, 79–88
   steps to build, 132–133
   strategy, 125–126
   technology, 85–86
International buyer program, 218
International Commercial Terms (Incoterms), 90, 216, 222, 266–268, 274–275
   2010, 275
   Carriage and insurance paid to (CIP), 276
   Carriage paid to (CPT), 276
   Cost and freight (CFR), 278
   Cost, insurance, and freight (CIF), 278
   Delivered at place (DAP), 277
   Delivered at terminal (DAT), 276
   Delivered duty paid (DDP), 277
   export sales, 75
   Ex works (EXW), 276
   Free alongside ship (FAS), 277
   Free carrier (FCA), 276
   Free on board (FOB), 277

International Distributors Association
(IDA), 267–268
International freight and trade
compliance, 265
freight forwarder and carrier,
268–269
INCO term, 266–268
insure shipment, 268
landed costs, 270–271
leverage FTA, 272
shipping/logistics, importance, 265
tracking shipments, 269–270
International Plant Protection Convention
(IPPC), 115
International trade administration, 218
International Traffic in Arms Regulations
(ITAR), 110
Inventory, 60
IPPC (International Plant Protection
Convention), 115
IPRs (intellectual property rights), 84–85,
90, 320–321
ITAR (International Traffic in Arms
Regulations), 110

J

Joint venture, 218

K

Kelly Raia, 274

L

Landed costs modeling, 91
calculator, 289
definition, 279–280
export sales, 77
importing from China, 280–289
SOP, 278–279
Leaders, 5
Leadership, 2, 192
athleticism, 7
versus management, 4–5
quality skills, 7–10
traits, 4
Learning process, 15
Legalization process, 115

Letter of credit, 116–117
Licensing, 218

M

Managed printing service (MPS), 185
Management, 2–3
versus leadership, 4–5
traits, 3–4
Mantra, 52
Marketing, business development, 37
Market research, primary/secondary,
220–221
Market survey, 218–219
Measurable process, 53
Mentoring effectiveness, team building,
195–196
Merchandise description/tariff
classification, 317–318
Merger and acquisition (M&A) activity, 38
Military conflicts, 183
Mining process, 173
Mitigation step, 28–29
MPS (managed printing service), 185
Multilateral development bank, 219

N

NAFTA (North American Free Trade
Agreement), 209, 219
National Telecommunications and
Information Administration
(NTIA), 153
Negotiation process, 130, 171
in 2018 and new world economy,
177–178
business management skill sets, 30–31
business needs, 177
case studies, 180–187
compromise and consensus, 175–176
culture, 175
global, 174–175
problem areas and actions, 178–180
prowess, 192
and purchasing/supply chain
management, 185–187
questions to management, 176–177
and strategic plan, 172–174
trust, 176–187

Network security, 201
North American Free Trade Agreement
(NAFTA), 209, 219
NTIA (National Telecommunications
and Information
Administration), 153

O

Office of Foreign Asset Control (OFAC),
114–115
Operations
in business management, 49–52
security, 202
Organizational skill sets, 226

P

Packing list. *See* Export packing list
PASQ (preassessment survey
questionnaire), 309–316
Payables, 58
People skills in business management,
36–37
Periodic auditing/monitoring
process, 298
Piggyback marketing, 219–220
Pitney Bowes company,
139–147
Planning process, 173–174
P&L (profit and loss) statement, 58
Preassessment survey questionnaire
(PASQ), 309–316
Preshipment inspections, 116
Prioritization skill sets, 226–227
Problem resolution, 24, 193
action plan, 26–27
assessment process, 25
closure, 29
mitigation, 28–29
outreach, 28
reassessment, 27
revision, 27
stop bleeding, 25
strategy, 26
Procurement management, 61–62
purchasing, 63–66
RFP tool, 67–68
risk management in, 68–70

role in, 61–66
single *versus* multiple source
strategies, 69
sourcing, 63
vendor management, 66–67
Profit and loss (P&L) statement, 58
Pro forma invoice, 220
Project management, 21–23, 192
Prospects, 44–46
Purchasing function, 63–66

Q

Qualitative analysis, 156
assessments, 198
characteristics, 156–157
criteria evaluation, 164
versus quantitative analysis,
157–160
Quality sales personnel attributes,
42–43
Quandary, 31
Quantitative analysis, 156
characteristics, 157
measures, 198–199
metrics and model, 164
versus qualitative analysis,
157–160
Quotation, 220

R

Reasonable care concept, 97
Receivables, 58
Recordkeeping requirements, 259–261,
298, 306
Record retention system, 108–109
Regional value content, 220
Reid, B., 146
Relevant process, 54
Remarketers, 220
Request for proposal (RFP) tool, 67–68,
184, 186
Request for quote (RFQ) process, 184
Revenue/expenses, 58
RFP (request for proposal) tool, 67–68,
184, 186
RFQ (request for quote) process, 184

S

Sales component, business development, 37
Sales representative, 220
Schedule B numbers, 113
Senior managements guides, 88–92
Sight drafts, 212, 221
Sky Pie, 307–308
SMART (specific, measurable, attainable, relevant, trackable), 172–173
SMART-C, 53
SMART goals, 238–241
SOPs (standard operating procedures), 89
Sourcing function, 63
Specific, measurable, attainable, relevant, trackable (SMART), 172–173
Specific process, 53
Standard operating procedures (SOPs), 89
Strategic plan, negotiation and, 172
   action, 174
   assessment, 173
   closure, 174
   goal setting, 172–173
   mining, 173
   planning, 173–174
   tweaking, 174
Strategic planning and goal setting, 238–242
Strategic planning as operational responsibility, 52
   attainable, 53
   collaboration, 54–55
   goals and deliverables, 53
   mantra, 52
   measurable, 53
   relevant, 54
   specific, 53
   time frame, 54
Strategy in dispute resolution, 26
Stress, reduction in, 224–226
Supply chain management, 62
Supply chain security, 104–106
Sustainable business model, 189–190
   communication training, 190
   cyber security. See Cyber security
   integrative management, 191–193
   steps, 190–191
   team initiatives, developing/managing, 194–197

T

Tactical execution, 3
Tariffs code, 221
Taxes, 60
Team building, 192, 194
   camaraderie, 194–195
   collaboration, 194
   cross company silos, 196
   effective delegation, 195
   mentoring effectiveness, 195–196
   results, 196
Team initiatives, developing/managing
   managing team, 197
   team building, 194–196
   team members, 196–197
Technology licensing agreement, 221–222
Terms of sale, 222
Time drafts, 212, 222
Time frame process, 54
Time management, 31–34, 224
   and communication, 35–36
   consequences, 224
   delegation skill sets, 34–35, 227–230
   organizational skill sets, 226
   prioritization skill sets, 226–227
   stress reduction in, 224–226
Trade compliance management
   basics, export/import, 294–295, 302
   elements, 291, 308–309
   EMCP, 295–300
   import compliance management program, 302–308
   issues in mergers/acquisitions, 293–294
   between service providers/shippers, 290–293
Trade compliance process
   with customs, 96
   export supply chain, 109–117
   import supply chain, 93–109
   issues, 77
   manager, 91
   and regulatory responsibilities, 92–117
Trade fair certification program, 222
Trademark, 222
Trade statistics, 222

Trading house, 222
Trust in negotiation, 176–187
Tweaking process, 174
Tweaking strategy, 236

U

Uniform resource locator (URL), 148
United States, export-import bank, 213
United States Principal Party in Interest
  (USPPI), 112–113
URL (uniform resource locator), 148
U.S. Agency for International
  Development, 223
U.S. Central Intelligence Agency, 223
U.S. Commercial Service, 223
U.S. Department of Agriculture (USDA),
  215, 223
U.S. Department of Commerce, 223
USPPI (United States Principal Party in
  Interest), 112–113
U.S. Small Business Administration, 223

U.S. Trade and Development Agency, 223
U.S. trade representative, 219

V

Valuation process, 318–319
Value-added tax (VAT), 288
Vendor management function,
  66–67
Vetting process, 44

W

Warehouse receipt, 223
Web
  address, 148
  host, 149–150
Work group *versus* team, 198

X

Xenon Corp., 231–232